Gordon and Jane Rietveld are a writer/artist/photographer team who have traveled extensively in the Greek islands. Gordon, a former advertising agency executive, specialized in tourism. Jane, listed in *Who's Who of American Women*, has written and illustrated nine books for young people, three of them Literary Guild selections.

gordon f. rietveld
jane rietveld

GREECE
aegean
island guide

Prentice-Hall Inc., Englewood Cliffs, N. J. 07632

Library of Congress Cataloging in Publication Data

Rietveld, Gordon F.
      Greece, Aegean island guide.

            "A Spectrum Book."
            Includes index.
            1. Islands of the Aegean—Description and
      travel—Guide-books. I. Rietveld, Jane.
      II. Title.
      DF895.R53   914.99'0476   81-19226
      ISBN 0-13-365015-4   AACR2
      ISBN 0-13-365007-3 (pbk.)

© 1982 by Gordon F. Rietveld and Jane Rietveld

A SPECTRUM BOOK

10   9   8   7   6   5   4   3   2   1

ISBN 0-13-365007-3 {PBK}

ISBN 0-13-365015-4

Printed in the United States of America

Editorial/production supervision by Maria Carella
Page layout by Marie Alexander
Manufacturing buyer: Barbara A. Frick

This Spectrum Book is available to businesses and organizations
at a special discount when ordered in large quantities.
For information, contact Prentice-Hall, Inc., General Publishing Division,
Special Sales, Englewood Cliffs, N. J. 07632.

Prentice-Hall International, Inc., *London*
Prentice-Hall of Australia Pty., Limited, *Sydney*
Prentice-Hall of Canada Inc., *Toronto*
Prentice-Hall of India Private, Limited, *New Delhi*
Prentice-Hall of Japan, Inc., *Tokyo*
Prentice-Hall of Southeast Asia Pte., Ltd., *Singapore*
Whitehall Books Limited, *Wellington, New Zealand*

contents

ACKNOWLEDGMENTS

The authors would like to thank
Constantin Drivas and Mariella Fan of
the Greek National Tourist Organiza-
tion in Athens; Platon Davakis and
John Efthimiou of the Chicago and
Los Angeles branches of the G.N.T.O.;
Athanasios Haritos, Greek Consular
Agent in Phoenix, Arizona; and
Lillian Bowman of Scottsdale, Ari-
zona, for their valuable assistance.

COVER PHOTOGRAPHS

Top row (left to right):
Rhodes: entrance to Fortress of the
    Knights
National flag of Greece, symbolic of
    Aegean island travel
Delos: temple columns near the Sacred
    Harbor

Below title (clockwise from left):
Mykonos: windmills at Cato Mylon
    Square
Patmos: net-mending time at Scala
    harborside
Thera (Santorini): chapel in town of
    Fira
Crete: hand-loomed crafts on display
    at Kritsa

I
general information

TRIP PLANNER

If you are ready to leave your present world and enter another for a completely rewarding vacation, then the Aegean Islands could be for you. An eminently successful trip should have a solid foundation of facts and plans. Once you are armed with this basic knowledge, you will be able to navigate through every day with a captain's confidence.

Each Aegean island has its own personality and milieu. The maps, words, and photographs in this book will help you become acquainted, and you can choose the islands that appeal to you the most.

The map of the Aegean at the opening of this part of the book can be used as a trip planner and recorder. Pencil in your prospective trip (in case you make changes) and ink in your actual trip. Here are a few suggestions as starters.

Sporades

Flights between Athens and Skiathos save hours. Once there, you can navigate to other Sporades islands.

Northeast Aegean

There is a ship passage to the Northeast Aegean from Piraeus, Kymi, or Ag. Constantinos. There are daily flights from Athens to Kavala or Alexandroupolis. From this northern part of the Aegean you can sail south to a wide choice of islands. Or from Samos you can sail, via Ikaria, to Paros. Now you are in the midst of the Cyclades, with its wide number of choices.

Dodecanese

There are daily flights from Athens to Mykonos. Don't pass up the side trip to Delos. From Mykonos you can sail to Patmos, where you have a choice of sailing to the Northeast Aegean islands, or south as far as Rhodes.

Fly to Rhodes and take an excursion boat to Simi. Fly to Karpathos. Continue to Crete by ship. This plan includes the charm of both small and large islands. Return to Athens by plane.

Cyclades

Options are seemingly endless in season. There is ample steamer service between the Middle and Eastern Cyclades. Western Cyclades have fewer options, although there are excursion boats from Sifnos to Paros in summer. Ships sailing south along the Western Cyclades go as far as Milos. From Milos you can get to Thera and Crete.

Crete

Perhaps the best known and most famous Aegean Island, Crete is just a few hours by plane from Athens. And after your visit, you can fly or sail northward to islands of your choice.

Other Options

Don't forget those little islands where ships stop once or twice a week. These are still the most "Greek" of all the islands.

The Time Element

It is wise to return to Athens at least one full day in advance of your departure flight. Uncertain weather conditions may affect ship schedules.

TRIP EXPENSE INFORMATION

Each year, the Greek government issues prices for ship travel, domestic air travel, train and bus fares, and restaurant and hotel rates. Because of these

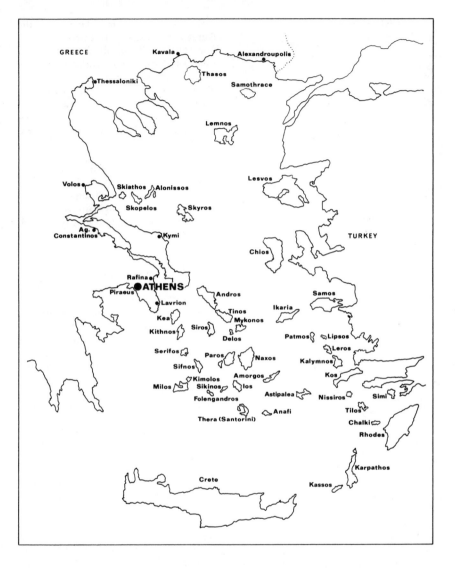

yearly changes, no prices are listed in this book. However, you can obtain all this information for the time of *your* trip by writing to the Greek National Tourist Organization and requesting it. For the address nearest to you, see the listing on pages 17–19. Allow several weeks for return delivery.

Foreign Exchange Rates

Contact your bank or daily newspaper for the foreign exchange rates. Daily listings give the current value of the drachma. You can "guestimate" your cost for lodging, travel, and food by multiplying drachmas by the published currency value.

Key to Island Maps in This Book

✈	Airport
●	Island Capital City
○	Village
•	Beach Facilities
□	Medieval, Archaelogical Site; Museum; Monastery; Caves
△	Mountain
▬▬▬	Main Road
▬▬	Secondary Road
⋯⋯	Footpath or Mule Track

ENTRY REQUIREMENTS AND REGULATIONS

Passports and Visas. All travelers must have a valid passport. Entry aboard a yacht is by Transit Visa obtained at the port of entry. Passport visas are required if crew members break their journey or spend nights ashore.

Customs. Airport arrival has a dual-flow system (red and green). Visitors with nothing to declare use the green line.

Importation and Exportation of Antiquities. Works of art may be imported free with declaration of value so they may be re-exported. It is forbidden to export antiquities or works of art unearthed or found in Greece. Castings and reproductions may be exported freely.

Cameras and Film. No entry restrictions. Before leaving your country,

register cameras and lenses at the Bureau of Customs International Airport Office. Bring all film with you. Leading brands are available in the islands, but expensive.

Vehicles. A four-month free-use card is issued by the Customs Authority for cars, trailers, motorcycles, side-cars, and mopeds. This card may be extended.

Currency. Unlimited import. For export: Drs. 750 in bank notes. All banks are authorized to buy foreign currency and traveler's checks at official rates set by the Bank of Greece. A passport is required to cash traveler's checks.

ATHENS

For most island travelers the arrival and starting point is Athens. Seen from the Acropolis, the city sprawls in angular concrete shapes over the plains of Attica. Down there is Syntagma Square, also known as Constitution Square, the city's hospitality center for its visitors. Here, too, in the National Bank of Greece, is the Greek National Tourist Organization (G.N.T.O.–E.O.T. in Greek). A helpful staff will answer questions, and give you free pamphlets and that all-important weekly schedule of ship sailings and fares.

While you are in Athens, it would be advantageous to spend several hours in the Archaeological Museum to see the many treasures that came from the islands you will be visiting. Summer hours: 7:30 A.M. to 7:30 P.M. Sundays and holidays: 10:30 A.M. to 4:30 P.M. Thursdays and Sundays are free admission.

SEA TRAVEL

Enormous, sleek white ships wait in silent elegance at the wharves in Piraeus, which is a thriving, busy city with a crusty, worn waterfront. Day-

Athens

time and nighttime departures are routine. The trip from Athens to Piraeus can be accomplished by taxi, subway, or surface bus.

In Athens there are travel agencies and shipping offices that sell tickets, many in the area of Syntagma Square. At the time of purchase, they will make a confirming call and tell you when you should be at the dock (usually several hours ahead of time). If you wait and purchase your ticket after boarding your ship, there is an additional charge of 20%.

There are many ticket and travel agencies in Piraeus, also, but if your ship leaves at an uncompromising hour it is better to have ticket in hand and board immediately.

Ship Schedules

The steamship information in this book was issued by the Ministry of Merchant Marine and by the Greek National Tourist Organization. Spring schedules start in April. Summer schedules begin about June 1 and end about September 15. After that date, sailings per week are fewer. This accounts for the book's listing (for example) "2–5 ships weekly."

Weekly shipping schedules are published each Tuesday and are available for the asking at the G.N.T.O. office in the National Bank of Greece in Syntagma Square in Athens, at the Athens East Airport, and in the G.N.T.O. offices in Piraeus, Crete, Rhodes, and Thessaloniki.

All schedules are subject to change. This is a protection against inclement weather, changes of cargo plans, and the many matters that enter into managing these enormous ships. It is unlikely that you will be inconvenienced since there is a wide choice of daily departures and Greek weather is ninety-nine percent obliging.

If you are an ardent pre-planner, you can request a sample shipping schedule from your nearest G.N.T.O., but you should know that it will be the calendar week's schedule that is in force.

Other Departure Ports for the Aegean Islands

Kavala: to Northeast Aegean Islands.
Thessaloniki: to Northeast Aegean and Dodecanese.
Volos, Kymi, Ag. Constantinos: to Sporades and Northeast Aegean.
Rafina: to Andros, Mykonos, Tinos.
Lavrion: to Kea.

Ship Accommodations

Tourist and Deck Classes. These are the cheapest. This ticket is for the outside upper decks and inside lounge. Many of the young crowd use these accommodations; nights are spent in sleeping bags.
Staterooms. A second-class, two-bunk stateroom may be shared by a couple, a four-bunk cabin by members of the same sex.
Second Class. This is a more comfortable lounge, and you can roam the deck, but not into first class. A stateroom is an added cost.
First Class. The cost is about three times that of tourist class and includes a stateroom. Lounges have music, bars, couches, and chairs that swivel.
Dining Aboard Ship. Dining rooms are most frequented by Greek businessmen and vacationing Greek families. It is never amiss to have your own food. Snack bars sell sandwiches, soft drinks, beer, and desserts such as *baklava* and packaged cookies.

Arrival at Port

A bus meets the ship if the island's main town is inland. Most islands have a few taxis. Scoot for these if the bus is not for you, and agree ahead of time on the fare.

Ticket to Next Island

Make arrangement for continuing your trip as soon as you can. Ship schedules are posted in shipping agency offices and Tourist Police offices. Departure times are not promised to the minute. The Aegean is its own master, and the ship captains follow its moods. When wind strength reaches Beaufort *strength 8*, all but the very largest ships are kept in port until the wind subsides.

Private Sailboats and Yachts

For some, this is the only way to "do" the Aegean. If this interests you, send for a free copy of *Greece for the Yachtsman* from your nearest G.N.T.O.

Excursion Boats

Many islands have elegant yachts or small launches available for excursion trips to nearby islands, usually allowing a stay of several hours.

AIR TRAVEL

Olympic Airways has exclusivity in serving the Aegean Islands and coastal mainland cities. Their service is year-round (a seasonal schedule, subject to change, is shown on the map as dotted lines).

Domestic air service is heavily booked in the summer months. For a firm commitment, see your travel agent before you leave home. Spring and fall flights are much less crowded, and bookings can be made after your arrival.

The Head Office in Athens is at 96 Syngrou Ave., tel: 92921. For reservations by phone, tel: 9232-323. Ticket office, 6 Othonos St., tel: 9292-444. Athens Hilton Hotel, tel: 9292-445. Flight information, tel: 9811-201/4.

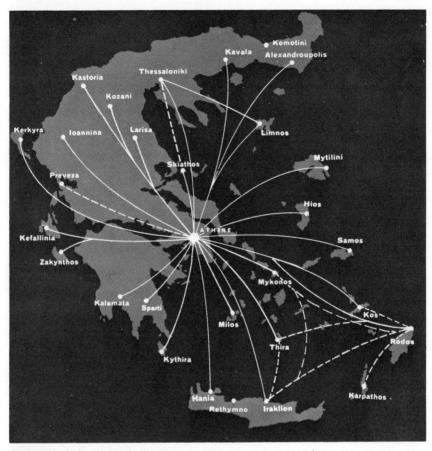

Olympic Airways domestic routes (*Map courtesy Olympic Airways*)

Other Olympic Airways offices are listed on the individual islands and coastal cities.

Bus service to the airport leaves the Olympic Airways downtown terminal at 96 Syngrou Ave., and goes directly to the West Terminal. Regular bus service is from the Othonos St. side of Syntagma Square. Buses leave every twenty minutes and go to the West Terminal.

Olympic Airways offers charter service in Piper Aztec five-seaters or by Alouette Helicopter. The helicopter service is available in case of an emergency departure from an island. This type of service is always handled through the Tourist or regular Police.

Island Arrivals and Departures

Airline buses meet all plane arrivals. Passengers are transported to the main office in the island's largest city. A fare is charged. Departures follow the reverse procedure.

It is wise to make reservations for

departure upon arrival if you intend to fly to your next destination.

BUS AND RAIL TRAVEL

The O.S.E. (Hellenic Railway Organization) operates buses and trains for mainland Greece. Its service is efficient and heavily used. It is best to arrive at a station early and obtain your ticket, especially for the more northerly towns. G.N.T.O. has schedules.

Bus Terminals for the Aegean Islands

Listed below are departure ports, number of buses daily, and the Athens bus terminal addresses.

Kavala: 3 buses daily. 100 Kifission St.
Thessaloniki: 6 buses daily. 100 Kifission St.
Volos: 12–18 buses daily. 260 Liossion St.
Kymi: 8–10 buses daily. 260 Liossion St.
Rafina: Hourly departures. 29 Mavromateon St.
Lavrion: 15 buses daily (by inland route to Cape Sounion). 29 Mavromateon St.

To reach the Kifission St. Terminal, take the No. 62 bus near Ommonia Square.

To reach the Liossion St. Terminal, take the No. 63/64 bus at the entrance to the National Gardens, Syntagma Square.

To reach Mavromateon St. station, take the No.12 bus (Syntagma Square). The station is near the National Archaeological Museum. (Other buses use that route, too.)

Trains

The railway has its main office at 1–3 Karolou St., tel: 5222.491. Inquire there, at the G.N.T.O., or at a tourist agency for information and fares.

LAND TRAVEL

Driving Your Own Car. There is an ample supply of ferryboats to accommodate cars. How practical this is will be your own decision, influenced by the adequacy of the island's network of roads. International driver's license needed.

Rent-a-Car, Mopeds, Bicycles. All but a few islands have rentals of these vehicles. Bring your own auto personal accident and liability insurance identification with you. Read the rental contract before you sign. *Note:* it is illegal to drive a moped between 2:00 A.M. and 6:00 A.M.

Buses. Modern buses serve the islanders and benefit the tourists. The buses run on schedules that are fairly rigid. If you miss the last one, you may have to stay overnight in whatever town you're in. On the small, less touristed islands the buses are apt to be old and complaining. Unpaved roads are like built-in vibrators.

Four-Legged Creatures. There are still places accessible only by mule. The islanders joggle along quite comfortably. Tempted?

"Mai Ta Podia." Greek for "on foot." The supreme delight. May you have many long and enjoyable walks.

ACCOMMODATIONS

In addition to the G.N.T.O. source for accommodations is the Hellenic Chamber of Commerce, 6 Arisdou St., Athens. They will send you information and make hotel reservations. You can write directly to a hotel of your choice, or use the services of your home town tourist agent.

In Athens you can go to the Reservation Office at 2 Karagiorgo St. (near Syntagma Square). This is especially feasible if you want Luxury, A- or B-class hotels. It should be noted that luxury hotels are exempt from government price regulations.

Reservations can be made on arrival at the East Terminal of the Athens Airport, and at the G.N.T.O. desk in the National Bank of Greece in Syntagma Square. Islands that have tourist agencies can make reservations for you on your next island. Very often, in such cases, you are met by the hotel's minibus. Some hotel managers also offer the "next island" reservation service.

All accommodations are classified from Luxury and A-grade through D- and E-grade. While this is an orderly arrangement for prices, it doesn't measure complete standards. Islands differ widely in their accommodations, and you are bound to have a variety of experiences. You may find the hospitality, novelty, and comfort of a room in a Greek home quite rewarding.

Bungalows. For longer stays, bungalows and villas are available, and can be rented through a local tourist agent. They range from modest to luxurious, with prices to fit. Some have maids for cooking and cleaning.

Pensions. A pension can be surprisingly comfortable or next to primitive. Prices are very reasonable for the traveler on a modest budget.

Youth Hostels. Membership cards are advised. They may be obtained from the Greek Youth Hostel Association, 4 Dragatsaniou St., Klafthmonos Square, Athens. There are Youth Hostels in Crete in Ag. Nikolaos, Iraklion, Sitia, and Ierapetra. The islands of Samos and Thera also have hostels.

Monasteries. In isolated areas, a monastery will provide shelter for the night. Men always; women not always.

Tourist Pavilions. These are located at tourist attractions and are supervised by the G.N.T.O. and local authorities. Some provide overnight lodging at exceptionally low costs.

Remote Areas. Accommodations can be spartan in remote villages. You may have to seek out the *Proedros*, the president of the community. If he is not approachable, go to the nearest café or taverna and state your need (sometimes by pantomime). If you are placed in a home for the night, what you pay may have to be "for the children" in order not to insult your host's hospitality.

Camping. This used to be an easy affair, but today it has become more strictly supervised. There is a minimum of official campsites on the islands. Tourist Police will usually cooperate in your request for a campsite if there is no intrusion on personal property. Strict ethical codes from the camper are, of course, expected.

Hawkers. These are Greek persons who wish to rent their rooms. They meet the ships. Their rooms are registered and meet G.N.T.O. specifications.

A Few Additional Facts. Midday is the usual checkout time. All the hotel rooms have a notice tacked to the inside entry door stating prices. These must not be exceeded. It is legal to charge a 10% tax for a stay of less than two nights. There is a 20% surcharge for the addition of a third bed. A 20% discount is allowed when a single person occupies a double room. Rates in spring and fall are lower than in midsummer.

Some hotels charge extra for the use of an air conditioner.

Note: Soap is provided only in the upper class hotels. For the men: Don't be surprised if sometimes you have to sit on your bed or a chair to use your electric shaver. Outlets are mostly in the baseboard near the bedside lamp socket. A converter is needed for 220 V.

CLIMATE AND CLOTHING

The most comfortable time of the year to travel in the islands is in the spring and fall. The weather is more ideal, reservations are easier to obtain, and more accommodations are available without reservations.

There are many travelers who have the entire summer to vagabond among the islands. Usually, these are the backpackers, who have learned wisely and well that the least amount of luggage makes the most comfortable traveling.

The "first timer" should know that traveling in the islands means very few porters or none at all. A remedy that helps this situation is to leave that handsome suitcase in your closet and substitute a canvas duffle bag or one of the new lightweight nylon bags. They're available in many shapes and sizes. Some canvas and awning shops will make a duffle to suit your needs. Clothes folded carefully unpack in a presentable state and it's amazing how much these bags can hold. The sides will always bulge a little for that added item.

Here is a test for the preparing traveler. Fill your selected bag with books or magazines weighing twenty to thirty pounds. Carry it for several blocks and up and down a few flights of stairs. Manageable? Add more weight or take some away until you've reached a weight you can handle. Camera bags, shoulder totes, etc., should be included in the test. Very often, a balanced weight on both sides of the body is most comfortable. When a workable weight has been determined, start planning your wardrobe within these restrictions.

Choice of wardrobe is a very personal thing. There are men who wear their Gucci or Pierre Cardin's, and those who are content with jeans and jerseys. There are women who like to look like fashion models, and those who could care less. Anything and everything in the way of clothes can be seen on the islands. Amidst all the tourist color flair will be the Greeks in their conservative, dark clothing. The garments that hang from the walls of their shops are strictly for tourists.

Practicality enters the picture. The weather influences what one wears. Starting with April, the Aegean climate is spring with a bit of caprice. Sunshine and winter rains have lured the countless wild flowers into bloom. Then one day a cold wind blasts at you in all this spring beauty. You'll be happy to have a warm sweater under a nylon windbreaker, and something on your head! The next day is overly warm. You'll want bare arms, lightweight clothing.

It's too cool for swimming in the Aegean in April. Still, the beaches are filled with sunbathers.

May is more consistently moderate, though when the wind comes up you'll want your sweater again, with or without your windbreaker. Days are warm, evenings cool.

The summer months of June, July, August, and part of September are warm to hot. A breezy evening will be more comfortable with a sweater.

In October and early November, you'll need sweaters in the morning and evening; days are mild.

Yes, it does rain occasionally. The lightest plastic poncho or raincoat is practical, something you can pack away and hope never to use.

You'll need a good walking shoe with thick soles to protect your feet on stony pathways, and swim gear. There are nude beaches on several of the islands.

The time and duration of your trip, plus the way you intend to spend your days and nights, will dictate the wardrobe you choose. Maybe you'll be wearing those Greek dresses, and use the Greek-type shoulder bag. If you are a man, perhaps you'll go for those jauntily-striped shirts. Other tourists will look at you and think, "That looks good on him (or her); maybe I'll buy one."

The photographs in this book were

taken in April, May, June, September, and October. As you can see, anything goes!

MANNERS, CUSTOMS, AND SOCIABILITY

Your entire trip could be classified as entertainment. People, places, and things, and not the least of which will be your experience with the Greeks.

If you are fortunate enough to be invited into a Greek home, accept by all means. The Greeks are noted for the warmth of their hospitality. Often, the greeting is an embrace and a kiss on the cheek. Small glasses of *ouzo* are served if the family can afford it. It is customary for the man guest to drink it in one gulp and the woman guest to sip it or just wet her lips. This is followed by a "spoon sweet," syrupy and fruity. A special tray with notches for spoons is passed. The oldest guest is served first. If you are the only guest, you may be the only one served regardless of the numbers of family members present. A glass of water is then served and raised as a toast. A simple one to remember is *"Yassis"* ("To your health"). The water, fortunately, takes away the sweet taste.

Sociability in villages is often more robust than in larger towns. Festivals may become very uninhibited. Eating from another's fork, perhaps with meat on the tines, is common. It may almost literally be thrust at your face. You are expected to take the meat in one bite and follow it with a gulp of wine. As a guest, special attention may be paid to you. It is best to get into the game and do as the others do. The entire procedure is done with good spirits verging on hilarity.

In small, remote villages you may not be spoken to until you speak first. Then, the results can be a bit overwhelming. People will approach to "inspect you," and if they know a little English, they will ask questions. Still, the traveler should remember that a lot of tourism changes a lot of simple customs, so seek out these experiences and enjoy as much as you can.

Music and Dancing. One could conjecture that the Greeks have music and dancing in their genes. Nothing can keep a Greek from expressing high spirits, a condition known as *Kefi*. The culmination of this joy and satisfaction finds its favorite expression in dance. Although dances include much improvisation, some basic forms remain. *Pedecto:* Has jumping, stamping, leaping, and hopping. As an aside, it should be mentioned that the Greek woman is expected to dance with dignity and skip the acrobatics. *Syrtos:* A joyous, peasant dance in 7/8 time, popular all over Greece. *Hassapiko:* Anthony Quinn did it in *Zorba*, and it has become a favorite. Done with arms outstretched, resembling wings, the dance is known as the eagle dance. It is slow-moving and introspective. One dances as if in a trance. Spectator applause is considered ill-mannered. *Syrtaki:* A most popular taverna dance. Here, men and women, arms around each other's shoulders, move with unity, eyes downcast; supposedly the dancers are quite lost in their celebration of wine and each other's company. The hand on the shoulder signals the next move.

The *bouzouki* and violin are descendants of the ancient lyre, Apollo's instrument. The clarinet evolved from the reed pipe used when Dionysos was worshipped. Sad to say, the juke box has become the most economical and practical source of music, but the joy and exhilaration remain the same.

FOOD AND DRINK

The traditional nontourist Greek cafe and taverna is patronized by males. It is their political forum and local club. Tourists are welcome, and if you speak

Greek and wish to enter into a conversation, they will willingly include you. Often a Greek who has returned from America will corner you and "bend your ear." Questions tend to be personal in nature. Don't be affronted, that's the Greek way. Greeks love to be in a crowd and spend free time talking. One suspects that conversations are often argumentative, judging by the heated emotions and gestures. It seems they are more interested in the complexity of their subject than in its solution. Men gossip and enjoy it, and they are particularly interested in the moral frailties of their fellow men.

After eating at the same restaurant several times, you will be recognized by the proprietor, who may come forward and shake hands. Inquiring about your health is *de rigueur*. "Welcome, glad to see you," may be the greeting; the parting, "Keep well."

In almost all island eating places you will go to the food counters, make your selection, return to your table, and have your food brought by the waiter. More formal hotel dining rooms and A- and B-class restaurants have menus, and waiters take your order. Two prices are listed in two columns. One is for the food, the second is for food plus a service charge. Theoretically, this eliminates tipping; if you add more, it is by choice. Most people do.

The *mikros*, the boy who brings the bread and beverages, is tipped by leaving a few drachmas on the table, not on the plate holding the bill.

Appetizers

Mezes. The word means "bits of food to whet the appetite." Custom dictates that they be served with *ouzo*, but they can be ordered separately. The bits include such food as olives, cheeses, pickled vegetables, smoked herring, crispy fried octopus, squid, shrimp, anchovies, bite-sized meat-balls, and tomato and cucumber slices. Superlative is the *taromosalata*, a pâté made with fish roe. This is heaped on bite-sized pieces of crusty bread and popped into the mouth.

Appetizers play an important role in Greek life, for they reflect the Greek's enjoyment of socializing and drinking at a taverna before dinner.

Soups

Soupa. Egg and lemon soup with a chicken broth base is a typical Greek soup. So are fish- and meat-based soups such as *youvarlakia* (meatball) and *kota me prasa* (chicken and leek soup). Fish soup, called *psarasoupa*, sometimes shrieks with garlic. Yogurt soup, *yiaourti soupa*, is an icy summer soup with the surprise of ground walnuts in it. Other less glamorous soups are made with lentils, *faki soupa*, or beans, *fassoulada soupa*. In most restaurants the soup is listed as "soup of the day," and seems to be a blend of whatever the cook has the most of.

Vegetables and Salads

Greeks love their fresh vegetables. In seasonal abundance are artichokes, carrots, eggplant (auberge), cabbage, lettuce, onion, leeks, zucchini, green beans, tomatoes, and potatoes. The tourist will experience potatoes *ad infinitum,* and always fried. The so-called Greek Salad will have tomatoes, cucumbers, olives, and feta cheese lavished with olive oil unless you say "ohi ladi" ("no oil"). "Just a little" is a gesture made with fingers indicating a small amount.

Other specialties: *Melitzanes yemistes,* a regal dish of lamb and a vegetable mélange.

Dolmathes, grape leaves filled with meat, rice, tomato, and spices, eaten plain or smothered with lemon sauce.

Spanakopitta, spinach pie: *phyllo* dough filled with spinach and feta cheese and served warm. Tourists walk down the street munching happily.

Yemistes Domates avegolemono. Tomatoes stuffed with onions, rice, beef, and pine nuts, baked and served with or without a lemon sauce.

Meats

Koto or *kotopoula* is chicken. Often whole birds, spit-roasted and served with a variety of sauces.

Lamb (*arni*) is the most commonly used meat, and is stewed, broiled, skewered, braised with every kind of vegetable, plus spit-roasted as a whole carcass.

Beef (*volthino* or *volthines*). Often served as steaks and stews embellished with nut and cheese variations, spices, and sauces. A favorite is meatballs, called *youvarlakia*. An American-type steak is usually disappointing. *Moussaka* is every tourist's standby: ground meat with eggplant, or other vegetables layered and topped with an egg sauce.

Pastas

There are more than thirty ways of combining pastas with sauces based on feta cheese, smoked sausage, vegetables, grated hard cheese, meats, eggs, fish, or any food the cook is inspired to use.

Fish

Barbounia (red mullet) and *maridhes* (whitebait) are the most common island fish. Octopus and squid are often prepared in a wine sauce. Baby squid is usually crisply fried.

Eggs and Cheese

If none of this appeals to you, there is always the omelette. Many kinds are available. Cheeses are limited. There is a Greek *gruyere*, blue cheese, hard yellow, and white cheeses. The feta is soft, crumbly, dry goat's cheese, very often eaten with olive oil poured over it.

Desserts

Those with a sweet tooth will find intense gratification in the sugary, syrupy, fruity, nutty desserts: *baklava*, a honeyed pastry with nuts; *galato-boureko*, custard with *phyllo* topping drenched with a spicy orange syrup; *halvah*, many ways to make it, but usually with walnuts, almonds, and pistachios; *kourabiedes*, a heavenly cookie that will shower you with powdered sugar; and *loukoumades*, honey puffs, deep-fried, drowned in honey, rescued and rolled in walnut pieces; *rizogalo*, a rice pudding, and yogurt with honey or fresh strawberries are also favorites.

Fruits

In their season, there will be apples, pears, peaches, oranges, cherries, melons, grapes, apricots, watermelons, and lemons.

Beverages

New to the tourist may be *ouzo* (anise-flavored) and *retsina*. *Ouzo* is served with water which, when added, clouds the drink. *Raki* is stronger than *ouzo* and, if that isn't strong enough, try *mournoraki*. *Retsina* is a resinated wine best drunk with a meal. It combines well with food flavors; at least, the Greeks think so. *Kokinelli* is another resinated wine rather like a rosé. If you want an unresinated wine, ask for *aretsinoto*. *Domestica*, light and fine, is available and moderately priced. *Malevizi* is a sweet dessert wine. It is always worth it to try the wine from barrels that line the walls of some tavernas and restaurants.

Brandy and beer (*birra*) drinkers will be well cared for. *Metaxa* brandy, for example, comes in various proofs (two to seven stars). Fix, Amstel, and

Henninger beer by the truckfuls arrive by ship constantly. So do the soft drinks, colas, and fruit juices. Bottled water is available. Tea (*tsai*) is a breakfast drink, as is decaffeinated coffee. Greek coffee, *cafedaki*, also known as Turkish coffee, is served in a small cup, and the grounds are allowed to settle; they are not for drinking. For sweet, ask for *gliko*. Medium is *metrio*, unsweetened is *sketo*.

Water

Bottled water is available, either plain or carbonated. When you purchase it at the grocery store be sure that the top is completely sealed. Many restaurant diners buy bottled water. Others ask for tap water. The only rule to follow is personal judgement or preference.

Picnic

Somewhere on the islands, try wandering off for a picnic. A flight bag can hold the "makings."

MONEY

The Greek currency unit is the drachma, abbreviated to drs. Drachma coins come in 20-, 10-, 5-, 2- and 1-unit pieces. Occasionally, you will see a 30-drs. unit.
Paper Money. Blue: 50 drachmas. *Red:* 100 drachmas. *Green:* 500 drachmas. *Brown:* 1,000 drachmas.
Arrival Currency. Some travelers feel more comfortable on arrival with at least a small amount of drachmas for minor expenses. These can generally be obtained at your local bank, prepackaged. However, you'll get at least 10% less than you'd receive abroad.

Travelers checks usually bring the highest rate of exchange. Banks, foreign exchange brokers, government tourist offices and issuing companies charge a modest 1.5% for currency con-

version. These offices are located at Greek airports, border crossings and port cities. Airport banks have daytime hours only.

METRIC CONVERSION*

LENGTHS AND WIDTHS

Inches $\times$ 25 = millimeters
Inches $\times$ 2.5 = centimeters
Feet $\times$ 30 = centimeters
Yards $\times$ 0.9 = meters
Miles $\times$ 1.6 = kilometers
Millimeters $\times$ 0.04 = inches
Centimeters $\times$ 0.4 = inches
Meters $\times$ 3.3 = feet
Meters $\times$ 1.1 = yards
Kilometers $\times$ 0.6 = miles

TEMPERATURE

Celsius to Fahrenheit: $\times$ 1.8 (+32)
Fahrenheit to Celsius: $\times$ 0.56 (−32)

WEIGHT

Ounces $\times$ 28 = grams
Pounds $\times$ 0.45 = kilograms
Grams $\times$ 0.035 = ounces
Kilograms $\times$ 2.2 = pounds

VOLUME

Pints $\times$ 0.47 = liters
Quarts $\times$ 0.95 = liters
Liters $\times$ 2.1 = pints
Liters $\times$ 1.06 = quarts

MINI-VOCABULARY

It is not too difficult to make yourself understood for basic needs. Most islanders who deal with tourists have already acquired a partial vocabulary of foreign words.

Salespeople will pencil the price of items on their wrapping paper near the cash register, and the exchange of money is done with smiles instead of words.

Here are a few words and phrases, with their phonetic pronunciations, to

*Approximate.

enhance your communications. Accented syllables are capitalized.

GENERAL

Please: pah-rah-kah-LOW
Thank you: ef-hah-ris-STOWE
You're welcome: pah-rah-kah-LOW
Thank you very much: ef-hah-ris-STOWE-po-LEE
Yes: NEH
No: OH-he
Good morning: kah-lee-MEH-rah
Good evening: kah-lee-SPEH-rah
Good night: kah-lee-NIK-ta
Hello (or) *goodbye:* YAH-sas
Excuse me: sig-NO-mee
Does someone speak English?: mil-EYE-kan-KNEES-an-glee-KAH?
It's O.K.: en-TA-xi
It's not O.K.: THEN-EE-ney-en-TA-xi
Today: SEE-meh-rah
Tomorrow: AH-vri-oh
Yesterday: ekh-TESS
Here: eh-THOUGH
There: eh-KEY
Big: meh-GHA-loss
Small: me-CROSS
What?: TEA?
When?: POH-teh?
Why?: yah-TEA?
What time is it?: TEE-OH-rah-EE-neh
Come: EH-lah
Go away!: FEE-yeh-ah-poh-THOUGH

"THANK YOU" is an important phrase in any language so, in case you have trouble memorizing the above, here is a simplified way of mastering "thank you" in Greek: F. Harry STOWE.

ISLAND TRAVEL

Where is the Tourist Police Office?: POU-EE-neh-ee-tou-ris-tea-KEY-ahs-tea-no-ME-ah?
Port: lee-MAH-knee
Bus: leh-oh-foh-REE-oh
Bus stop: STAH-sis
Please show me on the map: SAS-pah-rah-kah-LOW THEE-kseh-moo-stowe-KHAR-tea

I want a ticket to (name your island): THEH-low-EH-nah-tea-KEH-toe-yiah. . .
What time will the ship arrive?: TEA-OH-rah-ERR-heh-teh-toe-PLEA-oh?
I am lost: EH-hah-sah-toe-DROH-moh
I have lost. . .: EH-hah-sah. . .
Where is the policeman?: POU-EE-neh-ee-ahs-tea-noh-MEE-ah?
Where is the post office?: POU-EE-neh-toe-tah-he-droh-ME-oh?
Where can I telephone?: POU-boh-ROW-nah-tea-leh-foh-KNEE-soh?
Postage stamp: grah-mah-TOE-see-moh
I need a room with: THEH-low-though-MAH-tea-oh-meh:
one bed: EH-nah-kreh-VAH-tea
two beds: THEE-oh-kreh-VAH-tyah
three beds: TREE-AH-kreh-VAH-tya
I will stay: thah-ME-noh:
one week: ME-ah-ev-though-MAH-thah
one night: EH-nah-VRAH-thee
two nights: THEE-oh-VRAH-thee-ah
three nights: TREE-ah-VRAH-thee-ah
How much is this room?: POH-soh-toh-though-MAH-tea-oh
The bill, please: ton-loh-gah-rya-SMO-pah-rah-kah-LOW
I need: THEH-low:
a towel: peh-TSEH-tah
a water glass: EH-nah-poh-TEA-ree
another pillow: KEY-UH-low-mah-ksee-LAH-ree
another blanket: KEY-UH-lee-kou-VER-tah
clean sheets: kah-thah-RAH-sen-TOE-nya
a doctor: EH-na-yia-TROW

PICNIC ITEMS

Bread: psoh-ME
Cheese: tea-REE
Fish: PSAH-ree
Chicken: koh-TOH-pou-loh

Fruit: FRU-toe
Milk: GHAH-lah
Water: neh-ROW
Beer: BEE-rah
Wine: krah-SEE
Yogurt: yiah-OOR-tea
Lemonade: leh-moh-NAH-thah

MORE USEFUL FACTS

Tourist Police. The Tourist Police are the question-and-answer officials of the Greek National Tourist Organization. You'll find them at the docks when the ships arrive, or in nearby offices. You will know them by their trim uniforms with badges on the sleeve which indicate the language they speak. Handsome, affable, and with ready smiles, they will assist you in finding rooms in private homes, provide hotel and camping information, and help you with any tourist-type problems you may have. On islands where there are no Tourist Police, it is advisable to go to the regular police.

Health. Protective sunscreens, dark glasses, seasickness pills, headache pills, and a cure for diarrhea are a few of the basics. Mosquito repellents are needed in some areas. At night do not open your windows or doors if your lights are on. With lights off you are safe, and the annoying insects are not tempted to join you. If camping out, you may want to have a bug spray.

Before you leave home you could consider a short-term medical policy that covers illness and accidents. Keep all claim slips if the policy is used.

Greek hospitals are well-appointed, and islands have doctors and pharmacists. There is helicopter service to Athens if your problem is serious. Tourist Police or regular police handle this, but you must pay the bill.

Post Office (Tachidromio). The more populated islands have a main post office. On very sparsely populated islands the postal service may be in a bakery or café. Hours of service vary

according to need, but they are all closed during the siesta. Stamps (*grammatosima*) are sold at the post office, and also at kiosks. At the latter, you are expected to purchase a post card along with the stamp. Most islands have bright yellow post boxes; usually they are near the landing dock or on the main street.

Mail goes to Athens by boat, then by airmail. Post offices have free airmail stickers.

Telephone. All over Greece the telephone service is known as the OTE (Organism Telephikinonion Ellathos). Loosely translated, this means local and overseas telephone communication service. Very often it is in the post office, but separate from postal authority. Calls can be made direct or collect (reverse charges). Telegrams can be sent, and you can call direct abroad. Lines can be very busy, and unlimited patience is needed. Dial as fast as you can so no one interrupts.

Higher-class hotels have phones. As a courtesy, the manager will put through a call to the hotel on your next island, and make or confirm a reservation.

Electricity. 220 Volts A.C. Converter and/or adapter needed. Some islands have 110 D.C. Sockets are two and three pins.

Siesta. Hours are set by police authorities. Usually shops are open 8:00 A.M. to 1:30 P.M. and 5:00 to 8:00 P.M. Cafés are open until after midnight. Nightclubs are open from 9:00 P.M. to 5:00 A.M.

Greek Spelling. There is no standard formula for the spelling of Greek islands, towns, and places of tourist interest. This amounts to idiosyncrasies and a mass of contradictions. In this book we have used the spellings used on the individual islands, and this accounts for many of the differences you may find. Abbreviations help to simplify things. For example: Agios,

Aghios, Agias, and Aghias have become *Ag.* in this book.

If you are a Greek scholar you will know the correct term. If you are a happy-go-lucky vacationer you will have the information you need, plus the added interest of noting how many spellings a word can have.

G.N.T.O.
INFORMATION SOURCES

The following telephone numbers can be used when calling from the U.S.A. to the country listed. For other international dialing, readers should consult the operator or local phone directory.

USA

New York (Main Office):
Greek National Tourist Organization
645 Fifth Avenue
Olympic Tower (Fifth Floor)
New York, New York 10022
Tel. (212) 421-5777
Telex: 66.489

Chicago (Regional Office):
Greek National Tourist Organization
168 North Michigan Avenue
National Bank of Greece Building
Chicago, Illinois 60601
Tel. (312) 782-1084
Telex : 283.468

Los Angeles (Regional Office):
Greek National Tourist Organization
627 West Sixth Street
Los Angeles, California 90017
Tel. (213) 626-6696
Telex : 686.441

CANADA

Montreal (Regional Office):
Greek National Tourist Organization
2, Place Ville Marie
Suite 67, Essa Plaza
Montreal, Quebec H3B 2C9
Tel. (514) 871-1535
Telex : 60.021

EUROPE

UNITED KINGDOM & IRELAND
Greek National Tourist Organization
196-7 Regent Street
London, England WIR 8DR
Tel. (441) 7345.997
Telex : 21.122

FRANCE
Office National Hellénique du
Tourisme
3, Avenue de L'Opéra
Paris, France 75001
Tel. (331) 2606.534, 2606.575,
2605.022
Telex: 680.345

ITALY
Rome (Main Office):
Ente Nazionale Ellenico per il Turismo
Via L. Bissolati 78-80
Roma, Italy 00187
Tel. (396) 487.249, 487.301
Telex: 611.331
Milan (Regional Office):
Ente Nazionale Ellenica per il Turismo
Piazza Diaz 1 (Angolo via Rastrelli)
Milano, Italy
Tel. (392) 860.470, 860.477
Telex: 62.331

BELGIUM & LUXEMBOURG
Office National Hellénique du
Tourisme
62-66 Boulevard de l' Impératrice
Bruxelles, Belgium 1000
Tel. (322) 5130.206, 5132.712
Telex: 24.044

NETHERLANDS
Griekse Nationale Organizatie Voor
Toerisme
Leidsestraat 13
Amsterdam, Netherlands
Tel. (3120) 254.212, 254.213
Telex: 15.465

WEST GERMANY
Frankfurt (Main Office):
Griechische Zentrale Für Fremden-
verkehr
Neue Mainzer Strasse 22
6 Frankfurt/Main 1, West Germany

Tel. (49611) 236.562, 236.563
Telex: 412.034

Munich (Regional Office):
Griechische Zentrale Für Fremden-
verkehr
Pacelli Strasse 2
8000 München 2, West Germany
Tel. (4989) 222.035, 222.036
Telex: 528.126

AUSTRIA
Griechische Zentrale Für Fremden-
verkehr
Kärtner Ring 5
1015 Wein, Austria
Tel. (43222) 525.317, 555.318
Telex: 111.816

SWITZERLAND
Griechische Zentrale Für Fremden-
verkehr
Gottfried Keller Strasse 7
8001 Zürich, Switzerland
Tel. (411) 328.487
Telex: 57.720

SWEDEN
Grekiska Statens Turistbyrá
Grev Turegaten 2
P.O. Box 5298
10246 Stockholm 5, Sweden
Tel. (468) 211.113, 203.802, 208.061
Telex: 10.443

DENMARK
Det Graeske Turistbureau
Vester Fartmagsgade 3
DK 1606, Cöpenhagen

FINLAND
Kreikan Valtion Matkailutomist
150, Roobertinkatu 3-5 C 38
Helsinki 12, Finland

MIDDLE EAST
Bahrain
Greek National Tourist Organization
Canoo Building, 5th Floor
Manama, Bahrain
Tel. (973) 259.211, 259.212

ASIA
JAPAN
Greek National Tourist Organization
11, Mori Building, 2-6-4 Toranomon
Minato-Ku, Tokyo 105, Japan
Tel. (813) 5035.001, 5035.002
Telex: 222.5529

AUSTRALIA & NEW ZEALAND
Greek National Tourist Organization
51-57 Pitt Street
Sydney, N.S.W. 2000, Australia
Tel. (612) 2411.663, 2411.664
Telex: 25.209

SOUTH AFRICA
Greek National Tourist Organization
108 Fox Street
Homes Trust Building
Johannesburg, South Africa
Tel. (2711) 8342.551
Telex: 82.786

G.N.T.O.
INFORMATION SERVICES
IN GREECE
ATHENS
National Tourist Organization (EOT in
Greek) has its main office at 2 Amerikis
St., Athens 133, Greece, tel. (301)
3223.111-9, telex: 5832. *Information
Desks:* East Main Airport at Eliniko,
tel. 9799.500; National Bank of
Greece at 2 Karagiorgo Servias St.
(ground floor), tel. 32222.545; Port of
Piraeus at Directorate of Tourism, 105
Vassilisis Sofias St., tel. 4129.492 or
4121.400.

THESSALONIKI
34 Mitropoleos St.
Tel. (3031) 271.888, 222.935

KAVALA
2 Filelinon St.
Tel. (3051) 228.762, 222.425

VOLOS
Riga Feraiou Square
Tel. (30421) 23.500, 24.915

CRETE
Heraklion:
1 Xanthoudidou St.
Tel. (3081) 282.096
Information Office: tel. (3081)
222.487, 222.488

Hania:
6 Akti Tombazi
Tel. (30821) 26.426

DODECANESE ISLANDS
Rhodes:
Archbishop Makarios & Papagou Sts.
Tel. (30241) 23.255, 23.655

Kos:
Information desk at Akti Koundourioti
Tel. (30242) 28.724

II
the sporades

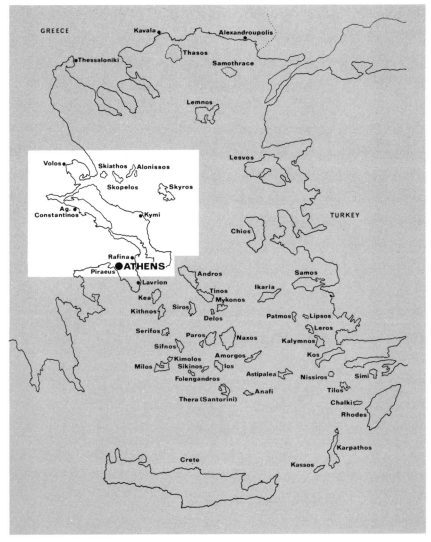

skiathos

GETTING THERE

By bus. From Athens to: Volos or Ag. Constantinos. (See Alkyon Travel Agency, 98 Academia St., if you wish to buy a combination bus and ship ticket.)

By train. From Athens to: Volos (via Lamia). Athens Ticket Office: 6 Sina St., tel. 36244025 or 3231368.

By ship. From Volos: 11 to 16 times weekly.

From Ag. Constantinos: 4 to 8 times weekly.

From Skopelos: 11 to 16 times weekly, via Kymi.

DEPARTURES

To Volos, Ag. Constantinos, and Skopelos: same ship schedules as above.

To islands of the Northeast Aegean: From Ag. Constantinos: 1 ship weekly.

AIR FLIGHTS

Daily except Thursday between Thessaloniki and Skiathos. Daily between Athens and Skiathos.

TOURIST TIPS

Skiathos has an area of 61 sq. km./24 sq. mi. Its population is 3,000. An air flight to Skiathos is the quickest for those who must budget their time. Make reservations ahead of time. In Skiathos, the airline bus will transport you to its Olympic office midtown. Or, if you have a reservation at an outlying hotel, its bus will whisk you to the hotel's private world.

For those with more leisure, a bus or train trip to Volos or Ag. Constantinos is a good way to see rural Greece. If you sail from Volos on a weekend, the Greek passengers will be in a festive mood. Dancing on deck in the morning? But, of course!

Skiathos has an excellent yacht and refueling station. There are several laundries and dry cleaning establishments. Calls to Volos and Athens can be dialed directly from the OTE. The town has a well-equipped clinic and pharmacy, staffed by a doctor and a nurse (tel. 42040). Schedules for local buses are posted on a bulletin board near the steamer landing dock. Taxis: tel. 42589, 42355, or 42758. See Tourist Police for rooms in private homes.

HOTELS*

Skiathos: (B) Alkyon. (C) Acti, Belvedere, Hotel San Remo, Koukounaries. (D) Hotel Avra. *Pensions:* Lazou, Mary's Guest House, Sarri. *Hostel:* Kira Dimitri.

Ahlaidas: (A) Esperides.

Tzaneria: (A) Nostos.

Koukounaries: (L) Skiathos Palace. (B) Xenia.

*See Part I, section on Accommodations, for explanation of hotel grades.

Apartment-hotel units and villas: Arrange through local tourist agencies or the Alkyon Tourist Agency, who represent the Sporades.

Megali Ammos: Hostels: Kamatarakias, Stamelos, Ella Pienaar.

HISTORY

11th Century B.C. Ancient settlement flourished, according to modern findings of surface pottery. *480 B.C.* Persian and Greek ships battle at sea. Island governed by Athens. *351 B.C.* About this time island minted its own money. *338 B.C.* Philip of Macedon took Skiathos. Devastated it upon leaving. *A.D. 325* Byzantine period began. Christianity gains a foothold. *1204* Island made a barony under the Ghizi family. *1400* Piracy rampant. Islanders moved to the Kastro, an impregnable fortress that became their main town. *1475* Turkish rule began. *1538* Barbarossa, the pirate, captured Skiathos. Three thousand islanders became slaves. *1745* People start to leave the Kastro and build their harbor town. *1807 Klephts* (guerrillas) plan Greek independence. First Greek flag is made. *1829* Greek independence begins. *1944* Many Allied soldiers were helped to escape by the Skiatotes.

SKIATHOS TOWN

When the Skiatotes came down from the Kastro, they chose a beautiful, natural bay on their small island and built their town between two pine-studded hills. Houses were painted white and roofed with red tile. Today, with the indigo blue bay as a frontage, brightly canopied cafés along the waterfront, and the green hills as a background, the town is smart and handsome.

The harbor faces southeast and southwest. At its corner is the islet,

Bourtzi, connected to the mainland by a narrow causeway. The Venetians used this area as a fortress; several ancient and benign cannons still point toward the sea. Below the fortress walls are huge, sun-warmed boulders, a favorite place for bikini-clad swimmers to sun idly or make arched dives into the sea. At night, within the fortress walls, and chaperoned by stately pine trees, disco dancers action-pack the hours.

Skiathos differs from most Aegean islands because of the English-speaking residents who own villas, live in them part of the year, then offer them for rent. Many of these homes are beach villas; others are "cliff hangers" with spectacular views. The presence of the English has given this Greek town an added dimension.

The waterfront (*paralia*) has a lazy, indulging kind of charm. The cafés have cushioned chairs for customers to sprawl in. Waiters hover to take your order for a cool drink or a delectable dessert. The latest English-language newspapers, magazines, and paperbacks are available. Your fellow tourists offer excellent people-watching. The luxury yachts are lined up in handsome array, and fishing boats chug in and out, momentarily roughing the smooth bay. There is no mistaking the aura of importance that hovers over Skiathos town, the result of its "in" reputation. Deciphered, its message could read, "Enjoy, enjoy!"

Dining and Entertainment

There are more than thirty cafes, tavernas, and restaurants for you to explore, all eager for your patronage.

The harbor frontage is a favorite spot to gather for breakfast. Here you will see tourists eating freshly baked buttered bread and yogurt smothered with honey, and drinking Turkish coffee.

Skiathos Town

At the corner opposite Bourtzi, there is a self-service cafeteria where you can buy bacon and eggs, orange juice, and milk. The cafeteria also has a bagged picnic-lunch service.

True Greek cuisine is plenteous and delectable. Seafood devotees should try VRACHOS restaurant above the harbor's west side, atop a flight of wide, shallow steps. Recommended for a starter is the *tzatziki* (cucumbers mashed with garlic and yogurt). Lobsters, prawns, and many kinds of fish, including *barbounia*, are good choices. An accompaniment could be thinly sliced, deep-fried eggplant, and, of course, the ubiquitous Greek salad of olives, tomatoes, and feta cheese.

MANDRAKI restaurant enjoys an excellent reputation. Spinach served with pine nuts and a cheese pastry called *tiriopita* are specialties.

FILIPAS restaurant blends olive oil, lemon juice, and herbs to embellish their sea bass, *synagrida*. Their stuffed green peppers, zucchini, tomatoes, or eggplant offer a substantial, tasty dish.

The town has more than a dozen bakeries. Try the *koulouris* (circular rolls topped with sesame seeds). Or *loukoumades* (small, crisp doughnuts sprinkled with cinnamon and deluged with honey). Then *baklava* or some almond candies—sinfully rich!

About seven in the evening the *volta* (promenade) starts along the waterfront. Search out the taverna with the most tempting plate of *mezes* (hors d'oeuvres). Grilled octopus, *taromosalata* (a pâté made with fish roe), with bread wedges, olives, and feta cheese is a good sample plate.

A favorite Skiathos drink is the Petraki Special, made with brandy and lemonade with added lemon juice. Local wines are St. Helena, Pallini, Achaia, and the sweet Mavrodaphne.

Dining is apt to be animated and extroverted. As you wander through the town, you may be attracted to the restaurants that have the most action: juke box music, laughter, loud voices, impromptu dancing. If you want a quiet atmosphere, keep on looking.

Chances are you will find that perfect little garden restaurant behind white, flowered walls, where tables cluster cozily under low trees bedecked with twinkling lights.

Nightclub life is informal and lively. Bourtzi has been mentioned. Near the steamer landing are several discos which open late at night, but go until dawn. The Bourgois, Scuna, and Porto Fino all have their dedicated followers. Megali Ammos, 1 km. from town, specializes in Greek dancing.

Skiathos Palace Hotel has a night-club, as does the Hotel Nostos. The Xeniá has a roof-top bar. Talagria has an open garden, *bouzouki* music, and dancing.

There are two movie houses. Programs are changed three times a week, and English films have Greek subtitles.

How about a moonlight sail on a warm night? Perhaps a swim? Star-studded sky, cool breeze. . .

Shopping

The inveterate shopper can anticipate hours of searching in the town's ninety gift shops. Tempting are such articles as antique silver buckles, intricately appliquéd folk costumes (old, but chic), exact hand-painted copies of Byzantine icons, batiks, embroideries, jewelry, hand-forged copperware, fishermen's caps—the list goes on and on.

Art galleries offer paintings and graphics. Antique dealers have scouted the island, and to browse in their shops is to see a visual history of the island's past.

Handwoven and embroidered linens are proudly shown by their creators, the price commensurate with the degree of skill involved in making them.

If you must have that old chest, that large rug, that immense copper tub, you will find the shopkeepers ready to ship it for you—at a price, of course.

Beaches

During the bathing season (from April to October), small boats go to the various beaches and to the island, Tsoungriaki. The large beaches have windsailing, speedboat, and water-skiing equipment for rent.

Skiathos is touted as a bathing resort and rightly so. It boasts seventy sandy beaches and coves with excellent, safe bathing and underwater swimming on its thirty miles of coastline. If you desire your own private beach, hire a boat owner to take you to it and pick you up later. Pay half when you leave and the remainder when you are delivered back to the harbor.

The bus provides regular service from town to Koukounaries Bay and back (total distance 11½ km./7 mi.). En route are the following bus-stop beaches:

Megali Ammos. Nearest to town (1 km./5/8 mi.), but least attractive. Taverna with Greek dancing.

Ahlaidas. Near Esperides Hotel (3½ km./2¼ mi.). Good snorkeling; wide, sandy beach. Huge plane tree for shade and picnic.

Kalamaki Peninsula. This area (5 km./ 3 mi.) has two beaches: *Tzaneria*, a small beach near a large number of holiday villas, and *Kanapitsa*, a larger beach with water skiing, small boats for hire, mini-sailers for children, and a taverna. On this headland are several bays and coves for you to explore.

Argyrolimnos and Kolios. These beaches are reached from the Tzaneria bus stop. An access road drops steeply to a path that divides. To the left is *Argyrolimnos*, a wide, sandy beach with plenty of pine shade and safe, good swimming. From here, you can climb and scramble your way around the headland to *Kolios*, located on a beautifully curved, shallow bay. Walk on to *Paraskevi* (2 km./1.2 mi.) for a bus back to town.

Koukounaries Beach

Megas Aselinos, on the north side of island, is an hour-and-a-half walk from the bus stop at Eikonistrias (7½ km./ 4½ mi.). Rocky, steep shelves provide access to water.

Troulos. (8 km./4.8 mi.). A wide, sandy, shallow beach. Taverna.

Mandraki. (10 km./6 mi.). A half-hour walk through shade woods to a big, sand-duned beach, unique on the island. Good snorkeling on the left.

Koukounaries. (11½ km./6.9 mi.). End of coastal bus line. Between the Xenia Hotel and the Skiathos Palace Hotel, this long, sweeping curve of a beach is claimed to be the best in Greece. The beach taverna serves meals, as do the hotels. Hotel dining requires proper cover-ups.

Ag. Eleni. A short walk from Koukounaries, accessible by car. A wide, sandy beach with fine views.

Kechria. A beautiful little beach recommended as a stop if you are on a boat trip around the island.

Tsoungriaki Island. Also known as Banana Beach. No cover-ups; in fact, no swimsuits. Nudity for one and all. This island has regular boat service. Make your own arrangements.

Lalaria. See *Excursions.*

Note: In season, there are daily boat trips to such beaches as Ahlaidas, Koukounaries, and Lalaria.

Excursions

Details such as prices and sailing hours are displayed on notice boards in front of the boats that make excursions. Moored along the waterfront, these boats generally make morning and afternoon trips, weather permitting.

Boats are available for rental, too, if you want to be on your own. Cars and jeeps, motor and rental bikes are also available.

There are daily boat trips to the islands of Skopelos and Alonissos. Skiathos has several grottos which can only be entered by a very small boat. According to reports, this is an "into this world" experience, almost unbelievable in its eerie effects.

A trip to *Lalaria Beach* and *the Kastro* is highly recommended. The stop at Lalaria Beach gives you time for a swim and a climb to the Kastro, a fortified, abandoned town, fronted by an unscalable cliff. It was here that the islanders sought refuge from marauding pirates, among them Barbarossa, the Turkish "Red Beard." Now overgrown with tall grasses and wild flowers, there remain a few foundations from the town's three-hundred homes and twenty-two churches. One intact church, near the footpath, is especially interesting. Note the willow-pattern china plates set into the walls, evidence that local seamen traveled far afield.

When your launch blasts its horn, you descend the steep path, take off your shoes, wade to the boat ramp, and motor away from this most beautiful, pebbled beach. The sea will be green, cerulean-streaked, changing to purple, and the sky a pale blue. The cut of the boat makes white waves. The breeze will be cool. You settle in your seat, completely absorbed in the moment.

Dedicated fishers can arrange expeditions with the harbor boat owners. Fish that may take your hook include red mullet, blackfish, red snapper, pike, hornfish, blacktail, and pagellus.

There are mule trips to *Evangelistria Monastery*. See a travel agent for arrangements.

For Naturalists and Hikers

Skiathos has pine forests, olive groves, magnificent scenery, well-watered valleys, and giant plane, poplar, and chestnut trees. In spring, there is a wealth of wild flowers. More than 250 species of birds can be seen between March and October. Marine life

Trail to Kastro

abounds in the myriad shoals. Trails are well marked and abundant.

The view from Ag. Fanourios offers a fine panorama of town and harbor, especially dramatic at sunset.

There is a 2½-hour hike to the Kastro on well-defined mule track.

Evangelistria Monastery, a fine church in Byzantine style, offers picnic possibilities.

Sea vistas unfold on a walk along the ridge of hills between Ahlaidas and Kolios.

Get off the bus at Tzaneria and follow the Kalamaki road around the peninsula close to the Kolios bus stop.

Festivals

July 25. Ag. Paraskevi (patron saint's festival). A 6½ km./3¾ mi. bus trip from town. Band playing, dancing, drinking, and Greek merriment!

August 15.   Evangelistria Monastery (Assumption of the Virgin Mary). It's a rugged walk to this place. Reserve your mule well ahead of time at a harborside tourist agency or gift shop. Feasts and celebrations.

August 27. Ag. Fanourios in Skiathos (special church service between 9:00 P.M. and 11:00 P.M. the night before).

Personal Comment

Several entrepreneurs developed Skiathos, starting in the sixties when the island didn't even have electricity. Their aim was to avoid mass tourism and to achieve an island with fewer rough corners, but with none of the essential flavor destroyed. Skiathos, today, is slick and smooth. Its flavor is intensified, and the tourist will find that here life's humdrum aspects take their place in the unconsidered background of the mind.

*Sedate Skopelos, although only seven miles
from its swinging sister-island, Skiathos,
refuses to imitate and instead
offers its own quiet charm and hospitality.*

skopelos

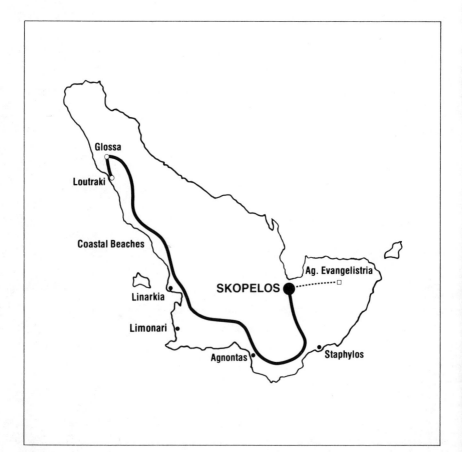

GETTING THERE

From Volos: 9 to 11 ships weekly.
From Kymi: 1 ship weekly.
From Skiathos: 11 to 14 ships weekly.
From Alonissos: 7 ships weekly.
From Ag. Constantinos: 4 to 7 ships weekly.

DEPARTURES

To Skiathos: 11 to 16 ships weekly.
To Ag. Constantinos: 4 ships weekly.
To Volos: 8 ships weekly.
To Alonissos: 8 to 15 ships weekly.
To Kymi: 2 to 4 ships weekly.
To Skyros: 1 ship weekly via Kymi.

TOURIST TIPS

Skopelos has an area of 96 sq. km./ 38 sq. mi. Its population is 4,500. No Tourist Police, but local Gendarmerie is very helpful. Apply there for room and camping information. The shipping ticket office is one block to the left of the landing pier. The bus station is next to the kiosk. Taxis and hotel vans meet arriving boats. The OTE is in the Post Office, which is closed weekends. There are several Tourist Agencies which book local hotels and make hotel reservations on other Sporades islands. There are several bus trips daily to the other end of the island. Skopelos Town is the official yacht station.

HOTELS*

Skopelos: (A) Mon Repose. (B) Rigas House. (C) Avra, Aeolis. (D) Amerika.
Pensions: Plaka, Bacopoulis, Kohitis, Lemonia.
Staphylos: Pension Stafylos. Rooms for rent.
Agnontas: Rooms for rent.
Loutraki: (D) Hotel Avrivi (Restaurant).

*See Part I, section on Accommodations, for explanation of hotel grades.

Panagia Evangelismos

HISTORY

Legend credits the Argonauts with founding the island. Later it was colonized by Cretans. In 1936, a grave was opened which contained funeral gifts showing it to be the royal burial place of Staphylos, a Minoan general. *596 B.C.* Islanders remained aloof from the Persian wars. *478 B.C.* Joined the Athens Alliance. *394 B.C.* Island coined its own copper money and paid dues to Athens. *340 B.C.* Philip of Macedon seized and plundered the island. *146 B.C.* Roman rule was established. *A.D. 330-1207* Byzantine period. Island used as a place of exile. Barbarossa, the pirate, menaced the islanders. *1538-1821* Weak Turkish domination. Island became self-governing. *1823* Island participated in naval battles against the Turks. *1830* Skopelos became part of Greece under the London pact.

SKOPELOS TOWN

The town is stunningly handsome and deserves its reputation as one of the most intriguing in the entire Aegean. Irregularly shaped rooftops are made of silvery-grey slate, and the whiteness of the houses is interspersed with accents of pale blue, ochre, and pink paint. Little arbors of brilliant summer flowers brighten the narrow streets that climb in amphitheater proportions from the harbor.

To walk in the upper town on a mellow summer evening is to witness a happy aspect of Greek life. As you pass the wide-open windows, you may catch a glimpse of a small front room with men and women crowded around a big, circular table complete with a lace tablecloth and a low, voluptuous bouquet of flowers. Chatter is fast, loud, and spiked with laughter.

As on most Aegean islands, the harbor frontage is the tourist's purlieu. The wide promenade is shaded by gnarled plane trees with bark as shriveled and grey as elephant hide.

Here you can sit in a comfortable chair and watch the fishing boats, the men playing backgammon or whacking sponges from muddy darkness to pristine cleanliness, the changing colors of the sea, cloud formations over the monasteries across the bay, the cautious interchange between the town's dogs and cats, and other components of island life.

If you are on the island on Sunday, the evening promenade (*volta*) is a distinctive sight. Dressed in their Sunday best, the townspeople walk the waterfront, then enjoy a meal at a restaurant. The town is still theirs; but you are a welcome guest, and they treat you with immense courtesy.

Dining and Entertainment

At first glance, the harbor appears to be a length of brightly colored awnings, shaded with restaurant tables and chairs which are color-keyed to prevent squabbles should a chair escape from home territory.

Skopelos Town

TAVERNA ANGEL and DIMITRI'S CAFE are representative of the town's food and drink. *Stefado* is a local specialty. This fancy version of beef stew rises above its peasant origins with halved walnuts and cubes of feta cheese added a few minutes before serving.

The taverna below the HOTEL AMERIKA is a favorite of tourists looking for sociability. Cassette music, wine, beer, *ouzo*, and brandy provide the basics.

Shopping

The pottery of Vassilios Rodis made an artistic impact years ago and is still sought out. Almost matte-black, his amphoras, jugs, and oil lamps copy production methods used centuries ago.

The local nuns make weavings in folk-style designs and wood inlaid objects. Glossa women excel in embroidery. The Archipelego Gift Shop has a sophisticated array of wall hangings, rugs, jewelry, and antiques.

Beaches

Paralia. The in-town beach is best around the harbor to the extreme east, and even then it does not compare with splendid beaches further afield.

Staphylos. Two miles from town you will find a beach where high pointed rocks rise from water of changing peacock hues. Spear fishers and scuba divers favor this area. A small *kafeneion* serves excellent fish.

Agnontas. The bus passes very near this sandy beach which is also a small port. Restaurant.

Limonari. After getting off the bus, you must walk down a winding road to a golden sand beach.

Linarkia. On the Bay of Panormos. This is a good beach, edged with white rocks and pine-dark hills. In Homer's time, triremes and galleons moored

here. Pirates used it. Today, yacht people consider it one of the best little harbors in the entire Aegean.

Coastal beaches. The bus passes fairly close to the sea, and there are sandy coves for several miles. Popular with hikers.

Excursions

The bus route that passes the beaches ends at the *Port of Loutraki*. The bus remains here for a few hours that coincide with ship arrivals. *Glossa*, the hill-hung village directly above Loutraki, also serves as an alternate port-of-call if the *meltemi* is blowing. Passengers are then taken by bus to Skopelos Town.

The *meltemi* is a phenomenon which you may or may not experience at some time while you are island-hopping. It's a howling wind that sweeps in from the sea, often with cloudlets scurrying overhead. It chops the sea into angry, lolloping, spitting whisps of spray. It bends trees, lashes leaves, swirls dust, rattles shutters, and sweeps up your balcony-hung swimming trunks and sends them forever from your sight. How do you handle this phenomenon? You can sit it out in some taverna, play backgammon, shut yourself in your hotel room, try to sleep, or read a book. It can last for hours. Hopefully, if you experience it, you'll be with someone you like. It's really rather exciting that way.

But back to Loutraki. The Hotel Avrivi is purported to have tasty food, or you can sit under their shady plane trees and wonder how the townspeople live in a quietude that seems unreal. If you become restless, climb back up to Glossa (an unexciting town, but the views are good).

Skopelos is a hiker's paradise. A local map shows all the back roads of this verdant, mountainous island. Europeans have been coming here for years. You see them leaving each newly minted day, knapsacks filled, eyes agleam with anticipation for a modest fourteen-mile hike, or more. Less vigorous travelers may enjoy an early morning walk harborside to watch the return of the *gri-gri* (fishermen). A mule ride to the *Monastery of Evangelistria* will take you through a landscape, heavy with the scent of oregano, to the lush monastery garden, heavy with the scent of jasmine and gardenia. The monastery chapel is filled with the scent of incense. In the anteroom handmade articles are for sale.

A 25-minute boat ride to the *Trypite grotto* may tempt you. A small island between Skopelos and Alonissos, *St. George*, has a monastery ruin and wild goats.

Ancient temples and walls dot the island. Guidebooks are available in the Skopelos bookstores.

Personal Comment

Skopelos and Skiathos have a friendly rivalry. They definitely have two different personalities. Perhaps you can live it up on Skiathos and rest up on Skopelos. Either way, we hope you'll also consider Alonissos, the next island of this group.

*Alonissos is an island where the traveler
is apt to give a sophisticated sigh
for the simple life.*

alonissos

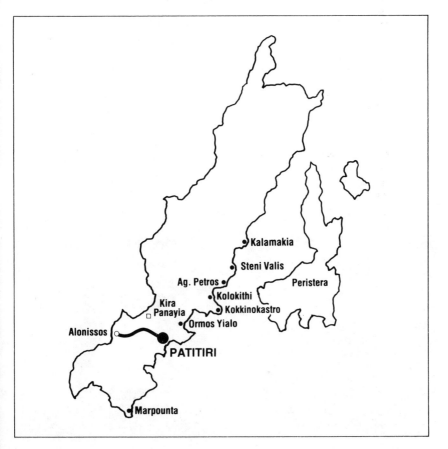

GETTING THERE

From Volos: 5 to 8 ships weekly.
From Kymi: 3 to 4 ships weekly.
From Skiathos: 8 to 16 ships weekly.
From Skopelos: 8 to 14 ships weekly.
From Skyros (via Kymi): 3 to 4 ships weekly.
From Ag. Constantinos: 2 ships weekly.

DEPARTURES

To Volos: 6 ships weekly.
To Kymi: 3 to 4 ships weekly.
To Skyros (via Kymi): 3 to 4 ships weekly.
To Ag. Constantinos: 2 ships weekly.
To Skiathos: 7 to 12 ships weekly.
To Skopelos: 7 to 13 ships weekly.

TOURIST TIPS

Alonissos has an area of 62 sq. km./ 25 sq. mi. Its population is 1,550. The ship ticket office is next to the landing pier. The island has six miles of minimal road. Transportation is mostly by donkey or *mia ta podia* (on foot). The Hotel Galaxy bus meets arriving guests. Hotel Marpounta guests will have a ten-minute boat ride from port. Boat rentals are available. The town has an OTE, a post office, and medical facilities. There are no Tourist Police; local Gendarmerie will assist. Camping only in outlying areas.

HOTELS*

Patitiri: (C) Galaxy (bungalows), Marpounta (bungalows), Hotel Alonissos, Kalogianni, Stavropolou. *Pensions:* Aragnostou. Chrisou, Kavos, Konstantinos. Many rooms to rent.
Steni Valis: *Hostels:* Theodorou, Mavriki.
Kalamakia: Pension Papavassiliou.
Monastery Kira Panayia: Accomodations for men and women.

*See Part I, section on Accommodations, for explanation of hotel grades.

Patitiri harbor

HISTORY

Cyclopean walls, fortifications, and charnel houses indicate ancient habitation. *A.D. 146–340* The island came under Athenian control. Philip of Macedon coveted the island, a fact that compelled the great orator, Demosthenes, to write his fiery speech about Alonissos. *340* The Byzantine period brought Christianity, and in the following years the island advanced into its greatest period of growth and prosperity. *1194–1453* Conquered by the Franks, who completed existing fortifications. *1453–1797* Submitted to the Turks. Island declined into insignificance. *Twentieth Century* Island has developed to its present economy of farming, fishing, and tourism.

Country woman

PATITIRI

Long, slender Alonissos gives a sense of distance from Skopelos and Skiathos despite its geographical closeness. Mainland Greeks like Alonissos and its peace. As one Athens businessman stated, "Alonissos is the way a Greek island should be!"

As your ship sails along the rocky coast prior to docking, you will see numerous sandy coves backed by tall pines and shrub-covered hills. There are ledges of slanting rock bordering the shores, just right for lying prone and luxuriating in Apollo's benevolent light. Sailboats and motorboats are moored nearby, for the coves and beaches are most easily reached via the water route.

The port town, Patitiri, has a new and rather modern appearance. Many of its inhabitants moved here and built homes after the island's capital city, Alonissos, was devastated by an earthquake in 1965.

Dining and Entertainment

Five cafés and tavernas share a beach

frontage under bright canopies and tree branches that shatter the sun's rays into flickering patterns. Oilcloth-covered tables and painted wood chairs are scattered in relaxed disarray. Here, lunch can last for hours, since there is so much waterfront activity to watch.

On this island you could eat the biggest lobster of your trip, served in splendor on a turkey-sized platter. The island is famous for its fish and seafood. A forty-boat fishing fleet goes out nightly and brings back the sea's gift of lobster, prawns, mullet, red snapper, blacktails, and *phangria*. Prawns baked with cheese and tomatoes are a specialty.

The evening entertainment for these waterfront eateries is local talent. Happy chatter blends with the music. If you are so moved, you can step from the patio onto the sand, cast off your shoes, and dance. Accompanying you will be the moon, which is making its own dancing glints on the darkened sea.

The handsome Hotel Galaxy has a restaurant, nightclub, and dancing. At

Marpounta there is a nightclub and restaurant. Because this complex is so heavily patronized by the English, it also has a "cozy little tea room." You can demolish daytime hunger pangs with the goodies available at the local Patitiri sweet shop.

Shopping

A third Archipelego shop has opened, and the selection of jewelry, clothing, and crafts is of their usual fine quality. There are Greek-style clothing shops next to the waterfront cafés.

Beaches

Awning-covered boats line up at the pier each morning ready to take you to the beaches. A share-in-the-fare arrangement can be made with those who wish to go to the same beach. Patitiri has its own beach, and others are ten to forty minutes away. Popular beaches are *Kolokithi, Steni Valis, Marpounta, Ormos Yialo, Kokkinokastro*, and *Kalamakia*. A picnic lunch is suggested.

Excursions

Venetian Castle. A fifty-minute walk through a countryside of brittle radiance and soft silence will bring you to the devastated capital town, *Alonissos*, and its Venetian ruins. The town has captured the fancy of a number of Germans, who are restoring areas of it

for their own use and to rent. In summer, there are two restaurants.

Kokkinokastro. Here, the antiquity buff can see the remains of this ancient city. There are walls, tombstones, and graves.

Around the island. This is a motorboat trip of four hours. Most dramatic to see are the precipitous cliffs on the northwestern coast.

Ag. Petros. Just south of Steni Valis, a sunken Byzantine ship is being explored.

Fishing

There is underwater spear-fishing for the over-eighteen crowd. The small island, Scantzoura, which is two hours away by boat, has caves harboring fish that sometimes weigh as much as eleven pounds. Local fishermen are ready to take you there or to their special nearby places. The herring-net method, fishing at night by gas lamp, and plain old pulling in the line are all fishing methods used.

Festivals

September 8. The yearly celebration of the Monastery of Kira Panayia.

Personal Comment

Alonissos is an island that is ideal for slowing down. It is a place where nature illuminates each passing hour.

The Greek poets and artists who have seen and loved Skyros have hoped that it will keep its great and moving simplicity forever.

skyros

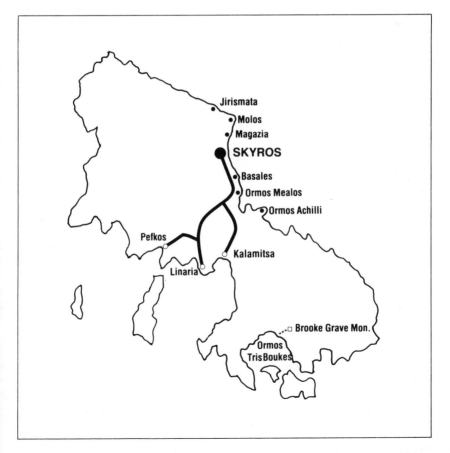

GETTING THERE

By bus. From Athens to Kymi: 3½-hour bus trip from main bus station, 260 Liossion St. Seats assigned.
By ship. From Kymi: 7 to 10 times weekly.
From Alonissos (via Kymi): 3 to 4 times weekly.
Note: From Kymi, 1 ship is scheduled weekly to the islands of the Northeastern Aegean.

DEPARTURES

To Kymi: 7 to 10 ships weekly.
To Alonissos (via Kymi): 3 to 4 ships weekly.
To Skopelos (via Kymi): 2 to 4 ships weekly.

TOURIST TIPS

Skyros has an area of 208 sq. km./83 sq. mi. Its population is 2,500. No Tourist Police, but local Gendarmerie will help you with room arrangements and camping permissions. Buses and taxis meet the boats at Linaria. No bikes, cars, or motorcycles are available for rent. The National and Commercial Banks of Greece have agents situated in commercial stores in the Chora. The post office, with OTE, is at the first bus stop on the main street. There are medical facilities. Siesta observed. For camping information, see below.

HOTELS*

Skyros (Chora): (D) Philippeos, Antonopoulou, Mantzourakis, Andrew, Kounadini.
Magazia Beach: (B) Xenia. (D) Aegean.
Pensions: Balotis, Panaria, Stephandis.
Basales Beach: Bungalows and private rooms to rent.

*See Part I, section on Accommodations, for explanation of hotel grades.

Note: The island has over a thousand rooms in private homes available to tourists. Many are decorated in intriguing island style. In July and August, the island is heavily booked with Greek vacationers.

CAMPING

Inquire at Pension Balotis near the Xenia Hotel. Campground is privately owned.

HISTORY

In prehistoric times, the cult of the ox, goat, and sheep was practiced. *476–475 B.C.* Island came under Athenian rule. *356 B.C.* Island became pro-Macedonian, but was unable to shed Athenian rule. *86 B.C.* Roman conquest. The island's multicolored marble was sent to Rome for use in statuary and building. *A.D. 343* Christianity introduced with the Byzantine period. Temples, idols, and shrines destroyed. Christian churches used these materials for their churches. *1175* Venetian fleet arrived. Island was given to the Ghizi clan, who made it into a pirate bastion. *1538* Barbarossa, the pirate, conquered it. Looting and burning. *1645–1649* Island suffered under the Frankish–Turkish wars. Turks became owners of the island, but very few Turks lived there. *1821* Revolution received with great enthusiasm. Island became a refuge for a vast number of uprooted Greeks from other areas.

Mythology
Achilles. According to prophesy, Achilles was to die in battle. Thetis, his mother, had dipped him in the river Styx to make him invulnerable, but failed to wet the heel by which she held him. On Skyros, in the court of King Lycomedes, Achilles was kept in the women's quarters dressed as a girl. The wily Odysseus discovered this and

Magazia Beach and Chora

persuaded Achilles to join the Trojan War. At Troy he was killed by Paris, who shot an arrow into Achilles' vulnerable heel.

Theseus. An illustrious hero in Greek mythology (in spite of his shabby treatment of Ariadne on Naxos), Theseus was removed from his Athenian throne because he was a Skyrian. He found refuge at the court of King Lycomedes, who secretly feared the presence and power of Theseus. On the pretext of showing him the view from the acropolis, Lycomedes pushed Theseus over the edge and to his death.

CHORA

Your ship will arrive at *Linaria*, a small fishing port with a few rental rooms.

Those who wish to go to the Chora and beaches will take the bus, which runs through a mixture of arid and verdant country until a sudden turn reveals an immense, unscalable-looking promontory topped by the remains of an acropolis. Spreading down the Chora's more gentle side is tier upon tier of white cubistic houses. The bus stops near the post office, and you are confronted with the fact that the only direction to go is up, or down by taxi to the Magazia beach where everything is on the level.

Settled in at last, you have many treats to enjoy. There is good reason why tourists, artists, and photographers are fascinated by this unusual Greek town. Angles and curves arrange themselves in endless variations, creating an architectural feast. The best time to enjoy it is during siesta when the streets are empty.

The early morning hours are quite different. About eight o'clock, the narrow main street is crowded with shoppers. Donkey vendors are assailed by women who can stridently argue the price of three beets or two zucchinis. Taverna keepers are doing a brisk business, and the men patrons are indulging in their favorite pastime of arguing. Three-wheeled delivery carts careen up and down the stony street. Children dart and yell; for them, the commotion is the best of games. Old men have found chairs from which to observe; old ladies gather on doorsteps, watch, spin wool, and embroider.

Acropolis. Keep climbing up the twisting streets, and eventually you will reach the top. Here, among the crumbled stones, are the beginnings of myth, fact, and lore that start with the Skyrian king Lycomedes, whose court was atop this promontory.

Moving down to another layer of history, you could visit the nearby church of St. George. An affable custodian has the key. She lives directly above the church courtyard. Proudly, she will show you the Byzantine church built in A.D. 895 (restored). She will point out the many icons, the carved wooden screen with Adam, Eve, and the serpent, and the miraculous icon of St. George.

Next on your sortie is the ruined Byzantine–Venetian castle with its carved lion of San Marco over the entry gate. Walking deep into the long arched corridor, it is not difficult to imagine the Ghizi brothers and their piratical gang astride their horses, clattering over the very steps upon which you stand.

Grouped together on the east side of town are the following three sights:

Faltaitz Museum. This is one of the richest and best-organized folk museums in all of Greece. It contains traditional and modern folk handicrafts, brass objects, costumes, ceramics, wood carvings, textiles, embroideries, and books. Closed Tuesdays.

Archaeological Museum. Small and very handsomely arranged, it contains island treasures dating back to 1200 B.C. Closed Tuesdays.

Rupert Brooke Memorial. A little *plaka* has an oversized bronze male figure memorializing the spirit of poetry and dedicated to the Englishman, Rupert Brooke, who is buried at Tris Boukes.

Dining and Entertainment

The cuisine of Skyros has been labeled "country food," which translates into commonplace, well-cooked Greek

Faltaitz Folk Art Museum

dishes. ANNA'S PLACE on the Chora main street attracts hearty eaters. Across the way is a patisserie where you can buy desserts and soft drinks. A few steps up the street and the tempting odor of spit-roasted chicken and *souvlaki* may make you pause at YIANNIS' and contemplate a purchase. DEMETRIO'S, at the kiosk, has fresh cheese pies daily. These are best eaten while hot. Across the way is a restaurant popular with the Greek residents. A sortie into the kitchen reveals kettles and pans of tempting-looking food.

Beach dining starts late and ends later. Except for the XENIA HOTEL, the nine beach restaurants are casual. Barefooted fishermen; barefooted tourists; impromptu dancing. Fish and lobsters are the specialties here.

On the stairway to the Chora, with lights you can't miss, is the DISCOTHEQUE ON THE ROCKS. On the beach is the disco SKYROPOULA. The Chora has two theaters. English films have Greek subtitles.

Shopping

Nicolos Pottery Shop. At the beach, next to the Xenia. Here, you will see pottery made and decorated.

Chora. Wood carving and furniture making. There are shops on the main street where you can watch the men at work.

Private homes. The women have streetside rooms to display their handicrafts. Open windows reveal women at their looms. See also page 44.

Beaches

If you choose to find accommodations down at the beach, your day will begin with a soft stillness, broken only by the rhythmic swish of waves on the shore. You open your shutters to a view of sea and sky whose radiance is known as the Aegean dazzle. Fishermen have beached their boats and are selling their fish and mending their nets. By ten o'clock, the bathers have staked out their day's territory with towels and umbrellas. Lazy hours stretch ahead of you unless you climb the hill to see the sights mentioned above.

Magazia Beach, on either side of the Xenia Hotel, is extensive, and the coastal road to the south as far as *Ormos Mealos* has little coves which offer more privacy. Good snorkeling is available. *Pefkos Bay*, near Linaria, is a favorite place for snorkeling and swimming.

Events and Festivals

Horse races of the little Skyros ponies.

Weddings: Dancing and feasting. Girls dress in local costume.

Carnivals: Pre-Easter celebrations. A colorful mix of pagan and Christian traditions.

Singing: Songs and instruments modeled on Byzantine forms.

Fairs: Usually held at small country chapels.

Personal Comment

Skyros rounds out an adventure in the Sporades by adding its distinctive personality. It has kept its traditions of craftsmanship alive and flourishing. Its folk art is unique in the Aegean. Add to that its attractive architecture, its beaches, and its antiquities, and you have an island offering a "souvenir" experience.

Island-crafted furnishings

The decorative and utilitarian objects in Skyrian homes date back for centuries. They were "relieved," often in an adventurous and bloody way, from ships from faraway places. The wealthy, upperclass Skyrians, many of them of the Ghizi clan, became avid collectors. Their caches represented an eloquent mark of wealth, social status, and even substitute money. This caused envy in the middle and lower class islanders, who began a long and ardent struggle to acquire these foreign objects. For many decades, Skyrians were actively involved in barter and trade. Eventually, all levels of society had representative collections.

The ultimate effect on the islanders was the development of a sense of beauty and a desire to create their own ceramics, furniture, weavings, and embroideries. Designs were interpreted with flair and originality; but you can still recognize adaptations of the originals from faraway countries. Along with the tourists, the Skyrians buy these newly made articles, for each new home must have its display of decorative and functional articles. Today, if all the objects in Skyros homes were in one museum, it would be the largest collection of ceramic and bronze art in the entire world.

III

the northeast aegean

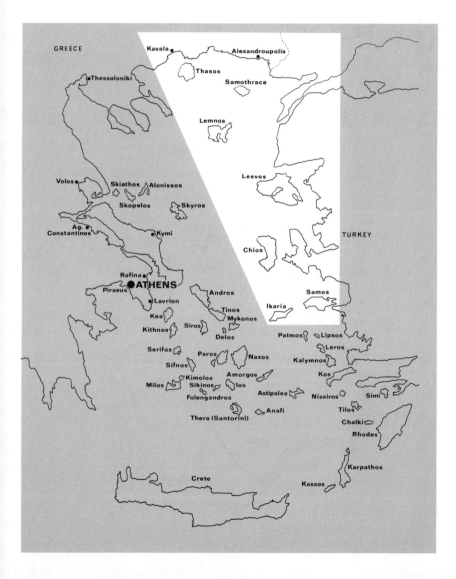

The magic of Pan, nymphs, and satyrs
remains in the vernal glens of Thasos.

thasos

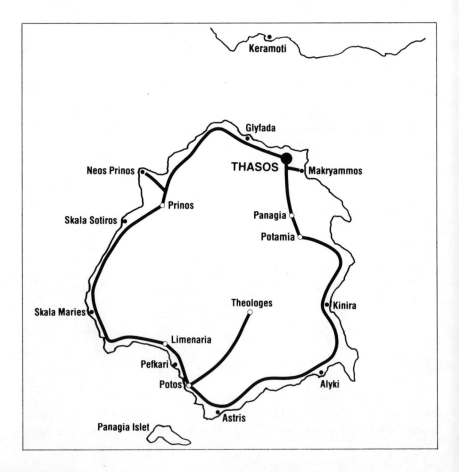

GETTING THERE

From Kavala: April and May: 6 to 7 crossings daily. June to October: 11 crossings daily.
From Keramoti: To Limenaria: 6 to 10 crossings daily. (Keramoti is a town east of Kavala.)

DEPARTURES

Reverse of above.

AIR FLIGHTS

From Athens: June 18 to October 7: daily to Kavala. Other times: Monday, Wednesday, Thursday, Friday.

TOURIST TIPS

Thasos has an area of 393 sq. km./157 sq. mi. Its population is 13,316. The Tourist Police are located in a small building at the landing dock. A harborside travel agency is one block to the east. Here, tours of the island to monasteries and special places of interest can be arranged, and general information is graciously given. Rent-a-Car facilities: tel. 21–535. There are medical facilities. Taxis and buses are stationed at the landing dock. Bus schedules are posted next to the Tourist Police office. Siesta observed. Camping is in designated areas only. Fishermen offer their boats for rent. There are banks, and a post office with an OTE on the main street facing the landing dock. Limenaria has a fine yacht harbor and facilities.

HOTELS*

Thasos: (A) Makryammos. (B) Xenia, Timoleon. (C) Angelika, Glyfada, Laios. (D) Akropolis, Amphipolis, Astir, Apollon, Galini, Linto, Palladion, Dionysos. Many rooms to rent.

*See Part I, section on Accommodations, for explanation of hotel grades.

Bird sculpture, Museum courtyard

HISTORY

8th Century B.C. Island's first inhabitants were Ionians. *6th Century B.C.* Island colonized by Phoenicians, who prospered by exploiting the gold and silver mines. *492 B.C.* Persians seized the island. *389 B.C.* Joined the Athens Alliance. *340 B.C.* Philip of Macedon seized the island. *196 B.C.* Thasos became a Roman state. *A.D. 330* The Byzantine period began and lasted until *1459* when the Turks conquered the island. Oppressive slavery and piracy. *1770–1774* Russian fleet occupied Thasos and exported its timber. *1813* Island given to Mohammed Ali, the Turk. He permitted the islanders almost full autonomy and self-government. *1916* Allied occupation. *1944* Liberation.

Mythology
Silenus, the son of Pan or Hermes, was a water spirit by origin. He possessed the special knowledge and wisdom inspired by wine drinking. He appears in many Bacchanal paintings. He had a number of sons by nymphs. In satyr plays these creatures, Sileni, unlike their wise old father, were portrayed as drunken and cowardly.

Famous People

Well-known inhabitants included Polygnotus, the painter; Stesimbrotus, the rhapsodist; and Theogenes, winner of more than one thousand athletic crowns.

THASOS TOWN (LIMEN)

Thasos Town, also known as Limen, is far greater in antiquity and more impressive than the mainland city of Kavala. Now, snugly interlaced among its well-preserved ruins, Limen has many visitors who are attracted by the pastoral spell of its green and mountainous terrain.

A favorite with tourists is the sky spectacular on summer evenings, most comfortably viewed from the harborside restaurants. While you enjoy a cool drink, face the sea and watch the sunset. A huge fire-red ball descends splendidly toward the horizon. A pathway of gold streaks the sea. The afterglow can be delicate or robust, depending on the sky's mood.

While this is taking place, young Greeks parade in couples or groups, mothers wheel babies in elaborate prams, older people sit back and watch. The mood is relaxed and serene. Even the dogs trot peacefully.

Suddenly there is music. Strings of outdoor lights brighten the restaurants. People turn away from the darkened sea, and the evening meal becomes the center of attention.

In-Town Sights

The fifth century B.C. grand wall surrounding Limen has the reputation of being the best-preserved in all of Europe. Tours start midway at the Ancient Naval Harbor. The path ascends the hill to a small theater, now used for drama festivals in July. Onward and upward, with stops for pine-framed views of the Aegean, and you reach the Acropolis. These remains include foundations of a Genoese Citadel and a Sanctuary of Pythian Apollo (or Athena). Next is a shady glen with a small, worn Hellenistic bas-relief of Pan piping to his goats.

The descent is arduous. There is a sixth century B.C. secret stairway. A large stone with two enormous eyes

Ancient naval harbor

will protect you from the Evil Eye. At ground level, you will come to the Gate of Silenus and a bas-relief of Silenus, protected by a wire enclosure. The wall ends at the harbor. (A guidebook, with much detailed information, is available.)

Harbor Stroll. Follow the road around the Ancient Naval Harbor along a shady parkway of fig trees, where the waves sing their endless chant. Town cats crouch in the tall grass to watch the wary seagulls strut the beach. At the far end is a shipbuilding yard where men saw planks in the old pit-saw method, frameworks of caiques stand in exquisitely formed skeletons, and there is the good smell of sawdust and drying wood.

Museum. The entry garden is embellished with numerous sculptured antiquities. The museum has five rooms. Room A has a twelve-foot-high *kouros* carrying a lamb, a bust of Pegasus and a particularly ugly one of Silenus, among other objects. Room B has sculptures of the Classical, Hellenistic, and Roman eras. Room C has religious signs, sculpture; Room D has pottery; and Room E has coins and signs from the fifth to the third centuries B.C. A small entrance fee is charged. Closed Tuesdays.

Agora. The best time to visit is early morning or late afternoon, when the sun's rays add a special artistry. Among other findings is a sacrificial hearth, its iron ring still attached. There are a few statues, altars, partial columns, and a sanctuary to Zeus. As with so many of these ruins, reconstruction of its original grandeur is left to the mind of the beholder.

"black wine," unique to Thasos. For dessert, just as unique, is *Karithaki*, delicious sweets, made with the famous Thasos honey.

If you wish to stray from Greek cuisine, try the VERONA PIZZA PARLOR a few doors west of the Angelika Hotel. Another place for a pleasant lunch is in the shade of huge plane trees on the west curve of the Ancient Naval Harbor. You'll find quick-fried foods, fresh salads, and lots of Greek hospitality. At the Makryammos Hotel, you can combine a swim and a meal in elaborate surroundings. Don't forget picnics in your private little beach cove: daytime, nighttime, anytime.

Dining and Entertainment

You can count on excellent fish, usually grilled in island-made olive oil. *Astabos*, lobster, can be very choice. The famous wines of antiquity are just a memory, but worthy of a try is

Shopping

There are many shops. Clothing drapes the outside walls and hangs on outside racks. Crafts, weaving, embroidery, and fine linen are much in evidence. Smiling Greeks stand in their door-

Morning shoppers

ways: "Come in, come in!" They are ready and proud to show their wares.

Beaches

The island has many unmarked beaches. The bus will stop to let you off and pick you up if you hail it. Fare is charged according to distance. Regular bus stops are made at the following beaches:

Makryammos. A beautiful setting, fine-grained white sand.

Glyfada. Near town, to the west.

Kinira. Very long stretch of rocky beach.

Alyki. Sand beach; coves; stunning scenery.

Astris. Nearly white sand.

Pefkari. Marvelous headland. Shade trees. Beach and taverna.

Excursions

Several buses each day make a round trip of the island. The good road passes through a grandly endowed countryside with acres of chestnut and olive trees, lush meadows, and about two hundred thousand bee hives. The inland mountain is Hypsarion, height

3,745 ft./1,127 m. Clockwise around the island (see map at the beginning of this chapter):

Panagia. Hotels: (D) Elvetia and Tris Piges. Two gushing fountains cool the air in the shade of plane trees. Markets sell walnuts and figs. Bundles of fresh oregano scent the air. Spinning is a specialty of the women. They gather in groups to spindle the wool; their deft fingers are quick, but not faster than their chatter.

Potamia. Very old houses, stone-roofed. The balconies have Turkish overhangs. The town is a good starting point to a trail that leads up to Mt. Hypsarion and ends in Theologes.

Kinira. (D) Hotel Gerda. The road becomes steep and provides dramatic views. You will look down at the sparkling sea, and rocks just made for sunbathing.

Alyki. Here there is an ancient marble quarry where long ago the Greeks carved out blocks of marble and sent them seaward. A modern marble quarry is nearby.

Monastery Archangelos. This can be a dazzle of sunstruck white. In spring, the wild flowers and red poppies wreath it like a blessing.

Panagia Islet. A favorite of spearfishing enthusiasts.

Potos. Road inland to the town of *Theologes,* where some pirate-proofed houses have gable watch-holes and back door escape routes. Here is the home of Hatzigiorgis, the patriot who raised the Greek flag on Thasos during the 1821 Revolution.

Pefkari. (See *Beaches*.) Rooms for rent and a beach hotel.

Limenaria. An industrial town built to house the employees of German companies which worked the island's mines. The harbor is a favorite of yacht people.

Skala Maries. On an access road to the port is a small chapel with outstanding wall paintings. A big celebration is held August 15. The Skala towns along the coast are all beach places. *Skala Sotiros* has villas on the sea. Rooms to rent.

Prinos. A left turn will bring you to Ioannidis Campground at Neos Prinos. Facilities for autos. Tents for rent. Pavilion.

Glyfada. Beach. From here, on a high curve in the road, you can see Limen across the bay. You'll head back to Limen unless you have decided some-where along the way to spend the night.

Personal Comment

The northernmost of the Aegean Islands, Thasos provides a pleasant interlude for travelers on their way to or from mainland Greece. It's a good starting point, too, for the string of islands that edge the Turkish coast all the way to Rhodes.

One of the most northerly Aegean Islands,
its ancient past involved secret cults,
its present offers wide-open hospitality.

lemnos

GETTING THERE

From Ag. Constantinos and Kymi: 1 ship weekly.
From Kavala: 3 ships weekly.
From Lesvos: 3 ships weekly.
From Thessaloniki: weekly ship to Rhodes and return.

DEPARTURES

To Kavala: 2 ships weekly.
To Lesvos: 2 ships weekly.
To Thessaloniki: see above.
To Samothrace: excursion boat or via Kavala.
To the Sporades: 1 weekly sailing via Ag. Constantinos and Kymi.

AIR FLIGHTS

Daily between Athens and Lemnos. Lemnos office: N. Garofalidi St.
Twice weekly between Thessaloniki and Lemnos.

TOURIST TIPS

Lemnos (Limnos) has an area of 477 sq. km./191 sq. mi. Its population is 23,000. The main town, Myrina, has no Tourist Police. Local police are to be contacted for any camping information. Bus schedules are posted in Venizlou Square. Buses depart twice daily for island towns and return the next day. There are no hotels in other parts of the island, although room rentals are available. There are taxis, Rent-a-Car services, and boats for hire. Some pensions have their own launches for fishing and pleasure, piloted by a member of the pension management. The museum staff has information regarding archaeological areas. Hospital and medical facilities are available. Siesta observed. Banks, post office, and OTE are on the main street. Yacht facilities are excellent.

HOTELS*

Myrina: (Deluxe) Akti Myrina Beach Bungalows. (C) Limnos, Sevdalis. (D) Actaeon. *Pensions:* Tsiyiannis, Mytilineou, Daskalou. Many rooms to rent.

HISTORY

In prehistoric times, according to Herodotus, the early inhabitants of the island were Tyrrhenian pirates, a few of whom Dionysos transformed into dolphins when they attempted to capture him off the coast of Naxos. (See chapter on Naxos.) In Neolithic times, Lemnos had the most advanced civilization in the entire Aegean. During the Bronze Age, the culture was of the Minoan–Mycenaean type. *1200 B.C.* Thaos, the Cretan general, became first king of Lemnos. *513 B.C.* Persians conquered island. *500 B.C.* Island became a colony of

*See Part I, section on Accommodations, for explanation of hotel grades.

Athens. Athenians arrived, and soon Lemnos became a follower of the life of Central Greece. *314-229 B.C.* Macedonia claimed the island. *A.D. 90* Leon, the pirate, made it his kingdom. *924* Island liberated and ruled by the Greek admiral, Rodinas. *1292* Louria, the Sicilian pirate, raided the island, but lost it to the Venetians. *1450* The Genoese Gattelusi clan extended their authority over Lemnos. *1460* It became a Turkish despotism. *1912* Freedom from the Turks.

Mythology

HEPHAISTOS

From morn / To noon he fell, from noon to dewy eve, / A Summer's day, and with the setting sun / Dropped from the zenith, like a falling / star / On Limnos, th' Aegean isle. —Paradise Lost, 1.742-6

Hephaistos was born in one of the exotic places of Mount Olympus where the gods lived. In a rash moment, he criticized Zeus, his father, about the way Zeus was treating his wife, Hera. Zeus promptly hurled his critic out of Olympus. Hephaistos fell on Limnos, breaking both legs. In the depths of a fiery mountain, he built a workshop among the molten metals. For himself, he made gold leg braces. He made the golden chariot of the sun, Hercules' breast plate, Zeus' scepter and throne (forgive and forget?), and many other beautiful objects contained in celestial spheres. He became the patron god of metalworkers, jewelers, and smiths. His cult existed until the Middle Ages.

The hamlet of Palaiopolis on a rockbound peninsula in the Bournia Bay, is the site of Hephaistia, the principal city in classical times.

THE CURSE OF APHRODITE

The goddess, Aphrodite, was chronically unfaithful to her husband, Hephaistos, causing much indignation among the women of the island. It reached a point where they refused to pay service to the goddess. She retaliated by making them repugnant to their husbands. The husbands began neglecting their wives, whereupon the wives murdered all of them.

This unhappy situation was changed when the ship, *Argo*, dropped anchor off the island. Jason and his Argonauts came ashore and into the welcoming arms of the frustrated women. The Argonauts stayed two years and successfully repopulated the island.

MYRINA

Near this port your ship will pass low-lying, bone-bare land forms, then enter a fine natural harbor with a ruined thirteenth century Venetian castle (known as Kastro) on a craggy promontory.

Even before the ship meets the pier, the waiting crowd of Lemnos men start a shouting repartee with the ship's deckhands, while the port officials efficiently direct the unloading and loading. Prior to departure, the ship's sound system fills the air with joyous music, and as the ship departs the men drift away until the next one is due.

The feel of Lemnos comes on strongly as one of relaxed isolation, quite devoid of any busy tourism. One does not come here for that kind of stimulation, although Myrina's luxury hotel has facilities to keep you as busy as you care to be.

The harbor frontage is the most active and colorful part of town. The breakwater curves its protective arm around a small harbor jammed with fishing caiques and small craft. The boats are painted a rich red, Greek blue, billiard-table green, and always trimmed with white. Piles of fishing nets add another blend of bright colors. There is space for yachts, and a

Myrina

station that provides fuel and yachting necessities.

The narrow main street leading away from the harbor is flanked by many small shops and markets. Along the stone-paved streets there are evidences of both newness and decay. Nowhere is there an overall finished look. Rubble is lived with, natural to an island built with one civilization amid, or atop, another. Some of its ruins predate those of Samothrace, and the island has an especially rich and delightful mythology.

In-Town Sites

The hike to the Venetian Castle ruin above the town starts at a path left of the small chapel, Santa Paraskevi. The ascending path has a huff-puff last one hundred feet; other than that, it is easy. The reward at the top is the magnificent view, ever changing with the moods of the day. It is especially dramatic to watch the sea stained saffron by the setting sun. Mt. Athos is to the west, Turkey to the east, and the sea is scattered with islands as pure in contour as primitive sculpture.

Museum. English-language signs provide easy directions to the museum, where a helpful staff answer your questions. Exhibits are labeled in Greek and Italian. The island's most important ruins were uncovered by Italian archaeologists; most are from Paliochni. Museum is closed Tuesdays. *Cathedral.* Near the museum is the cathedral, the pride of the townspeople. It has an elaborately decorated altar baluster, evidence of the islanders' continuous devotion to their Byzantine heritage.

Dining and Entertainment

The harbor-front cafés and restaurants have a family atmosphere, with the cooks holding court behind their well-stocked, refrigerated cases. Paper tablecloths, enormous bouquets of flowers, small children darting between tables, and happy-loud Greek voices contribute to an informality that projects hospitable warmth.

Lemnos is an island that has a plentitude of fleshy lobster, red mullet (which when grilled is called *barbouni*), and blue-spotted and gilthead

Seascape from Venetian Kastro, Myrina

breams. Figs, raisins, and almonds are plentiful, and the delicious bread is made from a special blend of Lemnos wheat.

Lemnos enjoys a reputation for strong, potent wines. Specialties are *Muscat de Lemnos* and *Vin Blanc Sec*.

Cafés PLATONIS and AVRA are popular with the locals, the best kind of recommendation. Beyond the town beach, at the far east side, is a fish taverna, TAKIS, which opens about nine at night. Outdoor dining is within a few yards of the lapping surf; especially attractive on a night with a full moon.

Since the island is a military base, expect to see many young men diners in uniform. For a bit of luxury dining, contact the AKTI MYRINA HOTEL (reservations required), which offers a set-price menu, disco, and bar.

Beaches

The town beach is convenient, and best at the south end. Short walks will

take you to many nearby coves, backed by huge boulders where sunbathing and swimming are a private affair. Hotel Akti Myrina has a swimming pool, plus an attractive curve of beach. For other beaches, see *Excursions.*

Excursions

Lemnos is almost split in two, and its general shape has been likened to that of a lop-sided butterfly. The Bay of Moudros, to the south, is where the ill-fated British Expeditionary Force set out for the Dardenelles in World War I. Bournia Bay, to the north, is a haven for small craft.

The ancients on Lemnos worshipped earth and fire, natural symbols of the island's volcanic origins. Today, as you travel through the denuded western part, the landscape has the chiseled, rugged contours of land that has been deranged and arrested in motion.

The eastern half has orchards and productive fields. An island specialty is plums, grown for prune drying. Luscious, dark blue, and plump, they are remote from their hard, wrinkled, dried-up counterparts.

From Myrina, you have a choice of roads leading to *Livadochori*, but do not exclude *Nea Koutali*, one of the island's most attractive spots. Here you'll find an enticing beach, thick pine woods leading down to it, and a taverna to pass a succession of agreeable moments.

Across the bay is *Moudros* and, to reach it, you must return to Livadochori. Moudros is the joint capital of the island, and offers good beaches, strong, local wine, and excellent shellfish.

Southeast of Moudros is *Paliochni*, the island's most important ruin. Superimposed settlements include ones from the Bronze Age (1500–1000 B.C.), Copper Age (pre-Mycenaean), and vestages of two Neolithic cities. (Lemnos is credited with having the first stone baths in the entire Aegean.)

Beyond Paliochni, a secondary road leads to the tip of the island where a sandy landscape has been nicknamed the Lemnos Sahara. Facing the sea is the monastery, *Ag. Soson*. September 7 is festival time.

Head back to Moudros again, and northeast through numerous villages and verdant countryside to *Kontopouli*. A minimal road leads to *Hephaistia* and a medieval castle ruin which came into importance after the decline of the Hephaistia cult. In classical times, this site was the principal city of Lemnos and paid a large tribute to Athens. Pre-Greek in origin, it came to a disastrous end in a landslide. An eighth century B.C. necropolis and a sanctuary have been excavated.

Devoted ruin seekers can find their way to *Khloi*, situated on the land bordering the deepest inlet of Bournia Bay. Excavated in 1937–39 by the Italians, this sanctuary preceded the one on Samothrace. The Cabeiri cult (see chapter on Samothrace) attracted many historically notable persons. The Lemnos inscriptions list Philip of Macedon as requesting initiation into the secret cult.

Near here is *Kokkinos*, famous for its Lemnion earth used as a tonic and astringent medicine. This earth was the *terra sigillata* of antiquity, considered an infallible cure for festering wounds. Myrina and Moudros are purported to still sell it. Today, on August 6 at the Feast of Christ the Savior, traditional digging is done by a priest.

Boat excursions are organized regularly for guests of the Hotel Akti Myrina, which owns a fifty-ton caique. Day trips to Samothrace, Thasos, Ag. Efstratios, and Mt. Athos are included. Prices available at the hotel or by contacting Head Office of Akti Myrina Hotel, 4 Nikis St., Athens 126, tel. (01) 3230249.

Personal Comment

Lemnos offers quietness, lazy days. The island will have a special attraction for those interested in archaeology, not for its extensive ruins, but rather for its illustrious past.

If you stay at the deluxe hotel, you will have every amenity and still be in a noncommercial, typically Greek world.

The lesser hotels and pensions will offer you the chance to be close to island life, and to be the recipient of the islander's frank genuineness and hospitality.

*In ancient times, a cult island
of pomp, style, and elegance.*

samothrace

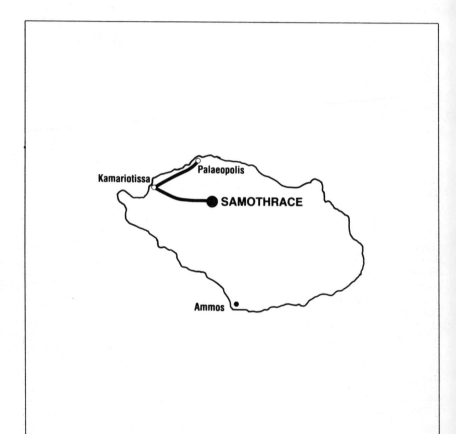

GETTING THERE

From Alexandroupolis: April to October: daily crossings.
From Kavala: 2 crossings weekly.
From Lemnos: by private caique.

DEPARTURES

To Alexandroupolis: April to October: daily crossings.
To Kavala: 2 crossings weekly.
To Lemnos: private caique, or via Kavala.

TOURIST TIPS

Samothrace (Samothraki) has an area of 180 sq. km./68 sq. mi. Its population is 3,000. You may wish to investigate tour possibilities in Kavala or Alexandroupolis. Winds and current buffet this round island which, according to Strabo, "rises aloft like a woman's breast." Nonpoetically speaking, it has a rocky, mountainous terrain with grey-green olive trees on the lower slopes. The chief occupation of the inhabitants is raising goats and sheep. The Chora has the post office and OTE, and there is a bus four times a day between the port and Chora. No tourist police. Camping allowed.

HOTELS*

Palaeopolis: (B) Xenia. Preference given to archaeologists.
Samothrace: (C) Akrouali. (E) Ilios. Many rooms to rent.

HISTORY

Island inhabited since Neolithic times. *8th-7th Centuries B.C.* Colonized by Greeks. *6th Century B.C.* Island flourished. Had a navy, its own silver coinage, a necropolis with encircling walls. *5th Century B.C.* Island's power declined, but the strength of its cult

*See Part I, section on Accommodations, for explanation of hotel grades.

kept it the North Aegean's chief center of religious life. *86 B.C.* Roman occupation. They rebuilt the sanctuary after pirate devastation. *A.D. 200* Following an earthquake, the island declined, although the cult existed until the end of the pagan era. *1441* Genoese Gattelusi clan came into control. *1457* Turkish rule. *1863* Discovery of the *Winged Victory. 1912* Island returned to Greece.

Famous People
Herodotus and King Lysander of Sparta were initiates. Plato and Aristophanes knew about, and spoke of, the Mysteries. It was in Palaeopolis that Philip of Macedon met Olympias, who became the mother of Alexander the Great. Aristarchus was born there. So was Dardanos, the legendary founder of Troy. Piso, father-in-law of Julius Caesar, was an initiate. Hadrian was a visitor, as was St. Paul on his way to Philippi.

ISLAND SIGHTS

Samothrace attracts the island-hopper who is curious about cults and ruins and is willing to brave a *sometimes* stormy sea to spend time on an island with very few tourist amenities. Adventurous persons will also investigate Ammos, a fine isolated beach to the south of the island and reached by boat. Here, sleeping on the sand is *de rigueur.* Also, there is Mt. Pfenari (height 5,200 ft./1,575 m.) to climb. According to the *Iliad,* it was from this summit that Poseidon watched the battlefields of Troy. On a clear day, you, too, can see these Trojan plains, plus many other islands lounging in the sea.

Landing is made at *Kamariotissa.* Directly upward is the *Chora,* braced against a steep tilt of land. A ruined Byzantine fortress crowns the top. Palaeopolis is the area of the museum

Palaeopolis (*Photo courtesy Greek National Tourist Organization*)

and the excavations, which extend over a promontory.

Museum. An English guidebook for museums and ruins is available. Included in the museum exhibits are reconstructions from available fragments, sculpture, and religious and votive objects. There are relief fragments of centaurs, fine-blown glassware, and tomb objects. Pottery reveals the sophistication of many of the initiates.

The Mysteries of the Caibeiri. The nature of the cult is still in dispute. However, one explanation gives credence to its centering on a group of deities of Phoenician or Phrygian origin. Rites were kept secret, and they evolved around fertility gods. The phallus was their symbol. Ceremonies took place by torchlight and were followed by banquets. During the summer, great festivals were held which included dramatic and religious rites. Initiation was open to any person.

Ruins. The ruins are well marked and

easy to find. Among them are: *Ptolemaini*, a monumental gateway to the *Sanctuary* where confessions were made. Baptisms took place at the south end of this building. The Rotunda, or *Arsinoeion*, is the largest round building of ancient Greece, 65 ft./20 m. in diameter. Here, public sacrifices were held. *Anaktoron* was the hall for initiation. The *Sacristy* was a place of enrollment. The *Temenos* was the site of the holy feasting. The *Hieron* was used for higher initiation ceremonies. In 1956, the five columns were reerected. The *Winged Victory* was found near the *Nike Fountain*. Nearby is the Western Hill, a medieval structure made with cannibalized Sanctuary materials.

Personal Comment

To go to this island amounts to a pilgrimage, even if you don't come away with an iron ring, a purple amulet around your neck, or a promise of worldly salvation.

*In an atmosphere of up-to-date, breezy vitality,
Lesvos still has the charisma associated
with its poets, musicians,
and intellectuals of the past.*

lesvos

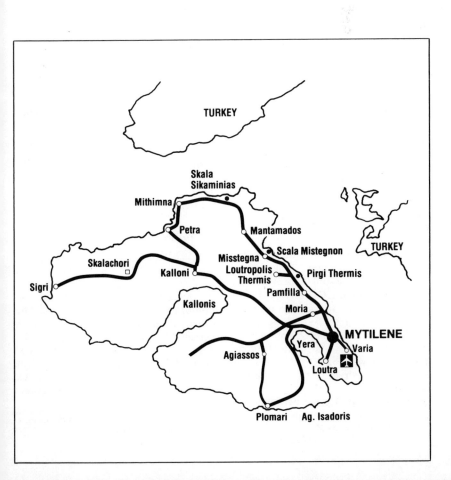

GETTING THERE

From Piraeus: 5 or 8 ships weekly, via Chios, return to Piraeus.

From Thessaloniki: Once weekly, en route to Rhodes, and return.

From Chios: 4 ships weekly.

From the Sporades: Ports Kymi and Ag. Constantinos: Each 1 ship weekly. (Lesvos is the last island on the Sporades route.)

DEPARTURES

To Turkey (Smyrna and Avalik): by caique, summer only.

To Piraeus: See above.

To Thessaloniki: 1 ship weekly.

To Chios: See above.

To Kymi and Ag. Constantinos: See above.

AIR FLIGHTS

Daily between Athens and Mytilene. Olympic Office: 13 Smyrnis St., Mytilene.

TOURIST TIPS

Lesvos (Lesbos) island has an area of 1,614 sq. km./630 sq. mi. The population is 123,000. The Tourist Police are located in the Custom House, to the right of the landing dock. Good coverage of the island is provided by public bus. Rent-a-Car service is available, and there are plenty of taxis. Near the landing dock are shipping and tourist agencies. There is a yacht refueling and supply station in Mytilene. There are several banks. Overseas calls can be dialed direct. Siesta is observed. No camping areas are designated. Inquire of local police for permission to camp near north harbor and small beach, Tsamakia, in Mytilene.

HOTELS*

Mytilene: (B) Xenia, Lesvion, Lesvos Beach (apartments), Blue Sea. (C) Rex, Sappho. *Pension:* Isadourou. Many rooms to rent.
Mithimna: (B) Delphinia. *Pensions:* Sea Horse, Romninakis. Rooms to rent.
Petra: (C) Petra.
Plomari: (C) Oceanis.
Sigri: (B) Nissiopi (pension).
Antissa: Moni Ipsolon Monastery. (E) Athina.
Thermi: (B) Blue Beach, Votsala (motel). (E) Saritza.

HISTORY

11th-10th Centuries B.C. Island settled by Aeolians. This most ancient and refined race left an indelible imprint in the arts, education, and culture. *8th-6th Centuries B.C.* Lesvos was the vanguard of civilization, with such personalities as Pittakos, one of the Seven Sages of antiquity; the lyrical poet Alkaios; Sappho, the ardent poetess; Terpander, father of Greek music; Arion, inventor of dithyrambic

*See Part I, section on Accommodations, for explanation of hotel grades.

poetry. *A.D. 405* Island fell to the Spartans and changed hands frequently until the Romans took over. Julius Caesar "won his spurs" during the Roman siege of Mytilene. *428* Peloponnesian War. Island revolted against Athens. Demodotus, son of Eucrates, prevailed upon Athens to revoke Athens' death sentence for the islanders. His speech is preserved in history as unique and of heroic dimensions. During the Middle Ages and Turkish rule the island changed masters often. The Crusaders and pirates plundered it. *1354* Genoese Gattelusi clan took over and a century of untroubled prosperity followed. The island was deeply involved in World War II.

Note: The two renegade Greek brothers Horuk and Khair ed-Din Barbarossa, who became corsairs and terrorized the Aegean, were born on Lesvos.

MYTILENE

More than ten million olive trees make a dense pattern of silvery-green, pine forests shade to darker green, and mountain tops emerge in craggy baldness on Lesvos, largest of the Aegean Islands after Crete and Euboea.

If you fly into the airport south of Mytilene, you will view two almost landlocked bays, Yera and Kallonis. Just before landing near grassy slopes cradling a few small hamlets, you will see that those black and white spots are grazing sheep. All is very bucolic and inviting.

Arrival by interisland steamer will be at a harbor that is rough-looking, worn, and busy with a thriving commerce. Beginning with the Genoese Fortress, the town's harbor curves around a deeply indented bay. Along the waterfront are numerous hotels,

Mytilene

cafes, shipping and exporter's offices, garages, patisseries, stores, restaurants, and banks. During busy daytime hours, there is continuous traffic, a passing show for the many seated streetside observers.

Mytilene has a flourishing economy and much wealth. It is a town of hodgepodge architecture often described as Asia Minor Baroque. The townspeople are friendly and helpful, although busy about their own affairs. There are a few in-town sights, but the real treasures are in other parts of the island.

In-Town Sights

The Byzantine Fortress, the Ancient Theatre, and the Archaeological and Popular Museums could occupy a day;

and do notice the almost inconspicuous miniature park on the waterfront, not too far from the landing dock. Here is a marble sculpture of Sappho, holding her lyre, and quite oblivious to the workaday world beneath her. Here is one of her verses: *A delicate sweet flame leaps within me / Like liquid fire. My eyes grow dim. / I see nothing before me: only I hear / A silent thunder.*

Dining and Entertainment

Exported, and a specialty of the island, is *ouzo*, touted to be a connoisseur's delight. The Bay of Kallonis provides the tasty sardines that are served boned, mashed, and fried as fritters in olive oil and garlic. The local wine is excellent.

Plato wrote: "Some say there are nine muses. How careless they are! Behold, Sappho of Lesvos is the tenth!" He also credits her with writing verses of impeccable purity and with a complete command of the language.

Traditionally, the town of Eressos is her place of birth, which is conjectured to have taken place sometime between 650 and 600 B.C. Small of stature, not beautiful, she held within her a flame of passion and tenderness that projected into her poetry. It is assumed that she presided over a school for young girls, whom she encouraged to write love songs. The word "lesbian" evolved from associations with her work. She was married, had children, and lived a long life. Today, we know her through a few surviving fragments of her writings. She introduced the metaphor into language with phrases never heard before: "White as milk;" "More precious than gold."

Sappho, Mytilene

The XENIA HOTEL has an inviting outdoor restaurant overlooking its swimming pool and a sea view of the Turkish coast. Ask the bus driver to let you off below the Xenia where a slightly steep, woodsy path will lead you upward to the hotel. Or a taxi will take you directly to the hotel's front entrance. For dining reservations telephone 22713 or 22717.

In-town restaurants and cafés are numerous. Spit-roasted chickens are a specialty of the ASTEPIA restaurant, portside.

Opposite the town hall, you'll find a rooftop, open-air movie theater. On the harbor is the handsome Municipal Theater. Programs of opera, classical music, and live theater are posted on the marquee.

Shopping

If you like collectables, search out the antique and secondhand shops back from the harbor. The island is known for its pottery, especially a water jug called the *koumaria*, superior for keeping water chilled.

Beaches

The town beach below the fortress has a taverna, but the really fine beaches are spread in sandy lengths and in tucked-away coves in other parts of the island. See *Excursions.*

Excursions

Mithimna. The fun-loving, lighthearted vacationer would do well to go straight to Mithimna and its neighboring attractions, *Petra* and *Scala Sikaminias.* Mithimna is built on a headland facing Cape Baba on the Turkish coast. It has exhilarating breezes, a long sandy beach, plenty of fishing, snorkeling, and a charm that was there long before it became slated as a rival of Mykonos, Skiathos, and Paros.

The Athens School of Fine Arts has sponsored a painting and pottery school here. Artists come to paint here and in surrounding areas. Writers live in residence, some from England and America.

A crenelated fortress built by the Gattelusi clan tops the hill. The town jumbles cozily on its slopes. Narrow

Mythimna

cobbled streets made for human and donkey, many shops with better-than-average souvenirs, many flower-potted balconies where you can eat, drink and enjoy the views, many spontaneous parties that go 'til dawn are some of the accouterments that become part of a delightful, hedonistic holiday.

Scala Sikaminias. There are two ways to get here. Most fun is by the excursion boat from Mithimna, filled with vacationers. Your guide will point out a cave where Achilles supposedly had a love affair while taking a respite from conflicts at Troy. Later, you will enter Scala's diminutive harbor that looks like a stage set. Octopus strung out to dry adds its decorative touch. If you come by car, it will be on the road that follows the north side of Mt. Lepetimnos into the town of Sikaminias and then down to the port.

Petra. The bus passes through this fishing village on its way to Mithimna. You may be tempted to return later and try the beach and waterfront cafés. In the evening, the departing fishing boats split and fracture the sundazzle of the sea. It is worth rising early to see them return when the black sea takes on the colors of dawn. One senses a good mood about this little village, and a feeling of severance from worldly affairs. *Petra* means "rock," and atop a large one is the *Church of Panayia Glykofiloussa* which, according to villagers, has a miracle-working icon.

One-Day Bus Trips from Mytilene

Agiassos. (Bus stay of two hours.) For protection against pirates, many of the town's houses were built with stone lower stories. Doors were made as small as possible. The streets are so narrow that many have been trellised with vines, making a sun-flecked, cool, and refreshing tunnel. The market square is the site of the principal church, which has a large basilica and a collection of icons, easily folk art at its best. Interior decoration overwhelms you with glitter.

In their own thoughtful Greek way, the townspeople have put a taverna opposite the church. Its enormous windows have a sweeping view of the square. Weaving and pottery are town specialties, and the pottery factory is worth a visit. If you still have time, you may wish to climb Mt. Olympus, which reaches 3,170 ft./950 m. Festival on August 14–15.

Plomari. (Last bus returns at 3:00 P.M.) Plomari is a nineteenth century town built by the islanders who returned after piracy was controlled. The island's famous *ouzo* is made here. The distillery is open to visitors when it is operating.

Fish restaurants on the waterfront are a drawing card for tourists. Those west of town have friendly, talkative proprietors, and a meal can turn into an occasion. Plomari is a town for wandering about, walking to the end of the breakwater for sunbathing, swimming off the rocks, and seeing picture-postcard views of the town. This trip is recommended for that slowed-down interlude sometimes needed on a trip.

Skalachori and Sigri. If you have never slept in a monastery or seen petrified wood, you may wish to cross the western side of the island for these experiences.

The road beyond Kalloni winds its way around Mt. Kouratsonas to Skalachori. A religious festival is held August 23. Near here is a trail to ancient *Antissa* on the coast, where legend states that the "singing" head of Orpheus was washed ashore. Beyond modern Antissa is the *Moni Ipsilou Monastery* on Mt. Ordimnos. Perched on a bare and rocky peak, it stands solidly against the vast blue sky. Accommodations are available for men and women. Down from the heights, still through a lunarlike landscape, you will suddenly see

Sigri come into view, backed by the blue blessing of the sea. It's a red-roofed town, houses squarely built on stony ground. A feeling of isolation pervades it. Splendid beach, Turkish fortress nearby. Artists come to Sigri to capture its drama.

Other Excursions

Varia. A short bus ride south of Mytilene will take you to the Moussio (Museum) Theofilou on the outskirts of Varia. (Theophilos is the island's equivalent to France's Rousseau.)

For the antiquary who is adept at the game of seek and find, there are many interesting places on the coastal road to the north:

Mytilene to Mantamados (40 km./ 25 mi.) The hot baths of *Loutra Kourtzi* date back to Roman times and are just north of the city. A short distance beyond is a by-road leading to *Moria*. Here are several fine Roman arches. Back on the coastal road and beyond *Pamfilla* is *Thermi*, a prehistoric site. Five cities, one on top of the other, have been excavated.

Pirgi Thermis, to the north, has a track to *Pehagia Troulloti*, a fifteenth century Byzantine church. The coastal road leads west to *Loutroupolis Thermis*, a major spa recommended as far back as Claudius.

Misstegna has traces of ancient *Aigeiros*. *Skala Mistegnon* is a fishing port; stop for lunch and a swim. Along the bay of *Makregialou*, the road follows the sea more closely before it turns inland to *Mantamados*. Near here is the church of Taxiarkhon, with a most unusual carved black-wood icon. Mantamados is where *koumaria*, the water jug, is made.

You are now in mountain country and must decide whether to drive north on a challenging road to *Skala Sikaminias* (see section on Mithimna in *Excursions*) or return to Mytilene.

Personal Comment

Lesvos is scenically superb. Good roads curve sinuously among the valleys and foothills, rising to cool pine forests and bare mountains offering extravagant views. Each day will have an astonishing power to enchant. Fortunate is the traveler with a car, but it is easy to cover the island by bus, vagabonding from day to day.

chios

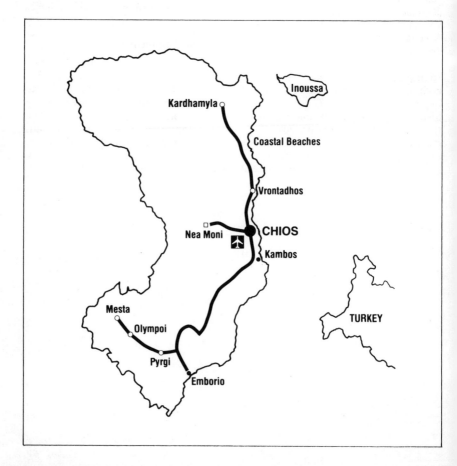

GETTING THERE

From Piraeus: 3 to 5 ships weekly, via Mytilene, return to Piraeus.
From Samos: Local boat, twice weekly.
From Thessaloniki: Chios is on the weekly route to Rhodes, with return.
From Psara: 3 ships weekly.

DEPARTURES

To Piraeus: See above.
To Samos: Local boat, 2 times weekly.
To Lesvos: Return by Thessaloniki–Rhodes Line.
To Tsesme, Turkey, and Inoussa: Daily, in season.
To Psara: 3 ships weekly.

AIR FLIGHTS

Daily except Tuesday. Office: Prokymaia Hiou St.

TOURIST TIPS

Chios (Hios) has an area of 858 sq. km./343 sq. mi. Its population is 54,000. Tourist Police are located at 35 Neorion St., tel. 0271–26555. Ship and airline offices are clustered midway on the harborfront. The bus terminal angles away from Vounaki Square on Od. F. deCoulans St. There is adequate bus service to scenic and historical island settings. Be sure to check return schedules. Cars can be rented from Chandris Tours, which provides guided visits to scenic places, monasteries, and workshops as well. Siesta observed. For rooms and camping information see Tourist Police. Island has yacht facilities.

HOTELS*

Chios: (B) Chandris, Xenia, Aktaeon. (C) Kyma. (D) Pekion, Filoxenia,

*See Part I, section on Accommodations, for explanation of hotel grades.

Haghioi Apostioi, Pyrgi

Palladion, Pelineon. *Pensions:* K. Bolla, Hotel Rodo.
Kardhamyla: (B) Kardhamyla.
Inoussa Island: (D) Prassonissia.

HISTORY

2600-2000 B.C. Proto–Helladic period. *1600-1100 B.C.* Mycenaean period. *800 B.C.* Ionian colonization. *493 B.C.* Persian destruction of Chios. *146 B.C.* Roman rule. Poverty, famine. *A.D. 312* Beginning of Christianity. Some degree of recovery. *961* Captured by the Byzantines. *1042-1055* Reign of Monamachus. Foundation of Nea Moni. Citadel built. *1204* Venetian occupation. *1261* Genoese occupation. Giustianini clan rules for nearly two hundred years. Prosperity. *1566* Piali Pasha captures island. Turkish rule begins. *1822* Uprising. Turks massacre 25,000 islanders. *1912* Liberation of Chios by Greek fleet.

CHIOS TOWN

Of all islands in this group, Chios has the strongest feeling of the Levant. Although the waterfront buildings are modern, the narrow back streets have strong Turkish design and ambience.

Here is an agglomerate of shops and living quarters that support an ancient and traditional way of life. Vounaki Square, a short walk inland from the mid-area of the waterfront, has coffee houses and sweet shops. From early morning until late evening, Greek men gather to eat, drink, and conduct business affairs in the comfortable disarray of outdoor tables and chairs.

The most exciting time in this area is morning market hours. The streets, both north and south of the Square, are jam-packed with shoppers. As many men as women partake of this social-domestic ritual. String bags bulge with luscious fruits and vegetables; freshly baked breads and freshly ground coffee send out tantalizing aromas. *Souvlaki* stands do a thriving business. Meat hangs from hooks, bins of fish glint silver. Strident Greek voices mingle with cassette music played at full volume. Promptly at noon everything closes. Canvas and plastic cover the fruit and vegetable stands. Fish bins are cleared, and iron grills come down over shop windows. The streets empty of people. The siesta begins.

In-Town Sites

Kastro. The vaulted entrance to this fortified citadel is at the north side of Vounaki Square, above the moat and close to the Town Hall (Porto Maggiore). Seek out the ruins of the *Giustianini palace*, the *Turkish cemetery* with tombstones of artistic and historical interest, and the *Church of St. George* on the main street. In the north corner of the Kastro are derelict Turkish baths with low domes. The north tower can be climbed for a commanding view of the sea, the gun embrasures, and the moat. The sea wall has not been changed since the Genoese period.

Haplotaria. Leading away from Vounaki Square to the south is Haplotaria, an old commercial street, once the religious and intellectual center of Chios. Today, you will find here the *Korais Library*, which houses the Ethnological and Folklore Museum. Island costumes, local handicrafts, embroidery, and weaving are among the articles of interest. Closed Sundays.

Museum. Chios has a handsome new museum built of rough-cut native stone. It occupies several levels with patio gardens interspersed among them. Located at the south end of town, it is a few blocks up from the harbor and opposite the school. It is recommended to those who enjoy seeing treasures of the past in cool, serene surroundings. Entrance fee. Closed Tuesdays.

Dining and Entertainment

The dining room of the HOTEL CHANDRIS showcases one of the best overall views of the sea, harbor activities, the town, and mountains, all accompanied by flocks of swallows that swoop and dart to the choreography of their own design. Food here is directed toward the tourist palate. For strictly Greek–Turkish food, seek out the small restaurants in the older areas. Chios has a unique specialty: *mastika*, similar to *ouzo* or *arak*. It also boasts a liqueur known as *mastiche*, often used as a flavoring in cakes and cookies. In general, seafoods are the best buy and tastiest choice.

Not to be missed is the waterfront promenade or *volta*. The activity begins about 6:30 or 7:00 P.M. A long area of the waterfront is roped off to vehicular traffic. Several hundred chairs and small tables, stacked during the day, are placed streetside in neat rows. Ouzo and plates of *mezes* are standards on the menu. Greek women make an appearance, either in pairs or with their husbands and children. If alone, they are wheeling a child in a pram. Except for the early morning hours, women are conspicuous by their absence in public places.

While you promenade, cast a glance at the plates of *mezes* and choose the taverna that offers the most tempting. Your promenade completed, join the Greeks who are enjoying each other and themselves. About 9:30 or 10 o'clock, they begin to drift away, and the waiters restack the tables with chairs. The waterfront becomes a quiet and deserted place.

Shopping

Next to the Olympic Airline Office is the Inta antique store, occupying a second and third floor. A visit here is a glimpse into Chios' past. Bargain if you see an object you must have.

Beaches

Bus is available to beaches *Bella Vista* and *Konteri*, both close to town. Near *Homer's Stone* are beaches *Nagos* and *Vikhada*. There is an excursion boat to beaches on *Inoussa Island*, and an attractive beach at *Emborio*. Near *Kardhamyla*, the summer resort of *Pashaspring* is rapidly becoming popular.

Excursions

Kambos. Nowhere in the Aegean Islands is there an area quite like the Kambos, which lies directly south of the city. Surrounded by high walls, the land has a dense network of roads and thick groves of citrus. As early as the fourteenth century, the aristo-

cratic families of Chios had second homes as private estates here. Numbering about two hundred, the houses were elaborate, with colorful courtyards and fountains, shaded by avenues of trees and situated to ensure complete privacy. Today, only a few examples of this remarkable architecture survive, although the citrus orchards are productive. The curious tourist may visit a number of better-preserved estates, monuments, and a few notable churches. See a travel agent for assistance.

Homer's Stone. A short distance north of Chios is the straggly town of *Vrontadhos*, and on its north outskirts is the Stone of Homer. For this reason the scholar may find sufficient reason to go there, knowing full well that at least seven or eight other areas claim Homer as their own. In ancient times, a clan calling themselves *Homeridai* lived on Chios; the reference to Chios in the Homeric Hymn to Apollo has a certain bearing.

The tourist who is able to romanticize can imagine bearded, old, blinded, laurel-wreathed Homer sitting on the rock and singing his immortal songs about Troy and his adventures of Odysseus to a raptly listening audience.

Nea Moni. Situated on Mt. Provation, 2,500 ft./743 m. above sea level, and 13½ km./8½ mi. from town. (Reached by taxi, by conducted tour or rented car, and on Sundays, by bus twice daily as far as the little town of Karies.) The Byzantine mosaics in this nine-hundred-year-old church are unique in the Aegean and are considered to be of international importance. Richly embellished and decorated, monumental and austere, displaying a lively use of vivid blues, dark reds, turquoise, pinks, blacks, and large areas of skillfully applied gold, they are enhanced by the play of natural light. The subject matter of the mosaics is the cycle of the life of Christ, and although fire and earthquake have caused the collapse of several mosaic areas (now being restored), those that remain are of compelling interest. *Note:* Skirts for women, please.

The Mastic Towns: Pyrgi, Olympoi, and Mesta. Mastic is a product of the evergreen shrub, *pistacia lenticus*, indigenous to much of the Mediterranean coast. Incisions are made into the bark, and the tree "weeps" crystal tears (sap) which fall into sand and harden. From this product, chewing gum and varnish, and the liqueur *mastica* were made. In classical times, the gum was considered a great delicacy and later was much in demand by the women of Turkish harems. Synthetics have replaced varnish, gum is no longer in demand, but the *mastica* maintains a steady production.

Pyrgi. The first town, Pyrgi, is the largest medieval town on Chios where life patterns remain mostly unchanged. Farming and stock-raising have stabilized the economy of this solidly built fifteenth and sixteenth century town. The facades around the center of the town are decorated with *xzsta* or *sgraffito*, a technique of engraving plaster into two-color bands of segmented, geometric motifs. Italian in origin, this type of decoration has been found in Padua and Naples. Bold, striking, pleasing to the eye, these designs shade from dark grey to white, all executed with skill and precision. The artisans seemed determined to make no two bands alike! This unique decor began under Turkish rule in the seventeenth century.

Pyrgi's hospitable main square (no restaurant, but tavernas provide plenty of liquid refreshment and nibblefoods) is dominated by the architecturally ambitious church of *Koimesustis Theotokon*, painted a baby blue with white *sgraffito*. The black-robed priests who frequent the square

Byzantine mosaic, Nea Moni

with other Greek men have an almost op-art setting for their visiting.

In the north corner of the square is a vaulted passage that leads to an important Byzantine church, *Haghioi Apostioi* (the keeper lives on the square). In the church, you will be asked to sign a guest book. Looking at the names and addresses proves that travelers from all over the world find their way to this remote spot.

Olympoi. About ten miles farther is the medieval town of Olympoi, with a few *sgraffito* buildings, but painted mostly in flat colors. After you enter the main gate, the streets become an intricate network. The defensive tower in the middle of town is in ruins, but its vaulted ground floor serves as a coffee house. A lucky spectacle to witness is a wedding feast in the community refectory.

Mesta. Less than three miles farther is

Mesta, the best preserved, the most solidly built, and perhaps the most stark and stony of the three medieval towns. Its arched and twisting streets are like tunnels with daylight filtering through intermittent openings in the vaulted ceilings. Built as a defense against pirates and earthquakes, it has repelled both, as well as Turks who came raiding for women.

The small main square is reputed to have the largest church on Chios. Elegant and with some fine sculptures, it features a charming blend of baroque and rococo styles.

Personal Comment

The island's two biggest attractions are Nea Moni and the Mastic Towns. Add to this the Kambos, and the tourist will have unforgettable memories.

Pyrgi

*Little Ikaria offers body repairs
and soul satisfactions.*

ikaria

GETTING THERE

From Piraeus: 6 ships weekly via Syros or Paros. Ship continues to Samos, returns via the same route to Piraeus. *From Thessaloniki:* 1 ship weekly on the Thessaloniki–Rhodes route.

DEPARTURES

To Piraeus: From Samos. See schedule listed above.
To Thessaloniki: 1 ship weekly (Thessaloniki–Rhodes route.)
To Fourni: Local excursion boat. Private arrangements.

HOTELS*

Ag. Kirikos: (D) Ilios. Many rooms and pensions.
Therma: (B) Georgios. (C) Anna, Galini, Apollon, Thermae. (D) Ikarion, Radion.
Therma Lefkades (Loutra): (A) Alifandis, Toula (hotel and bungalows). (C) Akti, Anna, Karras.
Note: Most of the hotels operate on a demi or complete pension basis. Pensions and rooms to rent.

TOURIST TIPS

Ikaria (Icaria) Island has an area of 267 sq. km./106 sq. mi. Its population is 9,000. No Tourist Police. You may need an interpreter for communication with regular police. Taxi and bus station is located at the landing dock. There are two daily bus services to the north coast of the island. The post office has the OTE. Ionian and National Banks of Greece have offices here. Shipping offices are in general stores. No bikes, cars, or mopeds are for rent. Siesta observed. Camping is allowed in designated areas, and there are yacht facilities, also.

*See Part I, section on Accommodations, for explanation of hotel grades.

HISTORY

Ikaria's history is illustrated by its few remains, including classical tombs and an archaic acropolis. A third century tower near *Faro* is a fine example. In antiquity, the island was known as Dolichi; the name changed when it was associated with Icarus, the first man in mythology to fly.

The art of the Byzantine period can be observed in the eleventh century church of *St. Irini* and a tenth century Kastro at *Kosoikia.*

The finds of the island are on exhibit during the school months in the Ag. Kirikos grade school.

Mythology
Daedalus, father of Icarus, built two pairs of wax and feather wings so they could escape from the Labyrinth on Crete. Daedalus told the boy *not* to fly too close to the sun's rays, for fear of the wax melting. Icarus flew too high; the wax melted, and he fell into the sea, and was drowned. Daedalus buried Icarus on the island, afterwards known as Icaria, and the Aegean around it is known as the Icarian Sea.

AG. KIRIKOS

Life appears to be very simple in this modest little port town, dominated by the elegant blue dome of the *Church of Ag. Nikolaos.* Why do tourists "jump ship" and linger here, sometimes for weeks? The sturdy Germans, Danes, Swiss, and English come for the island's superior beaches, the quiet, and the hiking, all culminating in a revitalizing vacation. The not-so-hardy visitors come for the therapy of the spas, which have springs known since ancient times for their powerful medicinal qualities.

Beaches

Therma. A beauty of a beach, served by excursion boat from Ag. Kirikos

Therma

every twenty minutes between 7:00 A.M. and 12 noon, and between 4:00 and 7:00 P.M. Therma edges a protected cove, banked by sheltering hills. It offers good swimming, plenty of hotels and restaurants, plus the therapy of the radioactive springs.
Evdilos. There is a bus twice daily. The island's only road stops at Evdilos. Your bus passes through spectacular mountain scenery with steep slopes dropping to wave-thrashed shores. Evdilos gentles down to comfortable levels, with sandy beaches offering space, light, and solitude. Here, the bus lingers for several hours before returning to Ag. Kirikos. There are tavernas and restaurants to serve your needs. Camping is permitted. Rooms are for rent.

Armenistis. Another older, slightly complaining bus will take you from Evdilos on an unpaved road. Armenistis has a pine-edged shore with sandy beaches. Camping is permitted. There are rooms for rent. From here, there are hikes to small inland villages for exploration of the island's history.
Therma Lefkades. Emphasis here is on spa therapy.

Festivals
July 17. Ag. Kirikos: feasts, speeches, folk dancing, music.

Personal Comment
This island has hidden charms to discover, and a simplicity that is refreshing. Beach enthusiasts would do well to investigate.

A mountainous, puissant island of forests, vineyards, running streams, and attractive towns that equates agreeably with the roll call of famous Samians of the ancient world.

samos

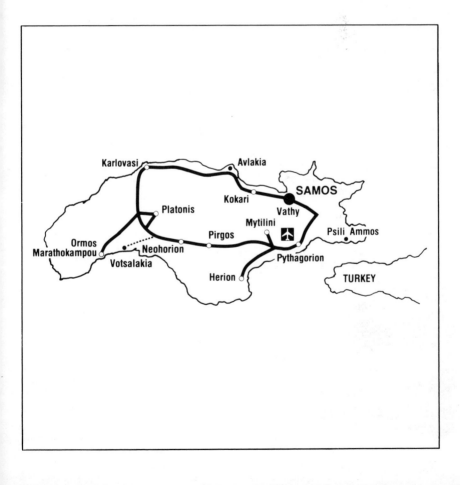

GETTING THERE

From Piraeus: 6 ships weekly, via Paros, Ikaria, and Karlovasi, or via Syros, Ikaria, and Karlovasi.
From Thessaloniki: Samos is on the Thessaloniki–Rhodes route. 1 ship weekly and return via Patmos.
From Patmos: Daily excursion boat in summer.
From Chios: Local bi-weekly boat between Samos and Chios.

DEPARTURES

To Piraeus: 6 ships weekly. Same route as above.
To Thessaloniki: Reverse of above.
To Kusadasi, Turkey: Excursion boats daily in season, also to Ephesus.
To Chios: 2 ships weekly.
To Patmos: Daily excursion boat in summer.
Note: Samos is also a departure island to the Cyclades (Siros or Paros).

AIR FLIGHTS

Between Athens and Samos daily. Samos Olympic Airline office: Them. Sofouli Ave., also Hotel Xenia. The airport is near Pythagorion.

Vathy harbor

TOURIST TIPS

Samos has an area of 468 sq. km./ 187 sq. mi. Its population is 32,000. Tourist Police are located next to the Post Office. The museum is next door. All front on a pleasant little park. Numerous taxis meet ship and plane arrivals. Rent-a-Car facilities are available. Use an English–Greek map since all road signs are in Greek. Many tour agencies are located on the Samos harborfront, offering tour arrangements for Turkey, island towns, and places of scenic interest. There is excellent public bus service to island towns; also a yacht supply station. National, Commercial, and Agriculture Banks of Greece have offices. Siesta observed.

HOTELS*

Samos: (B) Xenia, Samos. (C, D, E) Bella Vista, Ira, Ireon, Kohyli, Panthenon, Poleus. Many rooms to rent.
Kokari: (C) Venus, Tsamadou, Kokari Beach. Pensions and rooms.
Pythagorion: (B) Dorissa Bay. (C) Delfini, Aleandra. (D) Iraion.
Karlovasi: (B) Merope. (C) Morfeus.

HISTORY

670 B.C. Samians were rich from commerce and shipping. Ruled over the Asia Minor coast. *540 B.C.* The famous tyrant, Polycrates, came into power. There was a great leap forward in arts and learning. Temple of Hera, the Eupalinion Tunnel, and the Mole were constructed. After his death, the Persians dominated. *480–477 B.C.* Island joined the Athenian Naval Alliance. *129 B.C.* Roman rule. Island robbed of art, statues, treasures which were sent to Rome. *32 B.C.* Antony and Cleopatra set up headquarters in

*See Part I, section on Accommodations, for explanation of hotel grades.

Samos. *A.D. 400* Byzantine Empire began. *1120* Venice and Genoa rule. *1475* Turks conquer and plunder island. *1821* Flag of Revolution raised. *1912* Joined to Greece.

Famous People

Pythagoras, the mathematician and founder of philosophy and science, lived on Samos, as did Theodoros, architect of the Temple of Artemis at Ephesus and founder of the art of bronze casting. Rhoikas, chief architect of the Temple of Hera, was also a sculptor. Eupalinos (of Megara) engineered the water tunnel. Epicurus, philosopher, and Aristarchus, who theorized 1800 years before Copernicus that the earth revolved around the sun, lived here. Callistratus is credited with inventing the twenty-four-letter Greek alphabet. Aesop, who was not born on Samos, lived and authored his fables there.

SAMOS (VATHY)

The deep-water port at the north end of town accommodates all sizes of ships. The Tourist Bureau, a white building with wide stone steps, is at the end of the pier. A pleasant staff is there to help you. On one wall, a blackboard shows bus and shipping schedules.

The town has arranged itself in a pleasing pattern of red-tiled roofs and white and pastel-colored buildings accented by green foliage that spreads protectively or spikes upward with stately cypress trees. A gently curving bay is the town's frontage. From there, it nestles on slopes of amphitheater proportions. This makes for good walking among the upper streets, where stairways have a charming and sneaky way of leading one up, down, and around the old Turkish quarter.

At the waterfront is *Pythagora Square*, where an affable lion sculpture

Pythagora Square

is centered. Bright orange and blue chairs are arranged invitingly in front of the numerous tavernas and restaurants. Music comes from a centrally located sound system and is a conglomerate of Greek, rock, and unrecognizables. Here, one can pass the hours contentedly, savoring talk, silence, liquid refreshments, food, sights, and the endless activity that surrounds boats and fishermen.

The town makes a good home base from which to take bus trips around the island. It also has a few of its own attractions which should not be missed. *Archaeological Museum.* The cool-looking museum has two floors and is next to the Post Office and shaded by a little park. Open 9:00 A.M. to 1:00

P.M. and 4:00 P.M. to 6:00 P.M. Closed Tuesdays.

Among other objects here are terra cotta figurines from the eleventh century B.C., found on Samos. Imaginative in design, they depict animal and human forms. Here also are finds dating from the Roman occupation, an archaic bronze statuette, and an absolutely entrancing collection of griffin heads. Any craftsperson or designer of jewelry would find instant inspiration from the rich collection of numerous objects that are decorative, utilitarian, and even warlike.

Church of S. Spiridon. Next to the museum is an elaborately decorated church with some very charming, ingenious icons that offer a pleasing contrast to the museum's collection. *Byzantine Museum.* Tourists interested in the monasteries of Samos will see icons, crosses, codices, manuscripts, parchments. Many consecrated vessels, sacred vestments, and reliquaries in the Byzantine Museum, located on Oktovrion St., two blocks northwest of the boat harbor.

Dining and Entertainment

"Fill high the cup of Samian wine," wrote Byron, aware that the island was famous for its muscat grapes that make the sweet Samos wine. The island is not famous for a rousing, swinging night life, although a few discos have made an appearance in the larger towns; Pythagorion has the Surf Club. Most tourists are content to make a congenial evening meal last long into the night. Fresh fish is abundant and usually an excellent choice. Music is mostly juke box, unless the proprietor can afford the government tax put on live *bouzouki*. Dancing is spontaneous and can occur anywhere.

Samos closes down early of an evening, and on Sundays it becomes absolutely quiet. The only creatures on the streets are tourists, dogs, and cats.

Shopping

Samos has a good book store on the harbor for maps, postcards, and books in English. Pythagorion has the usual souvenirs, as does Karlovasi.

Beaches

Bus service is available to the following beaches, counterclockwise around the island: *Kokari,* a curving length of small pebbles. *Tsamadon,* close to the village of *Avlakia,* is a sheltered beach and a growing favorite with tourists. *Karlovasi* has a fine sand beach to the west. To the south of the island is *Votsalakia.* This is near the town of Ormos Marathokampou. The coast boasts three miles of warm, sandy beach protected from the *meltemi.* Between *Herion* and *Pythagorion,* along the Sacred Way, there are intermittent sandy beaches. The best are near the Temple of Hera and the castle at the west end of Pythagorion.

On the strait that separates Samos and Turkey is *Chrissi Ammos* (Psili Ammos), with views of Turkey that may almost lure you to its shores.

Excursions

Bus Station. Turn left at the narrow street at the northwest corner of the main square, Pythagora. One block in is *Square Nikoulaou,* the bus station. All seat tickets are purchased in the small office on your left as you approach the square. Passengers are not allowed to stand in the bus aisles, a policy not practiced on all islands. Usually, there are three buses a day to outlying towns, the last returning in the late afternoon.

Organized Tours. Soufouli St. follows

Kokari beach and boat builders

the waterfront; here are numerous multilingual tourist and shipping offices. The tour agencies sponsor day trips to Ephesus, Turkey, to groups of monasteries on Samos, and to island towns of scenic and historic interest.
Kokari. A twenty-minute bus ride will take you to this seaside village that offers fresh sights, new impressions, and, if you're lucky, some delicious, freshly caught shrimp. Shipbuilding is the main industry and, on a weekday, the sound of hammers and buzz saws mingles with the occasional lusty rooster crow.

The houses are unusually small and cling to the rocky terrain with barnacle strength. Vines enhance and brilliant flowers growing in olive cans bedeck these modest dwellings.

Tavernas, small hotels, and "Rooms to Let" homes line the waterfront

with its impressive length of clean, pebbly beach. Here, where the breeze is fresh and the sky a vast dome of blue, city life fades from the mind. Snugly tucked away in a small cove to the east of town is a group of tavernas and restaurants. Beer, *ouzo*, shrimp, fish, plus genial Greek hospitality may make you miss that last bus to Samos. Never mind. Up on the highway, there are cruising taxis just waiting for people like you. (Or, change your mind and stay overnight!)
Pythagorion. This little fishermen's village (formerly Tigani) has always been a favorite of yacht people, but since the advent of the nearby airport and the 177-room hotel, the pace of Pythagorion has become more lively. Pensions and guesthouses have opened the village to tourists. Cafes and restaurants line the harbor, shaded by bright awnings and interspersed with mulberry and tamarisk trees which soften the bluntness of the sun. Souvenir shops are plentiful and, as usual, their wares spill out over the narrow sidewalk. The fishermen still mend their nets and carry out their daily routine. Turkish caiques wait harborside to whisk you over to Turkey for a day or longer.

There is a charisma to the town that is undeniable, perhaps due to its glamorous past. It was here that Antony and Cleopatra "made merry" with a fabulous fling before Antony's great defeat in the battle with Octavius at Actium in 31 B.C.
Mole. As you sit portside, drinking your *ouzo* or eating your octopus, imagine this calm little harbor in the time of Polycrates (540 B.C.). The mole he was instrumental in building harbored the famous red ships of the Samian fleet, their captains ever alert to protect his city or to plunder some likely-looking ship passing through the Samos–Turkey channel. Today, the mole has the modern harbor built over it. You can walk on either of its

Pythagorion; Logothetes Castle at right

two long arms and look down into the crystal-clear water. Surely some of that marble below was there during Polycrates' reign.

Another thought to dwell on: famous Samians of the ancient world lived here long before Athens had Socrates and Plato.

Temple of Hera. If you can tear yourself away from the good beaches, the tavernas, cafés, and souvenir shopping, there are other historical sites with their share of allure. If you arrived by plane from Athens, you may have passed over a single, unaligned column of marble, all that remains of the great *Temple of Hera* other than the chunks of marble nestled in the tall grasses. The column is one of 160 in a temple that was 95 m./320 ft. wide by 47 m./160 ft. long.

Close by is the river Imbrasos, which is associated with Hera's birth. Her original Sanctuary has been traced to the Bronze Age and to the Pelasgians who worshipped her as the goddess who was the protectress of Samos. Mythology contends that

Jupiter threw down a wooden statue of Hera from Olympus, and that the hero of the Argonauts, Angaios, built a wooden temple to contain it.

The great temple of 525 B.C. was destroyed by fire; the second temple began under Polycrates was more elaborate, but unfortunately was never completed because of his death. The correct name of the site is *Kalonna*, and it is south of Pythagorion. If you feel moved to pay homage to Hera, wife of Zeus, protectress of Samos, Queen of Olympus, or if you just want to walk, this is a place to go.

Logothetes Castle in Pythagorion. On the site of the prehistoric town of Astypalaia, this castle is a pleasant walk to the far side of the harbor. It and the *Church of the Transfiguration* occupy the same hill.

Eupalinion Tunnel. Close to the airport and a half-hour's walk from Pythagorion is another wonder of the ancient world: the water tunnel engineering for Polycrates, completed in 524 B.C. and discovered by chance in 1882. Thousands of slaves labored for

fifteen years from opposite sides of the mountain. The final meeting was miscalculated with a minor error of 6 m./18 ft. in width and 3 m./9 ft. in height. The tunnel was meant to serve as an escape route and a water supply source in times of siege. Today, you can explore it, beginning in the hillside and going inward quite a distance.
City Wall. The wall climbs up the mountain, stretches east along the top, and returns to the sea near the monastery of *Panayia Spiliani.* Thirty-five towers have been traced, only the topmost part of the wall is preserved, and the views of the island and Turkey are worth the climb.
Island Tour. Although the island is only about 18 km./30 mi. long, it will take a long day to drive around it. The rugged center through *Pirgos, Neohorion, Platonis,* and to *Karlovasi,* on the coast, reveals an extraordinary fertility of vineyards, forest, and olive groves. Pirgos offers a good lunchtime stop among its pine-shaded terraces. Karlovasi is an industrial town. Inter-island ships stop there. The city sprawls into areas called *Neon Karlovasi, Meson Karlovasi, Paleo Karlovasi,* and *Port of Karlovasi.* At the bus stop (Neon), there are several excellent cáfes and restaurants, shops, and two theaters. Beyond the headland west of Meson Karlovasi, you will see some of the most dramatic scenery on the island; fjordlike ravines with majestic cliffs and crashing waves. Small tucked-away beaches are hard to resist.

From Karlovasi back to Samos, along the coast, is 64 km./40 mi. There are splendid views and numerous beaches. The drive along the northern coastline offers you the chance to make forays up into the hills and visit pictorial areas where friendly Greeks in their fields still stop their work to wave or even pose for a photo.
Mytilini, completing a triangle with Samos and Pythagorion, has a museum collection of fossils of large animals unearthed in that area. Samos mythology speaks of large and terrible beasts, the Minades, who lived on Samos.
Monasteries. In Samos, the tour agencies offer monastery visits that greatly ease the driving problem. (If you are on your own, be sure to check monastery hours to avoid disappointment.): Our Lady of Vrontiani (1560), Zoodehos Pigi (1756), Holy Cross (1592), Our Lady (1586), Prophet Ilias (1703), Our Lady of the River (tenth century), Holy Girdle (1695), Our Lady of Spilisni (1836), Holy Trinity (Modern), Annunciation (tenth century).

Personal Comment

An island of great historical prestige with adequate tourist amenities. Pythagorion is especially charming for those who prefer a light-hearted vacation. Those who enjoy the mystique of the past will have much historically hallowed ground to walk upon. A good "take-off" island for Ephesus.

IV
the dodecanese

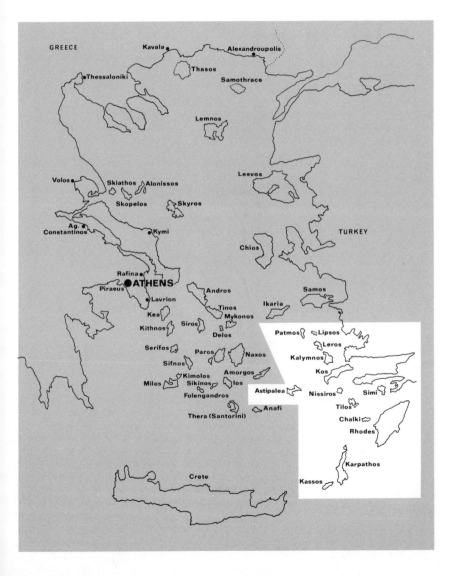

Tiny Patmos is a heart- and nerve-center
of Greek Orthodoxy.

patmos

GETTING THERE

From Piraeus: 6 ships weekly.
From Piraeus via Mykonos: 3 ships weekly.
From Rhodes via Kos, Kalymnos, Leros: 9 ships weekly.
From Thessaloniki: 1 ship weekly and return.

DEPARTURES

To Piraeus: 9 ships weekly, 3 via Mykonos.
To Samos: 1 ship weekly; daily excursion boat in summer.
To Rhodes via Leros, Kalymnos, Kos: 9 ships weekly.

TOURIST TIPS

Patmos has an area of 283 sq. km./ 113 sq. mi. Its population is 17,000. There are about 22 km./13 mi. of paved road through Patmos' spectacular landscape. Ships land at the port of Skala and, while the island does not have a Tourist Police, the local Gendarmerie is very helpful. Taxis meet arriving ships, and local men with two-wheeled carts volunteer luggage service. Shipping and tourist agents are in the main square. The OTE is next to the barber shop. Buses have regular service to the Monastery and to the island villages, scenic spots, and beaches. The bus and taxi station is at the wharf. It is always wise to check return hours before you depart for any destination. There is a yacht supply station.

HOTELS*

Skala: (B) Patmion (pension). (C) Astoria, Chris, Hotel Diethnes. (D) Rex. Many rooms in Skala. Inquire at Police Station for information on camping and rooms in outlying villages.
Grikou: (B) Xenia.

*See Part I, section on Accommodations, for explanation of hotel grades.

HISTORY

Fourteenth to eighth centuries B.C. Prehistoric period. Mycenaean and Geometric potsherds have been found dating from this era. *A.D. 1* St. John exiled on Patmos. *Seventh to eleventh centuries A.D.* Construction of the Monastery. *1300* Chora (upper town) built. Shipping and maritime activity established. *1600* Turkish domination. *1659* Morosini devastates Chora. *1713* Patmos School of Theology founded. *1812* Island was an active participant in the Greek revolution. *1912* Italian occupation. *1947* Liberation.

Saints and Monks
Patmos is considered to be one of the most sacred of the Aegean Islands. Here, in A.D. 95, St. John the Divine, by tradition identified with the Apostle John, was banished by the Romans. During his exile, he dictated *The Book of Revelation* to his disciple Prochoros. Immortality was given to the island by his words, "I, John, who also am your brother and companion in tribulation, and in the Kingdom and patience of Jesus Christ, was in this isle called Patmos. . . ."

In 1088, Emperor Alexius gave the island to a hermit-monk, Christodoulas, a saint unaware of most earthly perils but keenly aware of pirates. He masterminded the building of a nearly impregnable Fortress Monastery "as a school of virtue and always free from rights and laws." For those who had "unholy" purposes in mind, the Fortress had a balcony over the main gate from which boiling oil could be poured.

The Monastery grew rapidly in population and religious significance. In 1461, Pope Pius II took it under his protection. The Turks captured it in 1537 and made the monks pay an annual tribute. The Monastery continued to grow and prosper.

Down through the years, the monks have faced poverty, pirates, inter-

ference from authorities of the Orthodox Church, and all the hostilities
rampant in Aegean history. A typical
monk was a fighter, a builder, a collector of codices, a writer, a painter,
and collector of holy relics and icons.

Today, young monks receive train-
ing in theology, rhetoric, Latin,
ancient Greek, philosophy, and ec-
clesiastic music. (See the section on
Island Sights for more information on
monasteries worth visiting.)

SKALA (LOWER TOWN)

The ship harbor is in Skala, a small
town nestled into the curve of a fjord-
like channel, so protected it seems
more like a lake. Skala is a quiet,
friendly place where many Patmian
men spend time in the Square playing
backgammon or conversing. Very
often a black-robed priest will be part
of the group.

In this area are arcaded buildings
built in the Italian-colonial style, several restaurants, *kafeneions*, stores, the
police station, and a lovely Cycladic-
style church. At the harborside, yachts
and caiques rock gently at their moor-
ings. Yacht people are well acquainted
with this refueling station, and their
mast flags reveal countries from halfway around the world.

The more active hours for Skala are
in the early morning and late afternoon, when the Patmian women do
their errands. Other than then, they
stay in the area of their homes. A walk
through this part of town reveals
women sitting at their windows or in
groups on doorsteps. Busy hands do
the famous Patmian embroidery and
knitting.

If you are fortunate enough to have
a hotel with a waterfront balcony
room, you will have a box seat to the
daily drama of this slow-paced town.
Each day has its sound and light

Skala, view from Chora

performance. In a subdued cadence you will hear the deep male voices of the fishermen as they sit mending their nets, the chirping of birds, the buzz of an occasional motor scooter, children's laughter, the muffled put-put of a motorboat, or the deep tuba notes of the departing luxury cruisers.

The shimmering, pulsating light on the water has a vibrancy that slows only as evening falls. Then the light reflections turn to silver, and the gentle lapping of the water against the quay lulls the day to a quiet ending.

Dining and Entertainment

The second time you walk into a restaurant in Skala, the owner will probably come forward to greet you and shake your hand. This personal touch indicates the unrushed, non-commercial milieu of the island in early spring and fall. It also indicates that there is no plethora of eating places. Restaurants are informal, the food is simple, and featured are seasonal dishes. Vegetables are garden-fresh, fish is the day's catch.

The catch of lobster is an occasion. When a proud fisherman brings one into a restaurant, the Patmian men gather around and admire it. It is weighed and brought among the diners, who may bargain for it to grace their next meal.

The bakeries are worth exploring. One patisserie near the harbor has a captivating selection of Greek goodies, plus comfortable seating if you want coffee or tea.

Delicious nuts can be bought in the stores, and luscious black olives can be scooped from a can for that picnic of bread, wine, and feta cheese.

Juke box music blends with the balmy evenings and moonstruck white of this charming town. For lively, swing-a-long tourists the MELTEMI BAR and MELTEMI TAVERNA provide a fine fillip to end the day.

Shopping

In Skala, along the harbor, a spate of boutique shops has opened. In the Chora, near the entrance to the Monastery, is a rather unusual boutique and gift shop run by young non-Greek people who have brought a degree of sophistication to their gift-type articles. Inside the Monastery is a small shop that sells postcards of Monastery treasures and an excellent guidebook of the island should you be visiting "in depth."

Island Sights

The Monastery of St. John, the Theologian. The heavy polygonal Fortress Monastery looks more like a castle with its turrets and battlements. Its abrupt contours catch sunlight and shadow in stark patterns. The town of Chora, a cluster of white cubistic houses around its base, adds a dramatic finishing touch (see *Excursions*).

The Orthodox Easter Week is celebrated here with Greek enthusiasm and pomp, and Saint's Day, May 21, offers the faithful a chance for a very special visit.

Morning visiting hours for the Monastery are from 8:30 A.M. to 12:00 noon. There are three bus trips each morning from Skala to Chora. In the afternoon, four trips are scheduled, and the Monastery is open from 3:00 P.M. to 5:00 P.M. (Sunday, 8:00 A.M. to 12:00 noon). If you miss a 5:00 P.M. return bus to Skala, you will have to walk or call a taxi.

The Fortress Monastery is a fabricated world, complete unto itself. Here, religion is nourished, fostered, and kept healthily alert in order that its influence can reach all of Greece.

When you enter the worn stone gateway and walk into a narrow courtyard, you will see handsome, buttressed arches overhead. They reveal a celestial blue sky that im-

Monastery of St. John the Theologian

mediately gives you a sense of upward, unending space.

Two small chapels are dark, stained with the candle smoke of centuries, with flaked frescoes. The old, ornate furnishings are heavy and dark. Near here, the tour groups stand attentively, listening to priest guides.

Leading away from the court is a labyrinth of passageways. The refectory has long stone tables where the monks dine. If you come as an important guest, you will be seated here and served wine which the monks make.

The Treasury has centuries-old religious and artistic objects of great value. There are vestments embroidered with pearls, a superb crozier with sixty-two diamonds, benediction crosses, and icons galore.

The Library was founded in the eleventh century and contains some 800 manuscripts of different epochs and 2,000 books, among them thirty-three leaves of the Codex Porphyrius comprising most of the Gospel of St. Mark. In some devious manner 182 pages were spirited away to Leningrad. Oxford has some pages, too. Other valuables in the library are an eighth-century *Book of Job* and *Discourses of St. Gregory*.

Climb to the roof terraces and see still another world. Immediately about you is the dazzling white of the inner Monastery. Walkways, domes, bell tower, stairways, arched windows, crosses, balconies: all are architectural triumphs. The absolute final touch against all this whiteness will be a black-robed monk striding, his robes flared by the freshest of breezes.

From this vantage point you can see one of the vastest views anywhere in the Dodecanese. You can spin on your heel, turn full circle, and the view fans out from your spot. The horizon of the Aegean, an incredible blue, meets the blue from above, and they meld together perfectly.

Your eyes will sweep the contours of the island of Patmos. Distorted, irregular, barren, and largely arid; but, seen from the Monastery's height, the landscape is strikingly beautiful. When you leave, you will have experienced space; Greek space, powerful and peaceful.

The Monastery of the Apocalypse.

Situated about halfway between Chora and Skala, this building has chapels and cells built over and around the island's most important sanctuary, the Cave of the Revelation. The once-barren cave is now heavily furnished with ornate fixtures. A monk will lead you down steps through the Chapel of St. Anne. Tradition has it that here St. John heard the voice of God through a crack in the ceiling and dictated the resulting Revelations to his student, Prochorus.

Excursions and Beaches

Chora. The new road from Scala to Chora is blacktop all the way, and it winds back and forth among the craggy, gorse-covered hills. The old stony muletrack dispenses with such nonsense and heads as straight for Chora as possible. It's a 20-minute walk, faster by mule if it will trot.

Nowadays, the muletrack is still used by natives and curious tourists who have the time to linger along the way and enjoy the spectacular views. If you are interested, you should consider riding the bus up to Chora and then strolling down.

Your wandering through Chora may begin with any of several lanes. Ever changing in width, they will lead you through a maze. Buildings are painted a dazzling white. Some are old and stately, built by the island's famous seafarers of the past. Others are small and unpretentious, but still unique. The builders did not consciously strive for aesthetic levels, but attained them through innate artistry.

Churches are numerous. Many are simple vaulted buildings; others are twin-sized, with a small bell tower above the entrance. For the islanders, the church is elemental to their lives. They borrow money to build them, support them for a lifetime, even provide for maintenance that will be needed after their deaths. Saints become associated with the family name and share the fortune or misfortune of the family members.

Roof terrace, Fortress Monastery

There are several tavernas in the Chora. The one nearest the Monastery entrance seems to be the liveliest. You may see a Frenchman talking to two Australian girls; a young student priest come striding in, partake of his chosen refreshment, then stride out again; Germans, Belgians, Dutch, perhaps someone from Los Angeles. It is a worldly place, this most sacred island.

A motorboat trip around the oddly shaped island of Patmos offers unforgettable vistas: sandy bays, steep rock promontories, the phantasmagory of emerald-clear water, the island silhouettes of *Lipsi, Fourni, Samos, Ikaria, Amorgos, Leros, Kalymnos,* and the coast of Asia Minor.

Choose a calm day and a boatman who has an awning on his boat. Settle on a price beforehand. You can avoid the midday heat by starting early, having a long lunch hour and leisurely swims at several of the beaches, and then returning late in the afternoon and into sunset-time, when nature will provide an extravaganza of land shapes and shadows, sea and sky.

Starting north from Skala, the motorboat passes the Bay of Koumani. At *Aspri*, you may want to stop for your first swim, or proceed past the lighthouse of *Vamvakia* to the Meloi Bay which has a fine, sandy beach.

From here, you will go around the Cape of Phokia and arrive at *Kambos*. This little town caters to tourists with its excellent beach and hospitable tavernas. This area is green, fertile, and has orchards and vineyards.

Your boatman will steer east from Kambos and around the cape. A stop could be made at the island of *Kentronissi* if you wish to explore the ruins of a hermitage. After the Cape of Gheranou, you will come to *Apollou*, where a hermitage of the last century is situated atop a small promontory.

The courtyard has shady trees and, if the caretaker is there, you will be offered a cool drink.

The next stop is *Lambi*, in the middle of the northern coast. Its beach is famous for its diversity of pebbles. The spectrum of colors and shapes may tempt you to become a collector. Here, too, is a small taverna for a quick pick-me-up.

Next is *Livadi ton Kaloghiron*, an old hermitage with a tempting beach. The coast now becomes steep and greenless until you reach the Bay of Lefkes, the most fertile region of the entire island.

After sailing due south, you can say goodbye to your boatman at either the harbor of *Mericha* or at *Chochlakis* and walk back to Skala.

If you wish to complete the round trip of the island, you follow the coast along the steep west shore to the southernmost point of the island. At *Diafofti*, a farming area, there is another beach. As you sail north, you will see the big rock of *Kalikatsou*, the object of many conjectures. The rock surfaces are chiseled to room size; there are chiseled stairways, and even a hand-hewn water basin on top, all pointing to the existence of an old, crowded settlement.

An easy distance away is *Grikou* and the port of *Sapsila*, both with good beaches, then a peaceful ride back to Skala. During the summer months, there are excursion boats to many of the beaches described. You can hike to Grikou by muletrack, and to Lambi from Kambos. Bus and taxi service are available to the major towns of the island and many of the beaches.

Festivals

If you are on Patmos in August, be sure to check the date of the fair of

Skala harbor

Panayia on either the sixth or fifteenth of the month. On the morning of the fair day, a religious service is held in the Chora. That evening at Kambos, a nearby town, festivals are celebrated outdoors with local folk music, dances, and a tempting meal of fresh fish or baby goat. If the festival falls on the night of a full moon, the fun and games become Dionysion, to everyone's delight.

A harvest festival at Diafofti is held September 14.

Personal Comment

Patmos is the perfect rest stop between Kos and Mykonos. The fast pace of those two islands emphasizes the peace, serenity, and quietness of Patmos. Many travelers consider it the most beautiful of all the Aegean islands. Those who will not commit themselves that far will still never deny its charm. Convenient boat schedules can give you two to four days there, and longer if you choose.

Diana's Island, quiet and restful.

leros

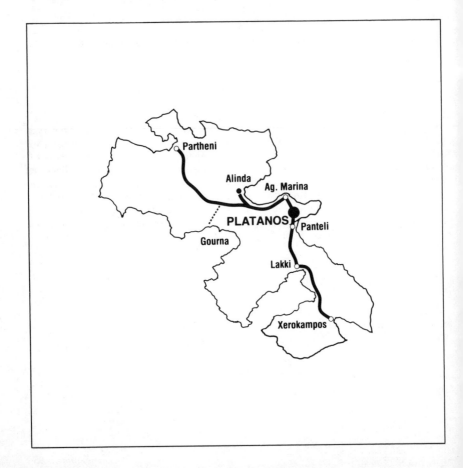

GETTING THERE

From Piraeus: Leros is on the Piraeus-Rhodes route, 5–9 ships weekly.
From Thessaloniki: 1 ship weekly.
From Kalymnos: Daily excursion boat.
From Patmos: Summer excursion boat.

DEPARTURES

Reverse of above.

TOURIST TIPS

Leros has an area of 52 sq. km./21 sq. mi. It has a population of 8,500. Regular police are stationed in the capital, Platanos. The island has good roads, taxi service, and bikes and mopeds for rent. Leros is a military base, which is the reason for the presence of all those handsome young Greeks. Siesta observed.

HOTELS*

Platanos: (C) Priklis.
Panteli: (C) Anemi, Panteli.
Alinda: (C) Alinda.
Lakki: (B) Zenon Angelou (pension), (C) Leros, Miramare. Many small pensions and rooms. See Police in Platanos.

HISTORY

Pelasgians were first inhabitants. *600 B.C.* Persian conquest. *431–404 B.C.* Spartan domination. *1 B.C.* Roman conquest. *A.D. 1300* Incorporated into the Byzantine Empire. *1306* The Venetian, Vinioli, sold the island to the Knights of St. John. *1522* Turks took over. *1912* Island became an Italian military base. *1948* Allied occupation. *1948* Return to Greece.

*See Part I, section on Accommodations, for explanation of hotel grades.

Mythology
Diana was an ancient Roman woodland goddess, a patroness of wild things and women. She was identified with the Greek goddess, Artemis.

ISLAND SIGHTS AND ACTIVITIES

Leros is one of nature's masterpieces of free form. Its hilly interior has sharp rises and deep plunges where lush foliage reaches to sand-fringed bays and coves.

Xerokampos, port for the excursion boat from Kalymnos, is a favorite with snorkelers, and its taverna is open all year. Taxis and a bus meet the arriving boats. The best way to see the island is by bus. The friendly driver makes a routine trip into a joy ride with his cheerful greetings to the islanders, who all seem to be old friends.

The island has six villages with a wide scale of tourist accommodations. Lakki, on the huge, cobalt blue bay, is fronted by bleak, white buildings nicknamed Italian-Extravaganza. The residential area is tree-shaded and quiet. *Platanos,* the island's capital, offers more tourist interest. The stores, the bank, museum, Town Hall, and tavernas cluster around a minute, tree-shaded *plateia.* Here, the taxis linger in the shade.

If you look up here, or perhaps from your hotel window, you will see the *Kastro*, another bastion of the Knights, who built it over a Byzantine castle. Inside this fortress, now used by the military, is a sacred, miraculous icon safely lodged beneath the roof of the gunpowder room. The fortress is closed to tourists, but the challenging climb to it promises an immense view.

From Platanos, the land drops sharply on both sides to hamlets, *Panteli* and *Ag. Marina.* Panteli, at sunset, is bathed in a golden glow. Fisher-

Xerokampos

men wind their nets, and families enjoy the early evening quiet. Later on, the taverna will be crowded with soldiers out of uniform, tourists, and the many expatriate Lerians with guests from such faraway places as Saudi Arabia and South America. Spit-roasted chickens, fresh fish, and countless bottles of wine induce a spirit of *kefi* (well-being) and unite the group into mellowness.

Ag. Marina, Alinda, and Partheni have attractive beaches where tavernas duplicate the scene just described. An extremely beautiful bay, Gourna, is reached by a short hike from the main road. It has an excellent beach, and its taverna is open during the summer months.

The island is unique in more than one respect: the Feast in Honor of Foreign Tourists in the village of Alinda on August 20 is a most tempting invitation.

Personal Comment

On your way to or from Kalymnos or Patmos, if you have the time, stop by.

kalymnos

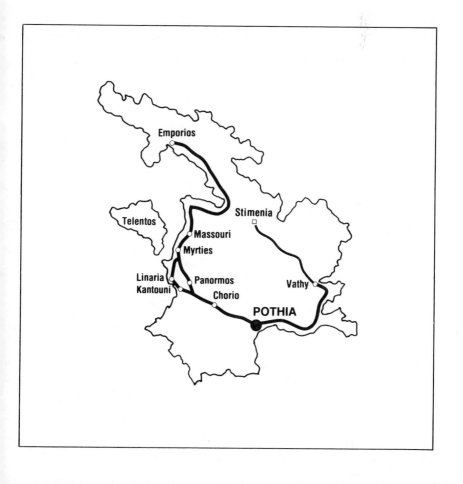

GETTING THERE

From Piraeus: 5 to 9 ships weekly.
From Kos: Daily excursion boats in summer.
From Rhodes: 5 to 9 ships weekly.

DEPARTURES

To Piraeus and Rhodes: Same as above.
To Leros and Kos: Daily excursion boats in summer.

TOURIST TIPS

Kalymnos (Calymnos) has an area of 109 sq. km./43 sq. mi. Its population is 4,250. Tourist Police are located to the right of the harbor in the half-domed, Italianate building. The post office is directly behind it. The OTE is beyond the taxi pool in Kypron Square. The island has one community bus which (at this time) travels only between Pothia and Vathy. Taxis are the main means of transportation. They assemble at Kypron Square, and the passenger waits until four or five others wish to go to the same destination. The modest fare is split. The same procedure is used for return trips. Bicycles and motorcycles are for rent.

The town has eleven travel agencies, and National, Ionian, and Agricultural Banks of Greece. There are a hospital and a clinic. Siesta is observed except for in all those harborside pastry shops. It is an excellent yacht harbor. Camping is permitted in certain areas.

HOTELS*

Pothia: (C) Olympic, Xenon Aris. (D) Thermes, Alma, Krystal. (E) Delfini. Many pensions and rooms.
Panormos: (C) Drosos, Katina Beach,

*See Part I, section on Accommodations, for explanation of hotel grades.

Kypreou, Plaza. Pensions and rooms.
Myrties: (C) Delfini, Atlantis, Marilena, Myrties.
Massouri: (C) Marias, Vallas.
Island has many pensions and rooms. See Tourist Police in Pothia.

HISTORY

Excavations of Pelasgic walls indicate that Pelasgians may have been the island's first inhabitants. Homer relates in the *Iliad* that Kalymnos, Kos, Kassos, Karpathos, Leros, and Nissiros sent a total of thirty ships to the siege of Troy. *447 B.C.* Island joined the Athenian League, although this did not keep the islanders from supporting the Spartans. Soon after this, they switched allegiance to Alexander the Great. *First Century A.D.* Roman conquest, followed through the centuries by invasions from Persians, Saracens, and the Crusaders. *1306* Knights of St. John established a satellite colony, although in *1522* they abandoned it to return to the defense of Rhodes. *1523* Suleiman, the Turk, took the island. Kalymnos claimed to be the first to take up arms against the Turks. (Other islands claim this, too.) *1912* Italian occupation. *1945* Allied occupation. *1948* Incorporated into Greece.

POTHIA (KALYMNOS TOWN)

Pothia is a noisy, gusty town bursting with good spirits. Along the harborside, traffic is active and, as usual, is a mixture of trucks, small vehicles, pedestrians, and four-legged creatures such as donkeys, dogs, and cats. The hundreds of sidewalk chairs are usually occupied, and liquid refreshments are dispersed early until late.

The occupying Italians left their mark in the form of several pretentious buildings and an open, morning

Pothia harbor

market that is a delight to those who enjoy the sights of luscious, fresh foods. Beyond the market, walking east, you reach an area that is reminiscent of Naples. Here, the fishermen's families live. Children are everywhere. They play among the rocks on the shore like water sprites; the boys foretell their future by sailing paper boats.

Mid-morning, along the harbor, beachbound tourists slap by on their rubber sandals, dressed in their briefest attire. Greek women, swimsuits covered by dresses and carrying sun protection parasols, are followed by broods of brown, nearly naked, rambunctious children. The town beach is on the far side of the landing pier and will suffice if it is impossible to get to the island's really great beaches.

At the edge of town is the boat building area, and beyond that an Italian-built thermal building, sometimes in operation but mostly not.

Knight's Castle. An enjoyable excursion (picnic suggested) is to the nearby Kastro Chrysocherias (photo page 100), where windmills and the ruins of the Knights of St. John are situated to give an enormous view of all about you.

Dining and Entertainment

After the sun goes down, tables are brought outside, and many are set for dining across the street next to the water. Those who choose to dine here can watch the fishermen prepare to go out for the night. Television sets are wheeled to taverna doorways, and Greek men pack together at small, outside tables to watch the soccer games. When a play excites or pleases them, they yell with delight.

STELIO'S Restaurant specializes in Greek and French food. *Poissurs* and *boulettes* share menu space with *moussaka* and roast lamb. SYRNOS, below the hotel Thermes, serves tasty

Kastro Chrysocherias

dolmathes, meatballs, and eggplant stew. Omelettes are served until 12:00 noon. The large Olympic Hotel has a pension-type, fixed menu.

For another kind of dining walk into the maze of streets behind the waterfront. Here, you will find tavernas with wine barrels lining the walls, *ouzo* and *retsina* arrayed on shelves. Alongside the booted, roughly dressed fishermen, you can eat *fasalia*, a bean dish blended with tomato puree, celery, garlic, and oil. When cold and thickened, it is cut in slabs, deep-fried, and served as *mezes*. Mackerel, fried as a steak, is served with lemon and oil. *Foosas*, for the brave, are a hairy sea-fruit with black and crimson meat, also served with lemon and oil.

In these tavernas, the talk is loud and the music is louder. Here, you may learn to drink like a fisherman. *"Si yeas"*: "To your health!"

For the disco enthusiasts, there is

Pothia harborside

DISCO JACKS, air-conditioned. Or the KORINA, near the sea, under pine trees with dancing on a concrete slab.

Shopping

Sponges, of course. All sizes and many shapes. One, in particular, suggests a brimmed hat. Wet and wrung out, it promises a cool head for a hot day. Pails of water stand near the sponge displays, an invitation to wet, squeeze, and try.

No more are the brave sponge fishermen crippled by their trade. Deepsea diving equipment is modern and safe, and the men are sent to a school to learn techniques; but, happily, the customs that surround their trade remain. Prior to their leaving each spring, the days are filled with parties, marriages, and christenings. Gangs of men prepare the ships. *Galetes*, sea biscuits, are prepared by the hundreds, and salted beef is stowed away. Departure day is accompanied by a religious service at the harbor, where a bishop and his attendants bless the ship, and the relatives and friends on the harborfront participate. When the roar of the engines signals departure, the crowd waves and yells good wishes. Months later, when the men return again, there are feasts, dances, marriages, and christenings. Every sponge fisherman is a hero, and he is eulogized as a *pallikaria* (strong man, hero). They even have their own song, *psara-poula*, bellowed to the accompaniment of stomping feet and sloshing glasses.

The island is known for its dark, thin, thyme honey. You'll see many beehives on the road to Vathy. Also, there is a white Kalymnian cheese that comes wrapped in herb-scented cloth.

If you collect gold jewelry, look for the myrtle design used on the island since Minoan times.

COASTAL BEACHES AND TOWNS

The middle-western coast of the island, near *Myrties*, is being developed as a resort area. (See map and hotel listing.) So far, it does not have a commercial appearance. Most hotels, pensions, and rooms are nestled in cool greenery and many flowers. The beaches are scattered along the coastal road in a landscape and seascape of undeniable grandeur.

Beach tavernas serve fresh fish and Greek dishes. If the evenings are too quiet, hop a taxi into town for a bit of hoopla.

Telentos. This is a part of the island that got away. In the sixth century B.C., an earthquake struck, and Telentos became an islet. A motor launch trip to it will give you a change of swimming coves, plus another view of Kalymnos.

Vathy. Vathy once had a population of 80,000. Today, its population is 700. It has become popular with Greek retirees seeking restful seclusion. For the tourist, it provides a pleasant bus trip to a little town that has a marina for yachts, excursion boats, and fishermen's caiques. Good beaches can be reached by boat. There is only one taverna, but more are on the town's schedule.

The valley leading into Vathy is a dense planting of tangerine, lemon, plum, and apple trees. Crops are marketed in Athens, where Vathy fruit is a favorite. In the spring, the whole valley is a froth of fragrant blossoms. Neat blue-and-white houses cluster in the nearby craggy hills along with little chapels and sheepherders' huts.

INLAND ISLAND TOWNS

Like most Aegean Islands, Kalymnos has vestiges of 3,000 years of history, and much of the island is still a sleeping museum of antiquity. For those who intend to do inland hiking, the purchase of a detailed map is suggested.

Damos. Up the valley from Vathy, Damos is an ancient city where the Kalymnians had their citadel and fortress in Hellenistic times. Today, it is a sprawling ruin. Houses are hewn out of rock; a few are now used as stables. You can still follow the Sacred Way from Damos, where fine jewelry of Minoan design was secreted in ancient tombs. Damos was destroyed by an earthquake in 1491, and today the devastated area has all the characteristics of a moonscape.

Emporios. The caves in the cliffs that encircle this hamlet are used by shepherds. Unusual is the ancient stairway in solid rock that leads upward to a grove where twisted fig trees are protected by walls incorporating hand-hewn Cyclopean blocks. Ruins of an acropolis and a citadel could date back as far as the times of Knossos and Troy.

Stimenia. Here are remains of a temple of Zeus similar to the one on Delphi.

Chorio. This is on the taxi route to Panormos. The town is less Italianized than Pothia, and the older areas have stairways that melt into the walls, corners that curve, and pavements that swell and dip. Above the town are flanked cliffs, watercourses choked with boulders, crumbled ruins, and abandoned caves which once served as escape places in the days of pirates. The mountains above are bleak and beautiful. A climb upward gives you a view of islands lying in a haze that melds the edge of sea and sky.

Festivals

July 27 is the day of the large annual fair, held in honor of Ag. Panteleimon. Local folk dances and a lively open-air banquet.

Personal Comment

You have a choice of staying at a quiet seaside town, or in a busy city. The fleet of taxis and the short distances provide you with the opportunity to share your daytime and nighttime hours at both places.

Kos is an island of classical greatness layered over with carefree tourism.

kos

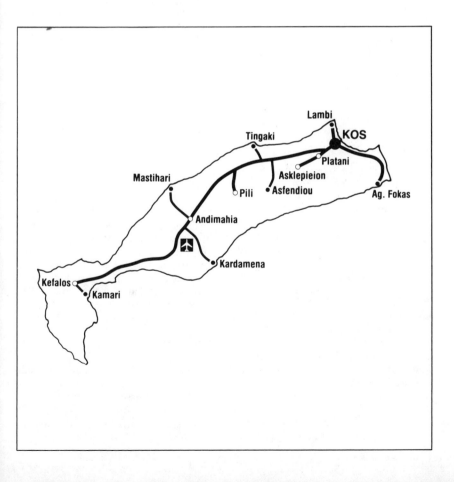

GETTING THERE

From Piraeus, direct: 1 ship weekly.
From Piraeus via Mykonos, Patmos, Leros, Kalymnos: 6 ships weekly.
From Piraeus via Patmos, Leros, Kalymnos: 4 ships weekly.
From Rhodes: 12 ships weekly.

DEPARTURES

To Piraeus: 11 ships weekly. Reverse of above.
To Piraeus via Amorgos: 2 ships weekly.
To Samos: 1 ship weekly.
To Nissiros: Daily excursion boats in summer.
To Rhodes: 11 ships weekly.

AIR FLIGHTS

Daily between Athens and Kos. Olympic Domestic office is at 22 Vasilios Pavlou Ave. Kos' airport at Andimahia is international.

TOURIST TIPS

Kos (Cos) has an area of 353 sq. km./ 141 sq. mi. Its population is 16,000. Tourist Police are located on Mandraki harborfront. Here you can obtain a free, keyed map of the city, bus schedules to island towns, and room rental assistance. Kos has twelve travel agencies. The OTE is at 8 Vironos St. The post office is two blocks back of the Agora, at 2 Leof. Vas Pavlou St. OTE here, too. Cars and more than a thousand bikes are available to rent. There are plenty of taxis. Taxi station is near the entrance to the Castle of the Knights. National and Ionian Banks of Greece have offices here. Shop owners observe the siesta, but most restaurants do not. There are telephone booths along the harborfront. The bus terminal is next to the Olympic Airline Office, a few blocks up from the harbor. No camping is allowed. There is a well-equipped yacht station. Small sea craft can be hired.

HOTELS*

Kos: (A) Atlantis, Continental Palace, Ramira Beach. (B) Alexandria, Dimitra Beach (Agios Fokas), Kos, Theoxenia. (C) Acropole, Christina, Ekaterini, Elli, Elisabeth, Iviskos, Koala, Koulias, Marie, Milva, Oscar, Veroniki, Zephyros.
Ag. Fokas: (B) Dimitri Beach.
Kardamena: (C) Panorma, Stelios.
Marmari: (A) Caravia Beach.
Many (D) and (E) hotels, plus pensions and rooms.

HISTORY

Fifteenth Century B.C. Island colonized by the Archaeans. *1184 B.C.* Islanders participated at Troy. After conquest, Kos hospitalized many injured fighters. *700 B.C.* Coalition with Rhodes. *600 B.C.* Conquered by Persians. *477 B.C.* Allied with Athenian Federation. *358-55 B.C.* Broke with Athens and allied with Alexander the Great. Island became very wealthy. Arts and sciences were developed. Byzantine period brought invasions from the Persians, Saracens, and the Crusaders. *A.D. 1315* Island sold to the Knights of St. John. *1525* Suleiman, the Turk, took the island. *1912-45* Italian occupation. *1948* Incorporated into Greece.

KOS TOWN

Hippocrates, whose practice of medicine included ridding the mind and psyche of stresses and strains, prob-

*See Part I, section on Accommodations, for explanation of hotel grades.

Kos harbor

ably would approve of the carefree pleasure-seekers who come to Kos. They arrive at a showplace harbor, lush with greenery and color accents of purple bougainvillea, scarlet hibiscus, and yard-high red geraniums. The salt air that comes off the sea keeps gently on the move. Coupled with the town's attractiveness is its citizens' broad and tolerant friendliness toward visitors.

Kos is small enough to explore superficially in a few hours. Several pencil-slim minarets and a few half-domes are architectural leftovers from the Turks. Greek and Turkish styles combine in the back business streets, which are somewhat reminiscent of Rhodes. Here are two cultures, for the Koan population is divided almost evenly between those of Muslim and those of Orthodox faith.

In-Town Sights

Castle of the Knights. This bastion is not to be missed. Entered via a bridge over Mandraki's palm-shaded avenue, the castle has a drawbridge and gateway. Here, among sculptural fragments, sepulchral monuments, and fine knightly escutcheons, you can wander and marvel at the building ambitions of the knights. In the great wall that surrounds the castle are openings where you can look down at the city, sea, and ships. An entrance fee is charged. Closed during siesta.

The Agora begins directly behind Hippocrates' Plane Tree. Propped to keep it from collapsing, it leafs bravely each spring. The fictional tradition that Hippocrates sat under it and dispensed wisdom will probably live longer than the tree.

Agora. Crisscross paths are deeply worn and lead to discoveries of fallen columns, broken pedestals, and beautifully carved sections of marble among the weeds, tall grasses, and towering cypress and palm trees. Quiet and deserted, today one wonders what it was like in 4-2 B.C. when the

Castle of the Knights

it. In Kos, living is for the moment (for all ages).

Because of the large influx of Europeans, foods tend to be less Greek, except for the beloved native specialties. The harborside restaurants have hundreds of outdoor tables, many placed as far into the street as the enormous overhanging tree branches allow. Cool and pleasant during the day, this same area becomes romantically attractive with twinkling tree lights at night. Posted menu cards feature *Chateau-briand*, "*Turnido Rossini*," "*Crepes Suzettes*," and a *Socrates' Special* that turns out to be beef flambé. You can order "Irisch" [*sic*] coffee, too.

A favorite place to congregate at all hours of the day or night is in Eftherias Square, where streetside tables are shaded by canopies and umbrellas. Here, various desserts and soft drinks

population of Kos Town was 160,000.
Museum. On Kazouli, the main square, is an elegant museum whose beauty enhances its treasures. Hippocrates has his own semicircular room. Among other objects are sculptures of the Hellenistic and Roman periods, plus a fine mosaic floor.
Ancient Greek and Roman Area. A few blocks up from the harbor is Grigoriou St. which leads to the Temple of Dionysos, the Gymnasium, Odeon, and the large number of Greek and Roman city ruins.

Dining and Entertainment

Kos does not have a formal *volta*, but about 6:30 each evening the downtown streets become a swarm of people. Chartered busloads of young men arrive from outlying towns; their youthful exuberance is clearly palpable. They're ready to be sociable, and the visiting female tourists know

Roman museum

can be consumed while you are people-watching and enjoying the silhouettes of the mosque and minaret.

You should consider hotel dining if you want to return to the formality of soup, salad, entrée, dessert, and coffee. HOTEL ALEXANDER is a good choice. HOTEL OSCAR has a Scandinavian ambience.

Kos has excellent wines: *Glafkos* (white), *Vereniki*, and *Apelli* (red), plus *Cair* (brut). Taverna-hopping can become a wine-tasting festival, which may include a cultural evening of listening to a Greek lad sing Greek poems set to music; it can also include dancing at discos and nightclubs as well as places that have girlie shows, live bands, and loud music.

Shopping

Ancient Kos was known for its fine, see-through silk, loved by the Roman women for its scandalous qualities. Today, Kos can offer its own variety of ceramics, much of it superior. However, most of the shops are overflowing with imports. Chinaware is featured from Germany, Czechoslovakia, and Bavaria. Better dress shops tend to have imports from Paris and Rome. The Italian shoes in the shop next to the Hotel Alexandria are outrageously smart in a whimsical way. Nikolesi's shop, next to the G.N.T.O., has handsome tailored men's and women's clothing made in Paris, but with a Greek label.

Beaches

Except for the harbor basin, Kos has beaches stretching for many miles on either side. Lambi, to the north, and Ag. Fokas, to the southeast, have restaurant facilities. Buses to the beaches leave the Kos bus station about 9:30 A.M. and return about 4:00 P.M. Beaches have pedalos, surfsail boats, kayaks, beach umbrellas,

and cots to rent. The beaches are heavily patronized. For other island beaches, see *Excursions.*

Excursions

A commercial bus tour of the island, in an air-conditioned bus, features the island's most scenic towns, a stop for a swim and a fish taverna lunch, and a return to Kos about 5:30 P.M. The regular island bus schedule is listed in the G.N.T.O. office. The tour includes:

Asfendiou. This is a mountain town with clusters of homes in three areas. The houses have kept their traditional appearances, and the town is known for its outdoor ovens for baking bread.

Tingaki. Swimming and sunbathing here, plus a fish taverna, are attractions.

Pili. A swing off the main highway to see the remains of a Byzantine church with fourteenth-century frescoes.

Andimahia. Inside the medieval castle are ruined houses, two churches, and several ancient reservoirs. The airport is near this village.

Kardamena. Here are long lengths of beaches, tavernas to enjoy, and a pottery factory to visit. Kardamena also has a large beach hotel complex.

Mastihari. A small fishing hamlet to investigate. Nearby is Marmari.

Kefalos. The long tail of Kos island is volcanic country, where the first capital was once situated. Natural caves are nearby. An unnatural artificial grotto on the sea has a nightclub-taverna. Kamari, the town's port, has a fine beach.

Asklepieion. This is the main out-of-town historical site, 4 km./2½ mi. from town by bus, taxi, bike, or foot. The latter two methods enable you to enjoy welcome diversions along the way: a ceramic factory where you can watch the skilled women apply the pallid colors that turn brilliant after firing; an amazing Muslim cemetery

Asklepieion

at *Platani*; a roadside taverna where drinks can be sipped under the shade of a grape arbor; Kos children calling out, "Alloow, Alloow," smiles and waves.

The Asklepieion is three-terraced and partly reconstructed. Here, patients were treated in surroundings of elegance and opulence. Although Hippocrates died before the Asklepieion was built, his medical techniques were used. From the highest terrace, you can see the Turkish mainland and look down on terraces once embellished with fine Roman statuary, bubbling fountains, and noble buildings. If you came on a bike, you have a treat in store. The return to town is downhill all the way. A whizz of a ride!

Festivals

Visitors are welcome at these religious fairs: July 30: St. Source of Life, in Kos; August 6: St. Apostle, in Andimahia, Savior's Metamorphose, in Kos; August 15: St. Virgin of Cacabinari, in Kos; September 7: St. Virgin of Tsokalarion, in Kardamena.

Personal Comment

No culture shock on this touristed island, just larkish indulgence in a cosmopolitan atmosphere.

The island that blew its top.

nissiros

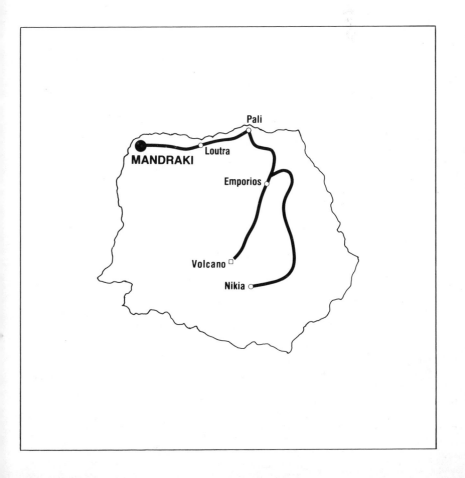

GETTING THERE

From Kos: Daily excursion boat in season.
From Piraeus: 1 ship weekly.
From Rhodes: 3 ships weekly.

DEPARTURES

To Piraeus, via Amorgos: 1 ship weekly.
To Dodecanese Islands on the Rhodes-Samos route: 1 ship weekly.

TOURIST TIPS

Nissiros (Nysiros) has an area of 43 sq. km./17 sq. mi. Its population is 1,300. Mandraki is the capital and port. English-speaking personnel are at the tourist information booth near the dock. Bus and taxi service are available on the island's five miles of road. There are sightseeing trips to the volcanic crater. Taxis take five persons; negotiate your price. Information regarding thermal baths can be had at the post office and Community House. Ionian and National Banks of Greece have offices here. There are local (not Tourist) police.

HOTELS

*Mandraki:** Three Brothers Hotel, Guest House Xenia, Community House.
Loutra: Thermal Spa.

HISTORY

Island was an Ionian colony and belonged successively to the Roman and Byzantine empires. *A.D. 1493* The Knights of St. John "liberated" it. *1573* Turkish rule began. *1914* Italians occupied it. *1945* The Allies, represented by the English, held it. *1948* Return to Greece.

*Category not listed.

Mythology
The island, according to Hellenic mythology, was formed during the Giants' war. The Giants persecuted Polyvotis by covering him and holding him under water with a huge rock detached from the island of Kos. In acute frustration, Polyvotis "blew," and the rock became a volcanic island.

ISLAND SIGHTS

Today, mythological eons later, Polyvotis' island has settled down. Lush vegetation grows in its mineral-rich overflow. The crater that he blew measures 4 km./2½ mi. in diameter, and the core approximates 225 m./250 yds. in diameter. Although the core looks like paved concrete, it is still hot, sulphuric, and dangerous. You will be standing safely at the edge, looking down.

Excursion boat landings are made at the island's main town, *Mandraki.* Here are restaurants for a luncheon interlude, several tavernas for libations, narrow streets to wander through, an outdoor museum, and the not-to-be-missed *Monastery of the Virgin Maria.* Two hundred steps lead to it and on the way are frequent rest enclosures carved in the rocks. Cool! At the top, an attendant will show you the Monastery's Madonna and Santos Chambers. Some of the icons were a gift from Catherine of Russia. Since the Monastery is enclosed within the Fortress of the Knights of St. John, you may wish to amble around the ramparts.

On the Holy Virgin's Day (Assumption), August 15, there is a big celebration. General merriment, dancing, songs along with church services, and processions are promised.

Nissiros has thermal baths; their therapeutic waters flow from volcanic springs which have been running for

Monastery of the Virgin Maria

hundreds of years. Loutra is the center of these baths, in case you have an ache or pain you wish to leave behind.

Nikia and *Emporios* are two other main towns. Emporios has volcanic caves to explore. (Ask locally for directions.) *Pali*, a fishing village, is a favorite with scuba enthusiasts.

Personal Comment

The daily excursion boat schedule allows four hours on the island. This is enough time to visit the island's main attractions and to capture its essence and charm. If you see the word "Kalesmenoi" chalked on the door of a home, it means that you are invited to a wedding. During July and August, the thermal spa is heavily booked. In spring and late summer, Nissiros is a place to relax and enjoy the hours that are strung together in sea and sky perfection.

*Simian motto: If a thing is worth doing,
it's worth sitting at a sunny
harborfront taverna and discussing it first.*

simi

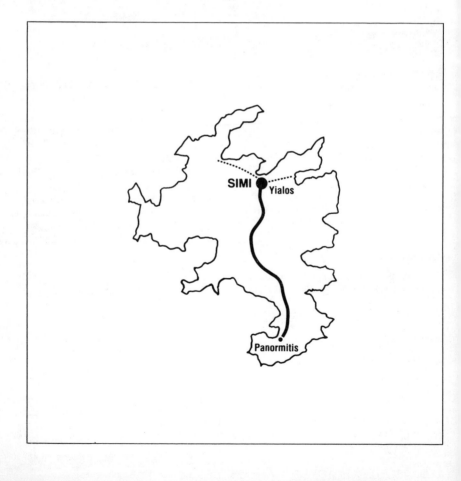

GETTING THERE

From Rhodes: 4 ships weekly. Also daily excursion boats.
From Piraeus: 2 ships weekly.
From Rhodes–Samos route: 1 ship weekly.

DEPARTURES

To Piraeus via Amorgos: 2 ships weekly.
To Samos: 1 ship weekly.
To Dodecanese Islands north to Kalymnos: 1 ship weekly.
To Rhodes: Daily excursion boat.

TOURIST TIPS

Simi (Symi) has an area of 84 sq. km./ 33 sq. mi. Its population is 2,500. Post office and Port Police are in the Italian building at the landing pier of Yialos. The post office has the OTE. Direct dialing is available from the A and B hotels. Travel agencies and ship agencies are situated in the winding streets near the Custom House. Personal cars are not allowed; motorcycles are frowned upon. Inquire about camping at the Town Hall. There is no underwater fishing. Boats are for hire. No Tourist Police, but local authorities in the town hall are very helpful. Siesta observed. Good yacht facilities.

HOTELS*

Yialos: (A) Aliki. (B) Nierus. Small villas to rent for one to two weeks. Many rooms in private homes plus a few (D) and (E) pensions. Inquire at the Town Hall.

HISTORY

Homer refers to King Nireus of Simi as the most handsome Greek next to Achilles. *480 B.C.* Island joined the

*See Part I, section on Accommodations, for explanation of hotel grades.

Athenian League. *412-11 B.C.* Spartans fought a victorious war against the Athenian fleet off the coast of Simi. *Roman-Byzantine Period.* Island closely bound to Rhodes as a defense outpost. Knights of St. John in direct control. *A.D. 1522* In exchange for privileges, Simi submitted to the Turks. *Seventeenth Century* Island became noted for its libraries and religious schools. *1821* Simi joined the Greek Revolution, although it remained under Turkish administration. *1869* Turks administered harsh restrictions. *1900-12* Severe depression. *World War II* When Germans withdrew from the island, they packed the church with munitions and blew it up; the church and surrounding homes were destroyed. Today, Simi is a National Monument.

Mythology
The god Glaucos, who constructed the ship, *Argo*, abducted Simi, the daughter of King Ialysos, and brought her to the island which he named after her.

ABOUT SIMI

Deep bays thrust into Simi's mountainous masses, which appear harsh and barren. It is difficult to believe that at the higher altitudes there are thick conifer forests, that winter rains revive the thyme, sage, and oregano into aromatic fragrance, and in spring there are poppies, wild orchids, rock roses, and crocus to enjoy as you hike to the Monastery Panormitis, or to some delightful cove for a picnic.

YIALOS (SIMI TOWN)

As your ship enters one of these fjord-like bays, you will see Yialos with its wide array of two- and three-storied buildings of neoclassic design. How

View of Yialos from Chora

and why neoclassicism was chosen remains a mystery, but the town is a harmony of facades with pedimented roofs and finely designed, fragile-looking balconies which, while sitting in them, give one the feeling of being sky-hung. Windows have ashlar stone surrounds; courtyards are paved with pebbles. On each side of the town, the mountains sweep down abruptly to the sea; at dusk, they turn purple-grey and blend with the sea's darker tones. In the morning, the sun paints the town golden.

The Second World War left deep scars in Yialos, and today the entire island is a National Monument. On a rock wall in town is a sculptured relief of an ancient ship with the inscription, loosely translated, "Today freedom spoke to me. Cease, twelve islands, from being pensive. 8th May, 1945." At a nearby restaurant, Les Katerin-ettes, is the sign, "The surrender of the Dodecanese to the Allies was signed in this house on the 8th of May, 1945."

Today, Yialos is not pensive. It is fast-paced theater with a continuous change of cast. First come the hundreds of day-trippers from Rhodes, arriving at 10:30 A.M. If the day is hot, they swim along the frontage of Yialos' two major hotels, then take a sortie through town, have lunch, and at 1:30 depart for the second half of their trip, a visit to the *Monastery Panormitis* on the other side of the island.

The town is very busy with these tourists and, when they leave, the emptiness turns to quietness until the siesta is over. Then the settled-in travelers and townspeople have their chance to be on stage. The audience that assembles may see an excited and noisy launching of a new boat that men have wheeled and pushed from the shipyard to the harbor center. It may be an admiring group of tourists staring at an extravagance of yachts or at a vehement Greek–Italian lady yelling at kids to stay away from her fruit stand; but assuredly it is groups of relaxed vacationers enjoying the exhilarating scene.

In-Town Sights

Chorio. The Chorio (upper town) is the oldest section of Yialos. It, and the Kastro above it, afforded protection in times of need. Five hundred easy steps will lead you to the Chorio and two hundred more will lead you through some of it. On the way up, you will see ruins from World War II incendiary bombs. Chorio streets and walkways are from two to twelve feet wide, with steps shortening the distance between them, and angling around huge plane trees and overgrown shrubs. The houses do not depart from the neoclassic style. If a new one is built, it follows the pattern, even if it means creating a false front. In the Square of the People's Union, *Laikes Omilos*, is a library with a rich and valuable collection. Nearby is a nineteenth century pharmacy, now a museum, complete with a nineteenth century operating room.

The museum and archaeological collection occupy an eminently handsome Simian mansion. (It takes persistence to find the person with the key.) Here are excellent collectables showing the affluence of the islanders from 1800 to 1900. There are a few Hellenistic sculptures and Byzantine objects. The Chorio has eleven churches. Look for Ag. Panteleimon and Ag. Georgios where, in black pebbles among white, is a courtyard mosaic of a fierce mermaid drowning the boat she holds like a small toy.

Kastro. When you reach the Kastro, you are, at last, on top. Here, you can read history into its walls, which suggest the passing of Byzantines, Franks, Italians, and Germans. Today, the jewel of the Kastro is the church of *Megali Panayia*. An icon of the Second Coming is an outstanding example of post-Byzantine painting. Nature's art is the view from the Kastro at sunset.

Restaurant row, Simi harbor

Kastro

Dining and Entertainment

Yialos is crowded with restaurants, many of them in remodeled harborside warehouses that were formerly used as such when sponge fishing was the island's main occupation. Now tourism has made deep inroads into the economy. Menus tend to be similar. Pastas, rice, or potatoes become the substructure for numerous fish, fowl, lamb, and vegetable combinations. The

Greek cucumbers, used in their namesake salad, have to be the crispest and mildest, their tomatoes the most succulent, their olive oil the purest, and their feta cheese the creamiest. One could make a meal of a salad, the good bread, and a bottle of wine—and many travelers do.

Conviviality in the tavernas is a rewarding way to pass the evening. GEORGIO'S in the Chorio has a vine-covered terrace for dancing, and you can look down on the harbor lights that are like flickering votive candles.

Shopping

The best buys are the interpretive island weavings of local scenes. There is some well-made local pottery. The usual boutiques have many articles from Rhodes. A Simi sponge is a lifetime remembrance.

Beaches

The walk to the in-town beach will bring you past the shipyards, a fascinating jumble of boats in repair and disrepair. Around the bend is a small, partly stony beach next to a concrete pavilion that is the summertime disco. The other alternative is to swim off the jetty in front of the town's two major hotels. Steps lead into the water. For other island beaches, see *Excursions.*

Excursions

Excursion boats line up mid-harbor waiting to take you to scenic coves for swims and picnics. Destinations are from twenty to fifty-five minutes away; the boat trip to the Monastery takes a full day.
Monastery of Panormitis. The island's new road will facilitate access to the other side of the island, where the eighteenth-century monastery has become a place of pilgrimage. To hike there takes about 5½ hours, and it is suggested you do so only as an early spring or fall jaunt. The Monastery has coped with as many as 5,000 pilgrims at one time. Its Greco-Russian Baroque architecture falls into that ambiguous category called ugly-beautiful. The Feast days of Patron Saints draw big crowds. The Sanctuary contains offerings from Simians who live in faraway countries. A treasure to look for is the magnificent iconostasis by Diaco Togliaduro of Kos.

Festivals

May 2. Ag. Athanasios (Chorio). This centers on a Byzantine custom, *Koukkoumas,* all about a maiden catching a husband. There is music, food, and dancing. Nine religious feasts between May and the end of August at various island monasteries, offer night-long festivities and a chance to learn some island dances.

Personal Comment

Before the trouble on Cyprus, little Simi was virtually unknown. When the excursion boats could no longer go to Cyprus, they came to Simi. Lucky Simi. Lucky tourists!

> *"I know no heaven in the earth*
> *More fair than Rhodes*
> *Or place more gay*
> *And strewn with flowers."*
> Lamartine (French poet), 1833

rhodes

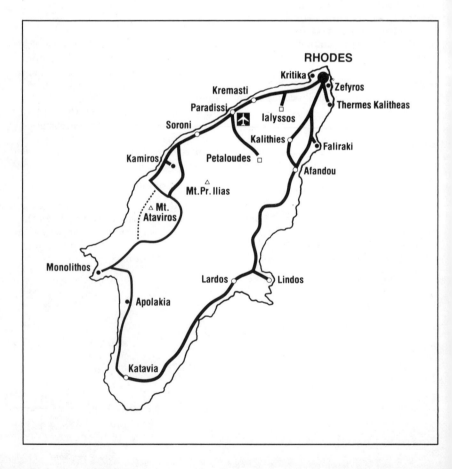

GETTING THERE

From Piraeus: 11 ships weekly (one direct).
From Crete: 2 to 3 ships weekly, via Karpathos.
From Samos and Islands of the Dodecanese: 12 ships weekly.
From Thessaloniki: 1 ship weekly (irregular).
Car Ferry service from Italy (March–November), France, Haifa, and Cyprus.

DEPARTURES

To Simi: Daily excursion boats.
To Crete, via Karpathos: 2 to 3 ships weekly.
To Dodecanese Islands north: 12 ships weekly.
To Piraeus: 11 ships weekly (one direct).

AIR FLIGHTS

Aphrodite, Old Town Museum

Daily between Athens and Rhodes. During the summer season, Olympic Domestic Airways has daily flights between Rhodes and Kos, Rhodes and Crete, Rhodes and Karpathos, Mykonos, and Thera. Rhodes airport is international. Direct flights from Italy, Germany, Austria, Holland, Belgium, Denmark, Sweden, Norway, Finland, Lebanon, U.S.A.

TOURIST TIPS

Rhodes (Rodos) has an area of 1,404 sq. km./561 sq. mi. Its population is 60,000. There is a G.N.T.O. desk at the Airport. The town office is at the corner of Archiepiskopou Makariou and Papagos St. The Tourist Police are located here, too. The G.N.T.O. desk has weekly shipping schedules of departures from Rhodes. Also available is an accommodations listing of Luxury, A, B, C, D hotels, and pensions. You can get room information from a helpful staff. There are hotels in Afandou, Faliraki, Ialissos, Kalithea, Kremasti, Kritika, Pr. Ilias, and Lindos.

You can also make a room reservation in Athens at a tourist agency or the G.N.T.O. office on Syntagma Square.

The OTE in Rhodes is in the Telephone Exchange building. National, Commercial, Ionian, and Popular Banks of Greece have offices. Car, bike, and moped rentals are available. Bus service to scenic areas. For private taxis, finalize a price before you start. There are many conducted tours of the island. Siesta observed except in eating places harborside. Excellent yacht supply station.

HOTELS*

Rhodes: (Deluxe) Grand Hotel. (A) Belvedere, Blue Sky, Cairo Palace, Chevaliers Palace, Ibiscus, Imperial, Kamiros, Mediterranean, Park, Regina,

*See Part I, section on Accommodations, for explanation of hotel grades.

Riviera, Sivarvast. (B) Acandia, Alexia, Amfitryon, Angela, Athina Palace, Cactus, Constantinos, Coral, Delfini, Despo, Esperia, Europa, Manaoussos, Olympic, Phoenix, Plaza, Spartelas, Stella (Pension), Thermae. (C) Achillon, Adonis, Aegli, Africa, Als, Amaryllis, Ambassadeur, Anthoula (Pension), Aphrodite, Arion, Astoria, Astron, Athinea (Pension), Atlantis, Caracas, Carina, Colossos, Diana, Diethnes, Dora (Pension) Egeon, El Greco, Elite, Embona, Flora, Florida, Galaxy, Helena, Hermes, Irene, Isabella, Laokoon, Lia (Pension), Lydia, Majestic, Mandraki, Marie, Massari (Pension), Mimosa, Minos, Moschos, New York, Noufara, Parthenon, Pavlidis, Perl, Petalouda, Phaaedra, Royal, Saronis, Savoy, Semiramis, Seve (Pension), Soleil, Sylvia, Tilos, Vassilia, Vellois, Victoria, Villa Rhodes, Żeus (Pension), Despina.

G.N.T.O. has listings of hotels in other areas of Rhodes. See *Tourist Tips.*

HISTORY

1400 B.C. Tribes from Asia Minor, Egypt, and Crete settled on the island. Phoenicians followed. *1200 B.C.* Dorians founded cities of Lindos, Ialissos, and Kamiros. *408 B.C.* New town, Rhodes, was created as capital. The city became great and rich. Nearly 80,000 inhabitants. *ca. 280 B.C.* One of the seven wonders of the ancient world, the Colossus, a bronze statue of Apollo was traditionally supposed to have stood astride the Mandraki Harbor entrance. In 225 B.C., an earthquake felled it. In A.D. 657, it was transported to Africa as scrap metal. *89 B.C.* Rhodes became a subject of Rome, followed by Byzantine, Persian, Saracen, Venetian, and Genoese incursions. *A.D. 1309-1522* Possessed by the Knights of St. John. *1522-1912* Turkish occupation. *1912-*

1944 Italian occupation. *1945-1947* British occupation. *1948* Returned to Greece.

Knights of St. John

In 1306, the Knights of St. John of Jerusalem, a charitable brotherhood founded to protect pilgrims on their way to the Holy Land, moved from Cyprus to Rhodes. They took the island by force after a two year siege. Their order was divided into Knights, Chaplains, and fighting Squires who followed the Knights into battle. They were of British, Italian, French, and Spanish nationalities, with French predominating. They were known as "Tongues," which designated their particular language.

The fortifications they built became a marvel of military architecture. Towers were placed strategically for the various "Tongues" to defend. In 1480, one hundred sixty Turkish ships blasted the Fortress with artillery. The Fortress held, and the Turks withdrew.

The Knights repaired the damage, increased the fortifications, and added parapets with firing platforms. Baffle plates strengthened the gates. The Fortress was no longer just massive, it was grandiose! A powerful fleet was assembled; the Knights grew wealthy through the expanded trade. Their naval power preyed on Turkish shipping and even assaulted the Moslem mainland at Smyrna.

In 1522 the Turk, Suleiman, attacked with one hundred thousand men and three hundred ships. A thousand cannons bombarded the Fortress. Massive assaults failed. Then, through internal treachery among the Knights, the Turks managed to secure a land position behind the Fortress and with continuous shelling the wall was breached. The Knights capitulated under honorable terms, and in January 1523, the Grand Master and one hundred eighty surviving Knights left

Rhodes and finally settled on Malta.

Under Turkish domination, the churches became mosques, a few scattered minarets pierced the sky, and the islanders reluctantly tolerated the new and strange culture.

The Italians captured the island in 1912. In 1947, it was officially returned to Greece. Since 1309, it had lacked true national identity.

CITY OF RHODES

If you arrive by plane, you will swoop low over an oval-shaped island of emerald green, edged in many places with fine sandy beaches. The city of Rhodes occupies the northern tip. The land southwest of it rises at one point to Mt. Ataviros, nearly 1,200 m./4,000 ft. high. Hills and valleys are lush with vegetation. Mythology suggests that the island sprang from the sea and became a gift to Apollo from Zeus. The myth is related to the fact. Rhodes originated from a volcanic explosion, and even today you can find seashells on its mountainsides.

In every possible way, the city of Rhodes is geared to tourism and, with few exceptions, visitors are treated with grace and style. With its Riviera touch, it deserves its name of "Flower City." Tree-lined streets, parks, gardens, lush blooming hibiscus, bougainvillea, and oleander thrive in its benign climate.

Arrival by interisland steamer is in the big commercial harbor next to the customs building and alongside the *Fortress of the Knights of St. John.* If you arrive by excursion boat, yacht, or caique, you will anchor in the delightfully situated Mandraki harbor with the two elegant deer aloft on slender columns, the *Fort of St. Nicholas* (1464), and a breakwater with several windmills.

Downtown Rhodes is a rather small area, and here you will find shipping and airline offices, travel and tour agencies, and many hotels and restaurants. Businesses observe siesta hours.

Mandraki Harbor. A day and nighttime focal point for tourists is the Mandraki Harbor area. You can promenade on the waterside and observe the luxury yachts with their watchdogs which roam stem to stern in devoted duty. Old, battered, campy boats, with wash hanging anywhere, often moor alongside the yachts in a relaxed intimacy.

The New Market, of stark white Turkish design, has cafes and patisseries on the harborside. Here you can sit with your Greek coffee, eat shamelessly rich cakes, sip *ouzo*, and watch the passers-by, or the ever-changing harbor activities.

Throughout the centuries Rhodes has experienced a number of architectural changes, but certainly the city owes many of its stylish waterfront buildings to the Italian reconstruction. Their buildings have a flamboyancy that has been called "Venetian Gothic." Outstanding are the Governor's Palace with its marble-decorated, arcade facade and the square campanile of the Cathedral.

The elegant minaret of the *Mosque of Murad Reis* is part of the waterfront complex.

Combining the Turkish, the Italian, and the massive, almost brutal strength of the Medieval Fortress, the result is a city of richly visual delight.

The Old Town and the Ramparts. The area within the ramparts (see p. 120, Knights of St. John) is like a museum, much of it in the open. The Collachium, or Castle of the Knights, is divided from the rest of the town by an inner wall. Here are the Inns of the various "Tongues," adorned with coats-of-arms. The palace, restored by the Italians, was readied as an ostentatious summer residence for Mussolini, but World War II stymied that. You'll

Fortress of the Knights of St. John

Entrance to Mandraki harbor

Fortress gate

find an Archaeological Museum, Hospital of the Knights, a Municipal Gallery, and a Museum of Decorative Arts.

Leaving these impressive edifices, one can walk into the shopping and living area of the town. Small enterprises line the streets. The living quarters above them often have the classic Turkish balconies. Walk the back streets for more nostalgia. Chances are you'll get lost, but you'll see people living in medieval surroundings. Aged walls, often buttressed, are brightened occasionally with whitewash and brilliant flowers.

Homes are narrow and dark, some with stone floors. Adults stand in doorways and smile at you as you pass. Cleanly dressed, healthy-looking children play in clearings once filled with the rubble of centuries.

Haven't we been on this street before? It's time to find a way out of the maze. Eventually, one rediscovers the main street of shops and restaurants and, for a moment, it is the flow of visitors who seem strange. You shake off the feeling of having visited the past and become a tourist again.

A tour of the ramparts is a must. Begin at the palace courtyard. If you are military-minded, you will get a defender's point of view: round and square towers, chapels, embrasures for artillery, guard rooms, parapets, and sculptures, plus one hundred fifty-one escutcheons of the Grand Masters. The width of the parapet for walking is forty-five feet.

The complete circuit takes about 1½ hours. A short-version guided tour, stopping at the Italian tower, takes about half an hour. Views of the Old Town and modern Rhodes are intriguing.

Acropolis. If you are "into ruins," you will not want to miss the Acropolis in Rhodes, although it suffers in comparison to others in the Aegean.

To the southwest of town, it occupies a gentle ridge called Mt. Smith, named after Admiral Sir Sidney Smith (1774–1840), who served on the island by keeping watch on the French fleet.

The Acropolis was partly excavated between 1924 and 1929. A stadium (restored) and a small theater of unusual square design are situated in an olive grove. The Temple of Pythian Apollo has a stylobate and occupies a higher terrace. The north ridge is the site of a Temple to Athena. Only a few foundations and column drums remain.

Dining and Entertainment

Dining is a big thing in Rhodes, and the restaurants, cafes, and tavernas go "all out" in their menus and decor. Some restaurants fly flags of the nations whose tourists they hope to attract, thus projecting a "just like home" feeling. Outstanding Greek dishes are served at the GRAND PALACE HOTEL, both as inspired buffets or as full dinners. The luxury and A-class hotels offer dining and dancing in quietly sumptuous atmospheres, featuring both Greek cuisine and European specialties. Decidedly informal are many downtown and semi-outdoor eating places. DEMETRIO'S TAVERNA, near the New Market, has whole lamb, pork, and chicken turning on the spits. Select the cut you wish and enjoy it with a salad, bread, and potatoes at an outside table. Typical of the night life is the COPA CABANA, quiet until 11:00 P.M., but by 1:00 A.M. going full tilt and continuing almost until dawn. Flowers are sold to the customers, who toss them at the entertainers. You may prefer a more robust gesture: breaking lightweight plates in ingenious ways (for instance, on the top of your head), then tossing them on the stage as a gesture of

Syrtaki dancers (*Photo courtesy Greek National Tourist Organization*)

appreciation. (You pay for the plates.)

Cafes and tavernas in the Old Town are lively at night, and any foods, from snacks to full-course dinners, can be eaten to the blast of music or a singer belting out a Greek song. Try NIKO'S BAR, on the main street, or NITTY'S on Apellou Street.

The white wines of Rhodes are recommended. You may wish to try the *Santa Laura. Ouzo* and *retsina* and beer, of course, are available.

Among the livelier nightclubs are the RHODIAN CELLAR, RHODINI, ISABELLA, GOLDEN BEACH, RO-MANTICA, and BELL PASSO. Disco, Greek dancing, and *bouzouki* are featured. During the day, if you yearn for *souvlaki*, go to the New Market (Nea Agora), where the huge interior has stands which sell this culinary curiosity. Here, too, are vegetable markets overflowing with colorful, tempting produce of the season.

Roulette and baccarat may be played in the marble halls of the Grand Hotel from 7:00 P.M. to 4:00 A.M. every night. In the lobby are slot machines, all waiting to gobble your drachmas.

The Sound and Light Festival of the castle, ramparts, and moats takes place from the first of April until the last of October. Check for performances in your language and try to see this "spectacular" from a comfortable seat in a boat for the dramatic water reflections. Tickets are available at travel agencies, the Rhodes tourist office, or the gate of the Municipal Gardens.

There are six outdoor movie houses. Greek dramas are presented in the Rhodian Municipal Theater, National Theater, and the Ancient Theater.

From July 5 to September 7, there is a Wine Festival in Rodini Park. The entrance fee includes all the wine you can drink. There is musical accompaniment from 7:00 P.M. to 1:00 A.M. Here, too, is the Greek Dance Festival. Agile Greeks in stunning native costumes do folk dances. Sit forward in the auditorium if flashing cameras annoy you.

Added to the natural attractiveness of Rodini Park is an intriguing zoo in a ravine setting.

Painting and handicraft exhibits change continuously. Many feast days and local fairs are held in nearby towns and can blossom into quite a celebration. For information, see the Tourist Police or a tour agent.

The Aquarium is for those who enjoy underwater life in the shape of exotic marine creatures. Night viewing downstairs among stone-walled tanks gives you the illusion of being underwater. Octopi, eels, starfish, and snail-like creatures may send you scampering up and out to the starlit sky and a stroll along the harbor.

Shopping

Rhodes is a duty-free port. Shops cater to buyers of designer clothes, fine jewelry, silverware, French perfume, and expensive leather goods. Notable Rhodian and Dodecanesian articles are Ikaros pottery, embroideries, and linens. More modest items available for the souvenir shopper are eight-track tapes of Greek music and dance tunes. In the Old Town, you will find brass and copper articles of every conceivable design. You can also find a variety of colorful enamel-on-copper plates and trays, very skillfully crafted.

Certainly try bargaining in the souvenir shops and places like the New Market; expect little or no success in a Gucci or Yves St. Laurent-type store (although one never knows).

Beaches

The public city beach is just north of Mandraki Harbor. It is wide, clear, but cluttered with an amazing collection of chintzy sun umbrellas and cots for sunning. If you participate, there is a fee.

Town beach

The huge hotels continue to be built along the west shoreline of modern Rhodes. Each has its own beach.

Zefyros, 1½ km./1 mi. south of the city on the east coast, is less crowded, less windy. At Kritika, on the west coast, there is a fine beach near the Poseidon Hotel.

Falaraki, forty minutes from Rhodes by bus, has a tourist pavilion and a splendid beach. Thermes Kalitheas, nearby, is another attractive beach in the Rhodes area. Buses leave from the K.T.E.L. terminal behind the New Market.

Excursions

Lindos. You may reach Lindos by motor coach or excursion boat. Either approach will be unforgettable.

From the road, you will see the crenelated hulk of the Fortress built by the Knights of St. John. Below, on its slopes amidst the greenery, is Lindos, a cluster of white houses, cubist in pattern. There is a nobility in the scene which quickens your interest, for you know that hidden in that Fortress high above the sea is the *Sanctuary of Athena Lindia*.

This legendary, warlike goddess, half-bird, half-female, could still the tempests, protect sailors and adventurers, and accompany them in spirit on their journeys and raids.

The approach by boat will give you a different view. The 350-foot cliff is sheared off as though it had been guillotined, and topping it in breathtaking white delicacy are the remaining columns of the temple.

Both approaches are blessed with the luminosity of Greek light, and the sensuous curve of the perfect little beach and harbor can only be made more beautiful if a sleek white yacht accents the Aegean blue.

Today, this traffickless town slumbers under the sun. Houses are decorated with twisted rope designs, arabesques, and often black and white pebbles form courtyard mosaics. Byzantine, Arabic, and native island decor attract the eyes as one wanders through the pattern of streets. The old Byzantine church has some fine mosaics and frescoes in its cool, shadowy interior.

Several outdoor restaurants offer local specialties, shade, and relaxation. If you are tempted to stay overnight, it is good to know that private rooms in homes are available. There are also several immense beach hotels a few miles away.

There are directional arrows to guide you to the Acropolis. Mules are available for those who prefer the easy way. For climbers, the long, stone stairway lessens the ruggedness of the

Lindos

Sanctuary of Athena Lindia

ating, with an underground chapel with fourteenth and fifteenth century frescoes and a ruined castle of the Knights. Nearby are late-Mycenaean geometric, archaic, and classical cemeteries.

Mt. Profitis Ilias. 51 km./32 mi. from Rhodes; thickly wooded. There are two hotels in Swiss-chalet style at 690 m./2,300 ft. A footpath leads to the summit. A feast day is scheduled in July. Check with a tourist agent for hotel accommodations.

Petaloudes. 21 km./13 mi. from Rhodes. Called the "Valley of the Butterflies." This offers a pleasant pathway walk with thousands of fluttering surprises. (Butterflies in mid-summer only.) Tourist pavilions.

Miramare Beach. On west coastal road near Rhodes. Good bathing, bunga-lows, bars, restaurants, tennis, and miniature golf.

Thermes Kalitheas. A fashionable spa. Often patronized by those seeking relief from kidney and liver ail-ments, diabetes, and arthritis. Caves of Hellenistic period, mock-Moorish buildings.

Mt. Ataviros. The climb takes about two hours and from the summit you can see the entire island. The summit has scanty remains of a Temple to Zeus. In the Byzantine era, it became the Church of St. John the Baptist. Votive offerings found at the scene are now in the Rhodes Museum.

climb. Once on top, you can wander on a summit that has kept its mystique from the fourth century B.C.

Other Things to Do and See

Car and moped travelers can tour the island on good-to-adequate roads. If you rent a taxi, be sure to finalize a price with the driver before you start your trip. Tours are available to most of the following places:

Kamiros. Homer's silvery Kamiros be-longs to the age before Pericles. Just 36 km./22½ mi. from Rhodes, it may be combined with a trip to Ialyssos. Kamiros has been called a "Little Pompeii." Once a place of splendor, it was rediscovered in 1859, after cen-turies of oblivion. In ancient times, the road between it and Rhodes was lined with statuary. The ruins occupy a hill that slopes toward the sea. There are stone foundations, no walkways. A picnic is suggested.

Ialyssos. Ruins here are minimal, but the *Monastery of Philerimos* is fascin-

Personal Comment

Days and nights can flow together seamlessly on this attractive, tourist-oriented island. To participate in all it has to offer, a week's stay is suggested. Less than that will require careful planning to make the most of every hour.

karpathos

GETTING THERE

From Piraeus: 2 to 3 ships weekly.
From Crete: 2 to 3 ships weekly.
From Rhodes: 2 to 3 ships weekly.

DEPARTURES

Reverse of above.

AIR FLIGHTS

Daily between Karpathos and Rhodes. On arrival in Karpathos, make departure reservations immediately (plane is small).

TOURIST TIPS

The island has an area of 257 sq. km./ 102 sq. mi. Its population is 1,363. The Tourist Police are stationed at the far end of the harbor street at a small park opposite the municipal buildings. Here, too, is the post office. The OTE building is nearby. The town has about a dozen taxis which meet arriving ships. The Olympic Airline Office is ñear the landing pier. Mopeds are for hire. The bus station is below the Karpathos Hotel. There are two bus trips to Aperi, Volada, and Othos in the morning, with immediate return. One trip to Aperi, Volada, Othos, and Piles is made in the afternoon. The bus returns the next day. (The same schedule operates for Menetes and Arkasa.) Camping is allowed on the island, but there are no facilities. The National Bank of Greece has offices here.

HOTELS*

Karpathos: (C) Porfyris, Romantica. (D) Karpathos, Anesis. (E) Zefyros. There are 35 (B) and (C) class rooms. See Tourist Police for information.
Amopi: (C) Golden Beach Hotel.

*See Part I, section on Accommodations, for explanation of hotel grades.

There are 22 (B) and (C) class rooms.
Arkasa: 10 (B) and (C) class rooms.
Olympos: 22 (B) and (C) class rooms.
Diafani: 22 (B) and (C) class rooms.

HISTORY

Karpathos was inhabited by Cretans, and the islanders took part in the Trojan War, according to Homer. *404 B.C.* Spartans subjugate island. *379 B.C.* Joined the Athenian Confederacy. *A.D. 42* Occupied by the Romans. *Fifth–Ninth Centuries A.D.* Saracens, Turks, corsairs, and Arabs held the island at various times. *1315* Knights of St. John secured the island for two years. *1317* Venetian occupation. *1538* Barbarossa, the pirate, captured the island for the Turks, who held it for four hundred years. *1821– 1833* Greek War of Independence. *1840* Treaty of London returned the island to the Turks. *1912* Italian rule. *1944* Occupied by the British. *1948* Returned to Greece.

KARPATHOS TOWN

After you have been in Karpathos (Pighadia) for a few days, you will observe that not only do the townspeople saunter down to see the ships arrive, but some of the tourists do, too. In a relaxed and slow-paced town, there can be high excitement over the sight of an arriving rototiller or an uncrated set of dining room chairs. The Greek men surround and admire that which interests them, the Greek women chatter and speculate until their curiosity is satisfied. For the tourist, after the bigness of Crete and Rhodes, this scene has freshness and vitality, and an intimacy that only a small island can have.

Although Karpathos is a modern town, there is an undeniable Italianate look along the waterfront. This

Karpathos Town

decorativeness goes well with the sight of a young Greek boy in lime-green shorts and a tangerine jersey, or a pretty girl sashaying by, purple shoes strapped above her ankles, wearing a golden yellow dress. You might see a stout man in a pink shirt and baggy blue trousers, or a black-and-white dog bounding down the street and flopping down next to a harborside table where uninhibited men are eating flaky, buttery *baklava*, walnut layer almost an inch thick and nestled in a spicy syrup. Time: 10:00 A.M.

This is a good time to explore the town. The country people have come down from the hills to do their shopping. Many of the women will be wearing native dress and they don't seem to mind the clicking of cameras. After the 11:30 A.M. freshly baked bread is ready, and quickly purchased, the streets quiet down. The backgammon players are deep into their games, and tourists who have rented mopeds are off over the hills, the Greek music blends with the construction noises from all the new buildings going up.

Another day in Karpathos. What to do? that is, besides enjoy the cordiality of sunshine, an inner harmony with the outside world, the fresh scene with no associations, or that delightful Greek ability to stare intently at nothing.

Climbers could ascend to the citadel above the town for the resplendent views of the little villages tucked into the magnificent folds of the island, knowing that where they stand was once the Acropolis to Athena of Lindos.

Dining and Entertainment

Restaurant DIACONIS, mid-way on Kolokotrou St., serves distinguished food in undistinguished surroundings. One should quickly add that the town's restaurants do not place undue emphasis on elegant appointments. Fish at Diaconis' includes *bakaliaros*, a light, flaky codfish in a crisp crust.

Island woman

The *souvlaki*, marinated in white wine, with lots of lemon, oregano, and garlic, is tenderly charcoal-broiled. If spinach is in season, you can order *spanakopitta*, an appetizer pie.

Dining at night along the harbor is brightened by lighting that is helped by the moon and stars. Here and there, pockets of brightness shine from the cafes and tavernas. Outdoor dining, with the gentle swishing of the waves a few feet from your table, is conducive to lingering far into the evening. Along with the tourists, the townspeople, mostly men, enjoy their evening's socializing. They crowd around tables,

heads bent forward earnestly in close attention to their discussions. Television sets with snowstorm images are completely ignored.

Shopping

There are several shops with impressive displays of gold jewelry, and fine coral and silver filigree jewelry. There is also an excellent shop with brass objects. All of these are located near the pastry and coffee shops facing the *plateia*.

Beaches

You will enjoy the sight of a splendid curve of beach at the northern edge of town. The island is blessed with sandy beaches and a sea floor that is tender to the feet. A convenient and attractive service, offered by the town's travel agent (office on the harbor street), is an excursion boat which will take you to a different beach each weekday for a fee. For these jaunts, you will need a picnic lunch.

The Hotel Golden Beach at *Amopi*, south of town (taxi or hike), has an idyllic beach, a bamboo-covered taverna, and a little chapel to add its blessing to the rocky coves and vast blue sky. All over the nearby hills is a small bush which, if a small piece is crumbled between the fingers, will give off a menthol scent that clears the head immediately. For those who venture further afield, there are other beaches. (These are described in *Excursions*.)

Excursions

It is simple and rewarding to take the bus ride to *Aperi*, *Volada*, and *Othos*. The bus will be crowded with the islanders who have completed their shopping, so sit on the bus driver's side to enjoy the dramatic vistas. The winding road ascends through the island's widest area with its great sweeps of rolling hills and stark rock walls, some split with ugly fissures. Here and there, you will get a glimpse of the sea, reassuring in its flat serenity. After traveling 8 km./5 mi., you will reach Aperi. Graves in this area have revealed coins dating from the time of Emperor Justinian. If you wish to see the town briefly, you can get off and catch the bus on its return trip. You can also hike on an unpaved road to the communities of *Mertonas* and *Katodio*, 6 km./4 mi. away. Nearby *Ahata* has a beautiful stretch of beach. Planning ahead could enable you to take a boat back to Karpathos.

Volada is about 450 m./1,500 ft. above sea level, and its claim to history lies in a proof that from this town came a small cypress tree donated to the Temple of Athena on the Acropolis in Athens while it was being built.

The morning bus trip ends at Othos, 12 km./8 mi. from Karpathos. The afternoon bus continues to *Piles* and remains to bring the villagers into town the next morning. Staying overnight enables you to explore Piles and its neighbor, *Steis*, two communities with vast views of the sea and the splendor of solitude.

If you elect to return from Othos, you will arrive back in Karpathos pleasantly massaged by the bus's vibrating springs and having had a full concert of Greek cassette music.

South of Karpathos are *Menetes* and *Arkasa*. The latter still has the charm of its long Venetian occupation and is considered by many to be the most attractive village on the island. Menetes can be reached on a paved road, but beyond that the stony road is especially hazardous to moped riders. *Finiki*, above Arkasa, is a fishing village and a favorite of holiday makers.

Those who stay in Arkasa during July and August (rooms available) may experience the hospitality of the Greek–Americans who have retired

there. Weddings are many, and they are festive occasions with much consumption of *retsina*, manifested, so we were told, by the way one must wade through the empty bottles to get out the door.

OLYMPOS

Many travelers come to the island to experience a visit to this town, the most interesting on the island. It has existed since 1420, settled by refugees who immediately isolated themselves from the rest of the world. So, it is a vast folkloric museum. Local dress, customs, social patterns, and houses are the same as they were hundreds of years ago. The women produce beautiful weavings and embroideries.

There are several ways to get there. You can take the two-hour boat ride to Diafani where there is taxi service to Olympos. Hiking takes about 1½ hours. From Karpathos you can take the bus to Volada, the start of a mountain trail for hiking to Spoa and Olympos (3–4 hours).

A surface road to Olympos may be finished by the time of your trip, and there will be bus service. Taxi fare from Karpathos is fairly reasonable if a party of four or five share the cost. On arrival in Olympos you can find rooms to rent.

There is good reason to call the village Olympos. While you are there, you will know why Zeus talked to the gods from Olympus. And, hopefully, you will "experience untroubled peace, a cloudless firmament on all sides, the white glory of sunshine, live, sleep and feast on nectar, and listen to Apollo's lyre."

Personal Comment

Karpathos is still one of the least visited Aegean Islands, where the Greek way of life hasn't drastically changed. At least, not yet.

other dodecanese islands

Among the Dodecanese Islands, there are several smaller ones*which offer a challenge to the curious traveler, or to those who are cruising in their own boats. Accommodations are in homes, hostels, and occasional inns. Island roads are minimal, usually dirt tracks fit only for man or beast. Small boats circumnavigate impassable land areas. Generally speaking, time spent on these islands is in the continuous present among simple scenes and happenings.

Lipsos (Lipsi)

Tiny Lipsos is near Patmos, and is on the twice-weekly Rhodes–Patmos route. A day's excursion from Patmos may suffice. Backpackers who stay will find excellent beaches, tavernas with reasonably priced food, and a friendly population of about six hundred islanders. To go to Leros from Lipsos, you will need the services of a fisherman who will put you ashore on the north end of the island near Partheni, where you can catch a bus.

*Refer to Dodecanese area map, page 85.

134

Tilos

Tilos is served by the north–south shipping route from Rhodes several times weekly. *Livadia*, the capital and port, has a guest house, hostel, and rooms in private homes. Livadia can be rather busy since the villagers come into town on the least provocation. Taverna life and ship arrivals are important to their lifestyle. Another big occasion is on July 27, when they congregate at the *Monastery Ag. Panteleiman* for their yearly feast day. Guest quarters are soon filled, but you may wish to be with the other islanders who sleep as close to the church as possible to absorb its mystical properties.

Megalo Chorio has a ruined medieval castle to explore. There are boats for hire and tracks to other villages where, on the way, a few scraggly grey ewes with curious yellow eyes will watch you furtively as you pass.

Chalki (Halki)

West of Rhodes is the tiny island of Chalki, served by the ship from Rhodes once weekly (with return). Life is very unhurried on this hilly

Waiting for a ship

island from which most of the populace has departed. Those who have elected to stay seem happily attuned to and content with the simplicity of their lives.

Above *Niborio*, the capital, a climb of 270 m./900 ft. will bring you to the *Horio* and its medieval castle. Built of Hellenic materials, it still shows ancient masonry. Inside is the church of *Ag. Nikolaos* with some fine, late-Byzantine frescoes.

September 14 is the islanders' lively folk festival at the *Monastery Stavros*. Love serenades are a specialty. Waterfront tavernas serve hearty food. Camping is permitted; there is a Public Hostel and rooms in private homes. Small boats are available to hire for chugging along the scalloped, sandy coast, where swimming is a private affair and the day is filled with a changing medley of Aegean moods.

Astipalea

If you are sailing west toward Amorgos, your ship will stop at Astipalea with its rough-hewn fortress, white domes protruding above its walls. *Periyialo*, the port town, wanders up the slope toward it in white, block-shaped houses. Except for about two hundred small shade trees among the houses, the town appears barren of foliage, and the surrounding hills have occasional sheer cliffs that drop to the sea.

Once you are inside the village, its charms make themselves known. Steep, narrow lanes wander between the cubistic houses, many with wooden balconies of criss-cross trellis-work. Venetian descendancy is proudly maintained in manner and customs, the heritage of the Quirini clan who ruled long and well.

The interior of the castle will appeal to those who like to mosey among narrow lanes, covered passages, and ruined buildings.

Livadi is rated as the most charming of the island's several seaside hamlets. If you decide to stay on Astipalea, you will be there until the next ship comes along, several days later.

Kassos (Cassos)

Emborio, the port, has a long jetty reaching into the sea, but if the Aegean is too capricious, the ship will bypass this little outpost island of the Archipelago.

Once prominent and densely populated, today life here has become very simple, with an occasional celebration of folk dancing, singing, and feasting.

Hikers will find places of sight-seeing interest. The cave, Selai, west of the village of *Ag. Marina*, has unusual stalactite formations. The villages of *Panayia, Arvantitohoi*, and *Poli* are as Greek as you could wish to find. The principal town, *Fri*, is where the wealthy seafarers lived, a reminder that Kasiot ships were the first to sail through the Suez and Panama canals.

Rooms are available in private homes, and Fri has two small hotels.

V
the cyclades

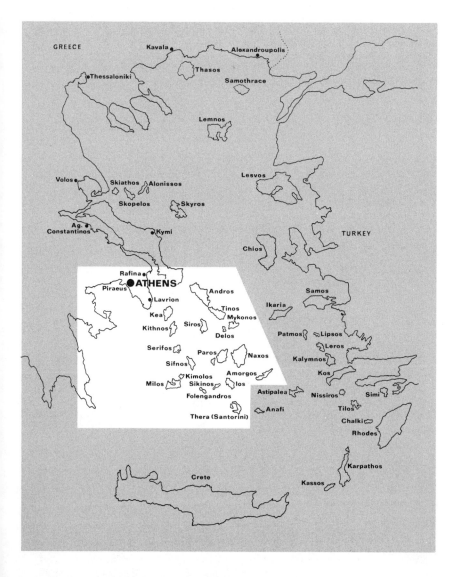

eastern cyclades

*Andros has all the accouterments
for a satisfying holiday.*

andros

GETTING THERE

By bus. From Athens to Rafina Port.
By ship. From Rafina to Gavrion: 14 times weekly.

DEPARTURES

To Rafina: 14 times weekly.
Note: Rafina is a departure port for sailings to Tinos, Mykonos, Siros, and Paros. Because it is an irregular line, see shipping clerk or travel agent about ticket.

TOURIST TIPS

In Athens the No. 12 bus from Syntagma Square, in front of the National Gardens, will take you close to Mavromateon bus terminal, 29 Mavromateon Square (near the Archaeological Museum). Buses leave the terminal hourly, and the trip to Rafina takes 1 to 1½ hours. When you buy your ship ticket from an Athens agency, be sure to obtain the sailing time and coordinate with the bus schedule.

Andros has an area of 350 sq. km./ 132 sq. mi. Its population is 10,497. Ships landing at Gavrion are met by buses which go to island towns. The local Gendarmerie will help with needed information in Gavrion, Batsi, Andros, and Korthion. Local stores cash traveler's checks, but for any extensive banking you will need to go to Andros or the branch bank in Korthion. Inquire locally for camping information. Siesta observed. Post office and OTE are in Andros Town.

HOTELS*

Gavrion: (B) Afrodite, Lykini. (E) Akteon, Athinaikon.
Batsi: (A) Olympic Villas (apartments), Irene's Villas. (B) Hotel Lyceum, Villa Love (apartments).

*See Part I, section on Accommodations, for explanation of hotel grades.

(C) Chryssi Akti. (D) Avra, Krinos.
Andros: (B) Paradise, Xenia, Villas Sophia. (C) Egli (Aegli), Helena, Korthion.
Apika: (B) Elena. (C) Pigis, Sariza.
Korthion: (A) Korthion. (C) Tryphonas.
The island has many beds available in private homes. See local gendarmerie in each town.

HISTORY

Island colonized by Ionians who built Palaiopolis. *480 B.C.* Island became subject to Athens, then to Philip of Macedon in 338 B.C. *200 B.C.* Captured by Romans. Ceded to Attalus of Pergamum. *First Century B.C.* Byzantine era began. Island heavily built with monasteries and churches. Pirates plague, and many tower dwellings were built as defenses. *A.D. 1207* The Venetian, Marco Dandolo, had the island as his fief. *1556* Island submitted willingly to Turks. *1823* Returned to mother country, Greece.

ABOUT ANDROS

Andros is a large island with lordly mountains, still snow-capped in March. In summer, their rugged tops snag the passing clouds. It is verdant and lush, and its gentle buffeting winds give the days a crisp felicity.

The three main tourist centers are *Gavrion, Batsi,* and *Andros Town. Apika* and *Korthion* are more remote and secluded.

GAVRION

Gavrion is a very busy port which you may enjoy if you like constant activity. If you intend to discover the island with daily bus trips, you may find it suitable.

Batsi Beach

BATSI

Batsi has a holiday atmosphere. Morning hours in the *plaka* are especially active: the loud and laughing voices of the Greek fishermen enjoying a morning libation, Greek housewives buying the day's food, and tourists lingering over their breakfasts under brightly colored awnings that bathe them in a luminous, flattering glow.

Batsi has enough tavernas and eating places for you to need a few days to make the rounds. For evening sky drama, try the restaurants on the terrace above the *plaka*.

One specialty, *phroutalia* (potato and sausage omelette, Andros-style), adds a fresh mint garnish for an extra flavor. The pizza restaurants on the *plaka* vie with each other for superiority of flavor. Stores sell snack food, fruit, potato chips, and soft drinks, good "makings" for beach picnics.

One disco, the *Maribout*, is a short walk up the hill from the plaka. If you dance long enough, you may hear a rooster's crow or donkey's bray announce the dawn.

In late morning, the tourists take to the beaches. Batsi's harbor beach has a sandy bottom, the kind of beach that invites you to take four or five big splashing steps and then belly flop into the water. North of town, there are rock shelves. Snorkelers like it here. A 45-minute walk south along the coastal cliff path will bring you to Ag. Marina. This beach has a taverna serving local specialties.

ANDROS TOWN

From Batsi and Gavrion there are three buses a day to Andros town. Schedules are planned to coincide with arrivals and ship departures. The bus ride takes one to one-and-a-half hours, and you will ride through a countryside of lofty mountain views, deep fertile valleys, and glimpses of the dazzling Aegean. On Andros, and on Kithnos, are mile after mile of slate stone hedges. The mind boggles at the thought of the lifting and fitting together of these stones, required to form territorial prerogatives.

The bus station at Andros is at the top of a hill, and you descend into town through its main street and a medieval fortress gate. Beyond this point, vehicular traffic is forbidden. The street is marble, and the buildings show strong Venetian influences, pride of upkeep, and a love of bright colors. Beside a lushly colored summer flower garden is the town's main cathedral, *Ag. Georgias*, enhanced by a brilliant blue dome. An elderly woman, dressed in black, may be sitting on a nearby bench. She smiles with pride as she sees you admire *her* church, while all around the sunlight is so bright that it makes the air shimmer.

Beyond this area, the town juts into the sea on a narrow strip of land. At its end is the windswept *Plateia Riva* with the *Maritime Museum*, a modern bronze sculpture of the *Unknown Sailor*, and the crumbled, eroded ruins of a Venetian castle that has succumbed to time and the thrashing waves.

Monument to *Unknown Sailor*

Andros folds up for the siesta. It appears deserted. The exception is the *Plateia Kairis* and its taverna-restaurant. Here, you can eat your midday meal under a spreading acacia tree and enjoy the view of the long, wide beach that curves out of sight.

The food is hearty: *youvarlakia*, meatballs flavored with cumin and garlic; *yemista*, vegetables stuffed with meat and rice, then baked; and many combinations of stews, plus the ever-tasty Greek salad.

Andros Town is a fine place to stay if you like an in-town atmosphere. On this side of the island, there are cool breezes even on the hottest days. Beaches are extensive, and the people are especially friendly.

Excursions

Korthion. If you take a bus trip to Korthion you will have ample time for

Ag. Georgias Cathedral

lunch and a swim, as well as for looking over the town's amenities. More remotely situated, it is in a vale surrounded by three mountains. The approach has a ruined Venetian fortress, and rows of gaunt, imposing towers. Cypress trees flourish, and the town is lush with olive and fig trees.

Apika. The famous Sariza mineral water is bottled here. It is a pleasant little village that attracts a large Greek vacation crowd in July and August.

Stenies. This is an old village with tall houses belonging to retired fishermen and seafaring men. Mainland Greek families have built their summer holiday homes nearby.

Menites. Gushing streams and cool breezes, lemon and quince jams, and walnut cakes made with honey are a few of the attractions of this mountain town. Here, too, are the square, lofty towers, a peculiarity of the island. When pirates came they were discouraged by boiling oil poured from above. No need for that today, and outer staircases have been added, windows installed, and comfort guaranteed for the dwellers.

Messaria. This town, in a fertile valley, has a church dating from 1157, of considerable merit and pure Byzantine in style. There are many dovecotes in the area.

Panachrantos Monastery. Built in 1608, the monastery nestles under a

Stairway to Palaiopolis

mountain ridge. It appears to be a brown village with a whitewashed church in its midst. Very often, huge misty clouds snag on it as they roll down the mountains. The church is beautiful with its Rhodian tiles, icons of saints in their silver embossed frames, and numerous other treasures. *Palaiopolis.* This archaeological site is known more for its attractive setting than for its extensive ruins. The island buses pass regularly; just say "Palaiopolis" to the driver and he will let you off. A second approach is by boat from Batsi to the small fishing port at the base of the ruin.

Palaiopolis was the ancient capital of the island. At its height, it was extensive and paid the same taxes to Athens as did Naxos and Paros. The site must have been ideal when it was complete, with its temples and public buildings. Rising up above it is Mt. Petalo, whose precipitous slopes send rushing streams down to the sea. The easy, wide staircase will take you through a hillside hamlet where homes have incorporated bits and pieces of classical distinction into their masonry.

The beautiful sculpture of Hermes of Andros, now in the Athens Archaeological Museum, came from the Palaiopolis site. You can still see the remains of a city wall, a few columns, and stones carved with letters. Much soil has washed down from the mountain and covered the area, and trees and flowers now add to the pleasantness of your visit.

Tavernas at the top and bottom of the ruins can take care of any thirst caused by your climbing endeavors. Many Batsi visitors come to the top taverna for an evening meal and juke box music.

Zagora. On the way to Korthion is this late-Geometric ruin. If the bus slows to a crawl, you can see the fortification wall and the remains of a sixth-century temple. Excavations are taking place, so if you have more than a casual interest, inquire about the hours.

Personal Comment

When you arrive at Gavrion port, it is satisfying to see the jostling, happy-looking, tanned crowd waiting to depart. It is almost tantamount to a guarantee of the good time awaiting you. Also, the island is a favorite vacation place for Athenians in July and August.

tinos

GETTING THERE

From Piraeus: 23 ships weekly, via Siros or direct.
From Rafina: 10 ships weekly.
From Mykonos: 26 ships weekly.

DEPARTURES

Reverse of above.

TOURIST TIPS

Tinos (Tenos) has an area of 195 sq. km./75 sq. mi. Its population is 8,236. Tourist Police are on duty during summer only. The island has bus service to outlying towns. Taxis and hotel buses meet the boats. No camping is designated as such, but during feast days the pilgrims sleep as near the church as possible, hoping that the healing powers of the icon will enter their bodies (see p. 146). Shops along the avenue to the church sell votive offerings, sometimes during siesta hours, depending on the crowds and their need to buy. For rooms and any

Dove sculpture in churchyard

Tinos harbor (*Photo courtesy Melanie Heims*)

camping information for other parts of the island see the Tourist Police. Siesta observed. There are yacht facilities.

HOTELS*

Tinos Town. (A) Tinos Beach. (B) Favie Souzane (pension), Theoxenia, Tinion. (C) Argo, Asteria, Avra, Delfinia, Flisvos, Galini, Leto, Meltemi, Oassis, Oceanis, Posseidonion. Many rooms available in private homes.

HISTORY

In ancient times, the island was called Ophiousa and was reputed to have many snakes, which Poseidon sent storks to eliminate. *480 B.C.* Islanders forced to fight against Greece by Xerxes' fleet. One of the Persian ships deserted from the battle of Salamis and informed the Greeks of the Persian plans. *A.D. 1207* Andrea Ghizi, a Venetian, captured Tinos. The long Venetian occupation caused the island to become the most Catholic of all the Cyclades. During this time, Tinos became celebrated for its doves and dovecotes. *1821* During the War of Independence, the Orthodox Greeks fought; the Catholic Greeks held aloof. *1822* Discovery of the miracle-working icon. *1940 (August 15)* During the Feast of Assumption, the Greek cruiser, *Helle*, was torpedoed in the Tinos harbor by a submarine of unknown nationality. War began between Greece and Italy.

TINOS TOWN

On no other Cycladic island does a street lead so directly upward or make such a positive religious statement as does the one that leads to the church of *Panayia Evangelistria*, Our Lady of Good Tidings.

*See Part I, section on Accommodations, for explanation of hotel grades.

The church exists today due to the discovery, in 1822, of a small Byzantine painting. Two workmen digging a well unearthed the small icon which, they claimed, was surrounded by a blue flame. Since antiquity, the presence of blue flame has haunted the Greek mind and is associated with earth myths. The first home of this miraculous icon was a small chapel where it began its career of healing the ill and afflicted. It soon found a new home, the resplendent Evangelistria. Some of the marble used to build this monumental edifice came from the Temple of Apollo on Delos where Greeks worshipped thousands of years ago.

An impressive staircase leads to the church and to a courtyard with pebble mosaics, shade trees, and porticoes. Inside the church the icon, once so modestly framed, is now so encrusted with emeralds, diamonds, rubies, and other jewels that one can only see the two small openings for the faces of the Virgin and Gabriel. The icon is protected by a glass plate which the worshipers may kiss. At night, it is put in a chromium-plated safe inside one of the church columns. Gradually, the icon's power has been accepted by the whole of Greece. It is protector of the nation and a symbol of national unity. It rules over the destinies of people and sailors in particular.

The church has its own museum of relics, silver and gold ex-votos (used candle holders), holy icons, and the all-important torpedo that sank the *Helles* on August 15, 1940 in Tinos harbor. Today, it is considered an important relic to remind the Greeks that the world "out there" can still harbor enemies.

The two main pilgrimage and feast days are March 25 and August 15. However, the Greeks do not adhere to pilgrimages just twice a year. When vacation time begins, usually in July and August, they come by the hun-

Church of Panayia Evangelistria

dreds to spend their days near the icon.

On the main street is a weaving school where young girls work at looms and complete yards of linen that show a high degree of skill.

Museum. The museum is built in dovecote style. One of its treasures is a seventh century B.C. colossal pithos (large storage jar) with five bands of frieze figures. Another 240 cm./8 ft.-high pithos has geometric designs. Andronikos Kyrrestes, a first century A.D. astronomer, is credited with the museum's sundial. Modern paintings and sculptures are in the upper room. Museum is closed Tuesdays.

Dining and Entertainment

Tinos has a sprightly harborfront life. Most hotels that line the waterfront have restaurant facilities. The blue- and green-canopied tavernas offer plain-cooked Greek food. Night life is most active during the pilgrimages,

when even illness and afflictions cannot keep those who have completed their devotions from enjoying themselves. Parades, dancing, drinking, and feasting are all a part of the scene.

Excursions

Tinos was celebrated for its doves, a table delicacy enjoyed by the ancients and throughout the Venetian occupation. On the farm holdings, the dovecote was usually next to the farmer's personal chapel. Today, as you travel throughout the island, you will see more than six hundred dovecotes, each in a different design.

Komi. If you fly between Athens and Mykonos, you will see how the little towns nestle into the green valleys. Local buses climb these hills with abandon and pass countless chapels flashing white in the sun. Komi, mid-island, is typical of these charming towns. For hikers there is a sandy beach, Kolibithra (Xolibithra), on the north coast beyond Komi.

Dovecote

Falatados. Set snugly in a hill basin, this town is considered the island's prettiest. All these small white villages reveal a strong Venetian influence, especially in the churches with their openwork belfries, lateral arches, and embellished facades. The vine is cultivated extensively. Tinos wine rates very high; the *retsina* and unresinated sweet wine are well worth your investigation as you travel throughout the island.

Xombourgo. This is the island's most important ruin. It is crowned with a ruined Venetian fortress, once pirate-and Turk-proof. There are also two ruined churches with half-towers of both Oriental and Italian design.

Personal Comment

This well-groomed, clean little island is well worth a stopover if you are sailing between Piraeus and Mykonos. One Greek lady on the ship going to Tinos said, "I've spent my vacation time on Tinos for the last twenty years. It keeps me healthy for the rest of the year."

Indubitably, Mykonos still reigns as "queen" of the Aegean, but whether you feel she is of royalty or of the theater is strictly a personal reaction.

mykonos

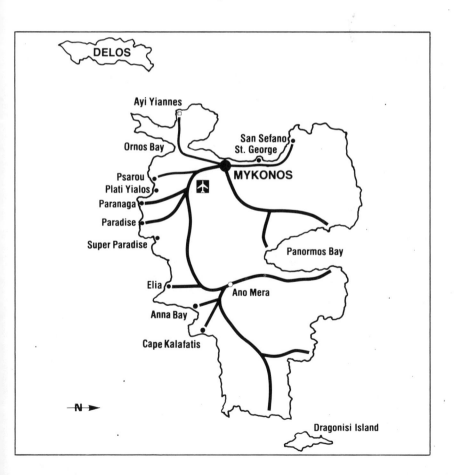

GETTING THERE

From Piraeus: 7 ships weekly via Siros and Tinos; 14 ships weekly via Tinos. *From Rhodes via Patmos and the Dodecanese Islands:* 6 ships weekly. *From Rafina:* 6 ships weekly (irregular line). *From Crete:* 1 ship weekly via Thera and Ios. *From Samos via Ikaria:* 1 ship weekly.

DEPARTURES

To Piraeus: 26 ships weekly.
To Patmos: 3 to 6 ships weekly.
To Crete via Ios and Thera: 1 ship weekly.
To Rafina: 6 ships weekly (irregular line).
To Ikaria and Samos: 1 ship weekly.

AIR FLIGHTS

Daily between Athens and Mykonos. Make flight reservations as early as possible.

TOURIST TIPS

Mykonos (Myconos) has an area of 37 sq. km./15 sq. mi. Its population is 4,000. Tourist Police operate between April and October. There are five travel agencies. Shipping offices are on the harborfront. The Olympic Office is near landing dock. Mopeds, bicycles, and jeeps are for rent. The town has four buses and fifteen taxis. Post office and banks are on the harbor street. Unauthorized camping is subject to fines. Campsite Paradise is 7 km./4 mi. out of town on the beach. There is an OTE, and most hotels have direct dialing. Tourist Police suggest that drinking water be purchased. Siesta observed except by a few restaurants. Excellent yacht harbor and facilities.

HOTELS*

Mykonos: (A) Ano Mera, Leto. (B) Aphrodite (beach), Alkistis (beach), Kouneli, Rhenia, Theoxenia. (C) Artemis, Bellou, Corfos, Magas, Manto, Marios, Mykonos, Mykonos Beach, Paralos, Petinos, Rohari, Sannis. Pensions Maroulens. Youth Hostel. Many rooms in private homes.

HISTORY

In antiquity, the island had two communities, Mykonos and Panormos. The latter has a few ruins of the medieval castle of Darga. In the Middle Ages, the Dukes of Naxos claimed the island, and it became a province of Tinos. In 1822, it repulsed a Turkish attack. The island came into prominence when tourism was developed for Delos.

MYKONOS TOWN

This town has a captivating charm. A person arriving without knowing the town at all, faced inward from a harbor street and told to meander and return in a few hours, will arrive bedazzled, bewitched, and happily entranced with the brief experience.

How does Mykonos achieve this charm? The answer, if there is any logical one, may be that Mykonos distracts you from your inner self, and, for the time being, you are completely caught in another force.

Mykonos is an architectural orchestration with melody that flows in unplanned harmony. One feels this in the streets that ramble without reason. They rise and fall, tilt to one side. Fortunately, the cobblestones are outlined in white. This keeps your feet solidly on the ground and delineates the verticality of the uneven, rounded, angled walls of sugar-cube whiteness.

*See Part I, section on Accommodations, for explanation of hotel grades.

Windmills at Cato Mylon Square

In-Town Sights

Mykonos Town

Paraportiani. A Cycladic gem, this chapel should be seen at various times of the day for a play of light and shadow. Moonlight provides an especially dramatic setting. Mykonos has more than two hundred fifty chapels, privately owned and cared for. Some stand alone, others snuggle between houses; there is one for every ten Mykoniots. Most of the chapels date back to the days when the fishing boats were engineless and anxious families vowed to build chapels to the Virgin if fishermen and boats were brought home safely. Today, these chapels are still used.

Museum. People who enjoy collectables will find the town's treasures of the past artfully displayed and proudly maintained by attendants. The attendants don't speak English. They point and pantomime smilingly.

Archaeological Museum. Here are important finds from the neighboring islands of Rheneia (425 B.C.), pertain-

Mykonos   151

Paraportiani

ing to purification rites. Also here are Delos pottery and a fine seventh century amphora (restored), showing scenes of the Trojan Horse and the massacre at Troy.

Dining and Entertainment

For daytime eating, the town caters to fast-food and snack-food enthusiasts. The bakery, a short distance from the taxi stand, has a line-up of tourists buying their apple, cheese, meat, spinach, or sausage pies. Doughnuts are for sale, too. Munch as you walk along. In fact, you can walk from one course to the next; and many do.

Evening dining starts late and is as glamorous as you care to make it. Beginning at the windmills is SPIROS' restaurant, featuring an elaborate selection of salads: *taromosalata*, mushroom, Russian, chicken, aubergine, fish, caviar, egg, and bean. One is tempted to try a helping of each. To go with this is grilled red mullet or swordfish. Here, you will be seated a few feet above the narrow beach with its lapping waves.

Next to Spiros is the PELICAN, with a very large area of tables. Here is served substantial food, such as roast suckling pig and an aubergine casserole. Beyond the Pelican is the Little Venice area. The SUNDOWN BAR is right at the water's edge. You'll recognize it by the octopus slung on a line. Charcoal-grilled, it becomes a delicacy. Their Greek wines feature *Caveros, Ellisar, Cinaroas, Laoura, Cabas*, plus the plebeian *ouzo* and beer.

The harbor restaurants are strung with lights. You have many choices here, but for elegance walk to the far end to the restaurant MYKONOS. Inside, it is invitingly conservative, with dark polished tables and chairs, and napkins looped perkily in tall glasses. Along with their well-seasoned Greek foods, they are proud of their seasonal fresh fruits and white figs from Corsica.

The many restaurants that crowd the area back of the harbor run the gamut from gourmet to hamburger. KOSTA'S GARDEN is romantic with its candlelight, flowers and leafy trees overhead. FISHERMAN'S TAVERN specializes in fish steaks. EL GRECO has an excellent menu with such foods as *sole meunière*, and lamb country-style (baked in *phyllo* and oven-roasted). Eggplant, stuffed with cheese and deep-fried, is another specialty.

Nighttime in Mykonos has Dionysian revelry in modern form. The discos start about ten o'clock and last into the early hours. Among the swirling lights, the rock sounds blare and escape from the door and windows to ricochet against nearby walls. The dancers seem mesmerized.

Small tavernas are crowded with people. At the MYKONOS BAR, they sit on cushioned wall seats, at low tables with drinks before them, and watch handsome, lithe young Greek men do authentic Greek dances: the *syrtaki, hasapiko, zeibecico, nisiotica, tsamico,* and *colamatiano*. All done with skill and pride.

Shopping

Not too many years ago, Mykonos was famous for its handloomed weaving, its rough-knit fishermen's sweaters, and its hand-dyed coarse yarn. These articles are still available, but you have to seek them in the shops that feature beautiful clothes for the beautiful people at commensurate prices.

During the day and until about eleven o'clock at night, the streets are hung with a bewildering and haphazard variety of clothing, basketry, shoulder bags, and even Petros the Pelican T-shirts. (Petros is a pet pelican who wanders among the tourists.) The busier souvenir shops are along the harborfront. Here are minor objects at minor prices.

The most interesting area clusters around Little Venice. The people who have these shops are mainly non-Greek artists, craftspeople, writers, and jewelers who have succumbed to the Mykonos charm, taken up residence, and earn their living by their talents. There are paintings and drawings of the Mykonos scene, posters depicting life in poetic, philosophical and artistic forms. Husband-and-wife teams join their talents to create unique jewelry, or embroidered and trimmed dresses that are collectors' items. Investigate the Gorgonos shop.

VERY SPECIAL

Hopefully, this young man will be wandering through the restaurant area when you visit the island.

Slender, dark-haired, and handsomely beautiful, he will pause beside a light-strung tree and begin to play his flute. The sweet, pure notes float into the shadowy night. Introspectively he plays, and from him comes an aura of enchantment. When he is finished, there is soft, appreciative applause. He steps back into the shadows and is gone from sight.

Has Pan returned to his woodland nymphs?

Almost anything of tourist interest can be purchased in Mykonos, from precious gems set in gold down to the bawdiest postcard.

Beaches

Buses leave the edge of town in the vicinity of the windmills. A board posts times and destinations.

Plati Yialos is the closest. Buses leave for it every half-hour. Taverna-restaurants, umbrellas and beach chairs, pedalos and surf-sail equipment are available here.

Psarou, a cove away, is reached from the road by skidding down a sandy hillside.

San Sefano, three miles north of town, is served by bus. There are two tavernas. You will pass *Tourlos* and *St. George* on your way. The bus driver will let you off if these beaches appeal to you. They also have tavernas.

Paradise and Super Paradise are nude beaches. Reach them by bus, then by boat.

Ornos Bay is a good hike from town, and has a sandy beach and hotel facilities.

Ano Mera is a hamlet near the center of the island. It provides access roads to coves and beaches. *Dragonisi*, a nearby islet, has eerie, macabre caves with an intriguing and shimmering blue light. Families of seals have taken up residence, but they don't mind visitors if they stay in their boats.

Personal Comment

There are those who say that Mykonos has "had it," that it is over-touristed, that it is no longer a truly Greek island. Regardless, try not to miss it. What is one more tourist, especially if it's *you*?

Plati Yialos beach

Ornos Bay

*"O Delos! Land of altars, land of prayers,
what sailor, what merchant of the Aegean
would dare to sail past your coast
in his fast ship?"*–Callimachus

delos

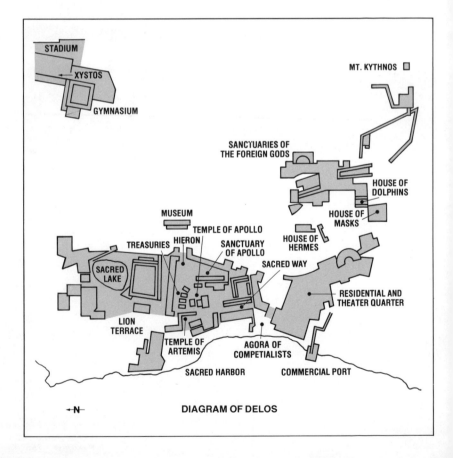

DIAGRAM OF DELOS

GETTING THERE

From Mykonos: Excursion launches and caiques departing daily, weather permitting. Half-hour trip.
From Tinos: Excursion launch calls at Mykonos and Delos, returns to Tinos. Check with Tinos ticket offices or your hotel for hours.

DEPARTURES

Boats remain at Delos, generally allowing you four hours for your visit. Confirm your departure before going ashore.

TOURIST TIPS

There is a modest admission charge. Sandwiches and soft drinks are available at the pavilion, or pack a picnic lunch. Souvenir guidebooks on Delos are available locally and in Mykonos stores. Worth investigating is a detailed account of the island written by the French archaeologist, Pierre Roussel. Sturdy walking shoes, dark glasses, and a hat are recommended for comfort. Many visitors come prepared for a refreshing swim, particularly during hot summer months.

HOTELS

A pavilion of four rooms is usually occupied in summer by the French archaeologists. Camping is permitted. No water.

HISTORY

Tenth–Ninth Centuries B.C. Ionians bring the cult of Leto to island. *Seventh Century B.C.* Festivals in honor of Apollo are held under the auspices of Naxos. *478 B.C.* Athenian Confederacy founded, a maritime league under the leadership of Athens. Treasury established. *426 B.C.* Purification rites. Decreed that all births and

Dionysiac relief

deaths must take place on nearby island, Rheneia. *422 B.C.* Athenians banished Delians on the pretext that they were impure and unworthy of the sacred island. *378 B.C.* Athenians institute a Second Athenian Confederacy. *315 B.C.* Egypt commands the Aegean. Delos enters its most prosperous commercial period. *250 B.C.* Romans move in. They dominate other foreign merchants and businessmen. *166 B.C.* Delos is made a free port. Romans remain masters. *146 B.C.* Corinthians settle on Delos. The great religious festivals become trade fairs on a heroic scale. Island handles slave trade. Beirut, Alexandria, and Tyre trade associations gain a foothold on the island. *88 B.C.* Island sacked by Mithridates, a bitter enemy of Rome. *69 B.C.* Athens sacked by Athenodoros, the pirate. *3 B.C.* Island put up for sale. No takers. From then on, it was ravaged by pirates, barbarians, and Knights of St. John of Jerusalem. It was used as a marble quarry by Turks and Venetians. *Seventeenth Century A.D.* Sir Kenelm Digby removed marble for Charles I. *1873* French began their excavations.

Mythology

In antiquity, Delos was a sacred island, for there was born the fairest of gods, Apollo of the golden hair. Before his birth, Delos was a free-floating, unimportant island, battered about by the Aegean seas. Leto, pregnant by Zeus and terrified of his jealous wife Hera, was without a safe place to give birth. Zeus commanded Poseidon, god of the seas, to anchor Delos. In a dramatic flourish, Poseidon made the island safe with columns that rose up from the sea. Here on Mt. Kythnos, according to one version, or by the Sacred Lake, according to another, Leto stood grasping a palm tree while Artemis, born the day before, assisted at her twin's birth. Thus was born Apollo, god of light and beauty. Later, he was given other attributes, such as god of music and reason, agriculture and stock raising, defender and savior. The Greeks, in their gratitude, built temples to him as far away as Didyma in Asia Minor.

Apollo brought a new concept of divinity into Greek life, and the temples were holy places and symbols of national unity.

Delos, as the greatest island in the Aegean, became a place of pilgrimage. Those who came to worship brought gifts of gold and silver and fine statuary to enhance the island's beauty. Every four years, the Delian festivals were held. Scenes from Apollo's life were reproduced in rhythmic choral dances. Competitions included wrestling, boxing, racing, javelin and discus throwing, and horse racing. Until the end of the fourth century B.C., these festivals were the greatest in Greece.

Homer's writings immortalized Apollo. His image remains as a champion of humanity against the forces of evil.

ABOUT DELOS

Delos is a small island with an area of about 5 sq. km./2 sq. mi. Here, you can roam acres and acres of ruins and call upon your abilities to imagine a past that no other Greek island can equal.

The French have been digging and dusting the ruins for more than one hundred years, and their splendid efforts will assist you greatly in your mental reconstruction of past glories.

Passengers disembark at a landing mole near the Sacred Harbor. On your arrival, you can sign up for a guided tour, wander as you please with your definitive guidebook, or just look around at your own level of enjoyment. A diagram of Delos' attractions on the first page of this chapter helps you get started.

Those who have camped overnight say that Delos by moonlight has a mysterious way of suggesting god-like ghosts in its shadows of smashed and broken marble. The nights are soft in comparison to the glare of the day. Before dawn the campers climb to the summit of Mt. Kythnos to watch the chrome-yellow sun come up and bring the dusky shapes of other islands into reality. Birds twitter, lizards slither, a shepherd and his sheep stir, and, in springtime, red poppies open wide to face the sun. The god-ghosts disappear.

RUINS

Following is a resumé of some of the island's ruins:

Sacred Harbor

North of the Sacred Harbor:
Agora of the Competialists. This is an open area near the landing mole. The Competialists were representatives of freedmen and slaves, who celebrated yearly the Roman festivals involving the gods of the crossroads. This area was embellished lavishly with monuments and statues.

Sacred Way. The Dromos, or Sacred Way, is a paved 13 m./42 ft.-wide road lined with statue bases at its beginning. To the east is the *Stoa of Philip,* which has a clearly visible dedication to Apollo by Philip of Macedon. One Doric column still stands. Originally, the stoa measured 70 m./234 ft. by 11 m./36 ft. and had sixteen columns.

Among other stoas in this area is the *Agora of the Delians,* which at one time had the Roman baths.

The Sanctuary of Apollo. At the end of the Sacred Way are three marble steps which lead to the main entrance of the Sanctuary, the most important site on Delos. The huge precinct encloses ruins of temples and altars, the remains of several thousand years of worship. Against the north wall is the base of the colossal statue of Apollo, made of Naxian marble. In archaic letters is the inscription, "I am the same marble, statue and base." Plutarch relates that a votive offering of a bronze palm tree, erected near the statue, was felled by a strong wind and took the statue with it.

Two other important temples along the Sacred Way are the *Temple of the Athenians,* 18 m./58 ft. by 11 m./37 ft. and the *Porinos Naos,* 15 m./51 ft. by 10 m./33 ft. The treasury of the Delian Confederacy was originally deposited here.

The Temple of Artemis. It is conjectured that a platform hewn into the rock may have been the tomb of two maidens, who brought the first offerings to Apollo. Many statues of Artemis, now in the museum, were found here.

The Hieron has a small gateway that leads to the museum. Outside the gate are several monuments in the form of a huge phallus, with Dionysiac reliefs on their pedestals.

The Museum. Athens has claimed many of the finest sculptures, but those in the Delos museum have the added value of belonging on their rightful island. Seeing the superb collection gives an increased dimension to all these ruins you have so diligently explored.

The Region of the Sacred Lake. A dried-up oval depression. At one time, it had sacred swans and geese, and the lake was associated with the cult of Apollo. The palm tree in its center commemorates the sacred palm to which Leto clung while giving birth to Apollo.

Terrace of the Lions. In the seventh century B.C., nine Naxian marble lions guarded this sacred area. Today, five remain. Down through the centuries, they have roared in open-mouthed silence, and their majesty endures.

Gymnasium and Stadium. Hikers and enthusiasts may wish to explore this northwest area. There are scant remains, plus a cluster of ancient houses.

South of the Sacred Harbor:

Harbor Area. Most of the remains of the Sacred Harbor are sanded up and under water. In archaic times, it was protected by a breakwater of granite blocks, 149 m./165 yds. long. In the third and second centuries B.C., Delos became a world market, and a commercial port was built alongside the Sacred Harbor. Warehouses followed the shoreline, built with their backs to the residential quarter.

The Residential and Theater Quarter. The shopping and business area grew around the new port. The residential area became densely populated. Crowded houses, on narrow twisting streets, spread upward to the Theater.

A typical Delian house had rooms built around a center court which was

Terrace of the Lions

embellished with marble columns and plastered, painted walls.

Theater. In the early third century B.C., the Theater held 3,500 spectators. Here, many of the festival events took place.

Notable Houses. To the southwest of the Theater is the *House of Masks*, with a mosaic showing Dionysos riding a panther. Across the way, the *House of Dolphins* has more fine mosaics.

Mt. Kythnos. The mount has prehistoric ruins, the remains of a sanctuary to Kythnian Zeus and Athena. Splendid view.

Sanctuary of Foreign Gods. On a long terrace are the sections devoted to the Egyptian and Syrian divinities. The Syrians, whose cult started in 120 B.C., worshipped Adad and Atargatis. After the cult was regularized by an Athenian priest, many of the orgiastic fertility rites were abandoned.

House of Hermes. Descending the ancient roadway, you will see the three-story house of Hermes built against a hill. The colonnades have been restored.

Personal Comment

"O Delos! Land of altars, land of prayers, what tourist, what island-hopper of the Aegean would dare to sail past your coast on his fast trip?" – With apologies to Callimachus.

middle cyclades

*Ermoupolis, Siros' main city, is a fascinating
combination of new industry and old elegance.*

siros

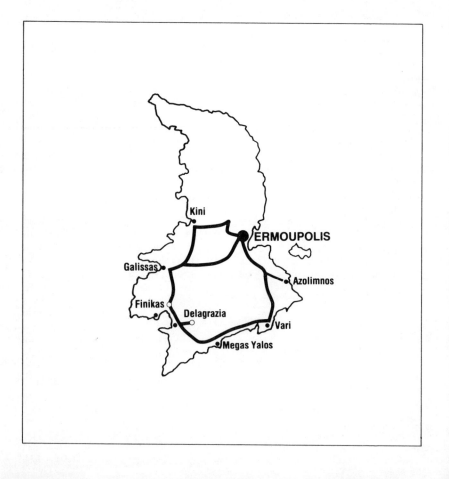

GETTING THERE

From Piraeus: 23 ships weekly.
From Paros, Naxos, and Thera: 13 ships weekly.
From Tinos and Mykonos: 7 ships weekly.
From Samos: 3 ships weekly.

DEPARTURES

Reverse of above.

TOURIST TIPS

Siros (Syros) has an area of 87 sq. km./35 sq. mi. Its population is 20,000. Regular Police are stationed on the west corner of Plateia Miaoulis, the main center of the city. On the harborfront, near the landing dock, is the Tourist Information Bureau. Personnel will help you obtain room reservations anywhere on the island, moped rentals, camping information, ship and bus schedules, and information on the various attractions of outlying towns. Taxis are available.

The public bus station is just beyond the Tourist Information Bureau. The OTE is on the east corner of Plateia Miaoulis. The Agricultural, National, and Commercial Banks of Greece are on the first street back of the harbor near the landing dock. Siesta observed. Yacht facilities available.

HOTELS*

Ermoupolis: (C) Europi, Nissaki, Kykladiko, Eleana, Hermes. (D) Akteon. (E) Averof, Mykonos, Chios, Helles.
Megas Yalos: (C) Aleandra.
Vari: Emily,[†] Bollas, Romantika, Domenica.
Finikas: Finikas,[†] Olympia.
Poseidonia: Dellagracia,[†] Poseidonia.

*See Part I, section on Accommodations, for explanation of hotel grades.
[†]No category listed. Inquire at Tourist Bureau.

HISTORY

Siros has minimal ancient sites. To the extreme north of the island is a marble strip running into the sea. On it are Roman and Byzantine inscriptions of prayers for good voyages. Old island coins show heads of Pan, goats, honey, and corn designs. *A.D. 1200–1300* The islanders built Ano (Upper) Siros to escape the pirate raids. *1556* The descendants of these Venetian and Genoese settlers came under the protection of the King of France. The French flag flew from the convent, and a strong French ambience was established. *1821* The massacre on Chios resulted in a massive immigration to Siros. These immigrants built the lower city, established a commerce that made the island the coal-bunkering center for packet ships. Islanders refused to participate in the Revolution, but received thousands of maimed and incapacitated refugees. Today, Siros is the most highly industrialized island in the Aegean and a connecting port for interisland travelers.

ERMOUPOLIS

Orthodox Greek and Roman Catholic churches crown the two hills of Ermoupolis. The population is divided almost equally in their loyalty and devotion. Leniency is permitted in matters of the heart. If two young people from separate "hills" wish to marry they may do so, providing a ceremony takes place in both churches.

Tier upon tier of pastel-colored houses cover the hills down to the busy harborfront. A walk along this *paralia* will take you past cafes, tavernas, bookstores, and specialty shops. Patisseries, with luscious window displays, may slow you to a stop. Further on is a shop that makes Turkish Delight, also known as *loukoumi*, a specialty of the island. At

Ermoupolis

the far end of the harbor are the shipyards with their cacophony of blasts, toots, rivet staccatos, whistles, and clangs. The hydraulic slip here is capable of lifting an interisland steamer out of the water. There are also two floating docks.

Backtrack a few blocks, and you will come to Market St., Odhos Ermou, where at 9:00 A.M. weekdays and Saturdays the awninged street will be crowded with Syriotes. Here are the fish stalls, the fresh fruits and vegetables, all a splendid harmony of color. In the open-fronted meat shops, the butchers wield cleavers with seeming abandon while curbside patrons sip their Turkish coffee and morning cognac.

This street will take you to the town's main square, Plateia Miaoulis, surrounded by colonnaded buildings and the impressive Town Hall. Unlike most town halls, this one is humanized by having much of its lower area given over to a cáfe that serves food and beverages to the people who gather each evening to stroll on the Plateia.

Veering to your right and starting uphill, by bus and taxi or by foot (only eight hundred steps), you will first pass the Opera House, modeled after Milan's La Scala. Reconstruction is in process. Pocket-sized parks of lush, overgrown greenery begin in this area among well-built nineteenth century mansions with intricately curved, wrought-iron balconies, massive doors with hand-shaped brass knockers, and much use of marble. You will pass the French Ecole des Frères and the large St. Sebastian Church. Here is the fashionable Neapolis quarter, with modern houses embellished with non-classical stonework, much marble, brass, and wrought iron.

The views along this promenade open to the ever-changing moods of the Aegean, and when you reach the top of the hill you will feel the crisp breezes that are heady and pure. Now you are in the old area of small houses and. narrow stepped streets, streets

Plateia Miaoulis

where only donkeys can traverse. Life and living seem far apart from the harbor town, lived more, within the aura and security of the big cathedral. To make your way down is a zigzag affair, but eventually you will be seaside again.

Dining and Entertainment

There are two theaters in town, both near Plateia Miaoulis, as well as taverna-nightclubs. Next to the OTE is a popular restaurant that has tablecloths, waiters in white coats, an attractive decor, and good food.

The many harborside cafes serve breakfasts that are substantial: French fries, sausage, pastries, cheese pies, potato omelettes, honey with toast or rolls, Turkish or decaffeinated coffee, even cognac or *ouzo*.

There are four discos in town; three have live *bouzouki*.

The tavernas are the main source of evening entertainment and, in their own Greek way, the patrons are the entertainers.

Beaches

In town, there is a small beach behind the Hotel Hermes where, if you can tolerate a few stones, you will soon reach sandy bottom. If the waves become too thrashing, the local bathers move north to Ag. Nickolas beach.

The best beaches are in outlying areas of *Vari, Megas Yalos, Finikas, Delagrazia, Kini,* and *Galissas*. At all these places there are restaurants, tavernas, stores, and nightclubs.

Personal Comment

Siros has a few secrets. European V.I.P.'s have found that there are quiet, restful, completely untouristed areas on the island where they can have a rewarding vacation. No doubt they hope to keep it that way. For the island-hopper who needs to go to Siros to make ship connections, it may be equally rewarding to stay at least a full day, longer if uncrowded beaches on other parts of the island have allure.

A pleasure-offering island where tourists wear minimal clothing and maximum suntans.

paros
antiparos

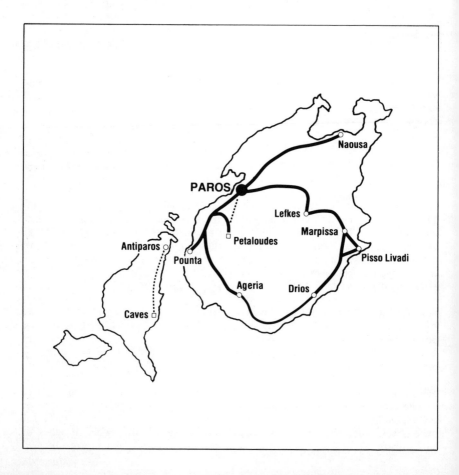

GETTING THERE

From Piraeus via Siros or Naxos: 3 to 11 ships weekly.
From Crete via Ios and Thera: 1 to 2 ships weekly.
From Samos via Ikaria: 2 to 3 ships weekly (summer season).

DEPARTURES

Reverse of above.
Excursion boat daily to Ios and Thera in summer.
Excursion boat daily to Antiparos in summer.
Excursion boat daily to Naxos or Mykonos in summer.
Excursion boat to Sifnos: 1 to 2 times weekly.

TOURIST TIPS

Paros has an area of 209 sq. km./ 81 sq. mi. Its population is 7,300. In the port town, Paroikia, the Tourist Police are stationed in the port windmill from May to October. Here, you can obtain free maps of the island and room information. Outside the windmill is a bulletin board with names of hotels and their phone numbers, plus bus schedules to island towns. Bus tickets are purchased aboard. The OTE is diagonally across the street.

No camping is permitted except in designated areas. Two campgrounds are north of town on the beach. Mopeds, bicycles, and jeeps are available to rent. National, Commercial, and Agricultural Banks of Greece have offices. Excellent yacht basin at Paroikia and Naousa. Siesta observed.

HOTELS*

Paros (Paroikia): (B) Xenia. (C) Alkyon, Argonatis, Asterias, Gorgy, Ermes, Paros, Stella.

*See Part I, section on Accommodations, for explanation of hotel grades.

Xenon: (C) Arian, Dilion.
Naousa: (B) Naousa (pension). (C) Ambelis, Atlantis, Galini, Drosia, Hippokambos, Mary, Minoa, Piperi (BG).
Marpissa: (B) Marpissa (pension). (C) Anesina, Leto, Logares.
Pisso Livadi: (C) Lito, Logaris, Piso Livadi, Viky.
Drios: (C) Avra, Julia, Ivi. (D) Drios. Many rooms in private homes.

HISTORY

Sixth–Third Centuries B.C. Neolithic period; findings reveal marble figures foreshadowing the famous Cycladic figures. *Third–Second Centuries B.C.* Mycenaean influence changed pottery styles. *1100–990 B.C.* Dark Age, followed by influx of Ionian culture from the East. *490–146 B.C.* Classical period. Island prospered as a marble center. *146 B.C.–Fourth Century A.D.* Roman period. Romans drained island of money and materials. *Fourth Century–A.D. 1207* Byzantine period. Pirate raids. Christianity introduced in the sixth century. Ekatontapyliani was built in the sixth century. *1207–1566* Venetian period. Sanudo dynasty ruled Paros. *1566–1821* Ottoman Empire. Pirates plunder island. Six thousand Parians sent to slave market in Anatola. *1821* Paros shared the fate of the Greek nation and won independence in the Greek revolution. It was also occupied in World War I and World War II.

PAROS (PAROIKIA)

A town fanning out from its port windmill, Paros promises, in some intrinsic way, to give you an entertaining time. It is friendly, refreshingly relaxed, and possessed of enough interesting sights to make you want to linger longer than you had planned.

Leading away from the windmill are the main streets, crossed by walk-

Paros residential street

exhibit includes fragments of the Archaic, Hellenistic, and Geometric periods. Inside, along with many other treasures, is a part of the famous *Parian Chronicle* which outlines Greek history before the time of Homer.

Acropolis. Rising from the main shopping street and fronted by the Kastro wall of column drums from ancient temples is a street that leads to an area mostly untouched by tourism. Worn marble steps lead to a blue-domed church, Konstandinou. Daylight is for seeing details; try dusk with night descending, balmy, a moon-paved, silver path on the inky-dark Aegean. Pure magic.

Dining and Entertainment

Paroikia has over one hundred first- and second-class restaurants, plus all those tavernas and "goody" places. There are waterfront eateries; midtown elegance; hotel-type set menu; chic and continental; small, dark, and candlelit; undistinguished and purely Greek.

ways that will intrigue the curious-minded. In pirate times, Paroikia's streets could be covered, and people could move about unseen.

The main shopping areas are centrally situated, interposed with Cycladic homes showing Venetian influences, fountains, and an upbeat and spritely view of island life.

In-Town Sights

Ekatontapyliani. The island's most important antiquity, also known as the *Church of the Hundred Doors*, wears its fame with complacent beauty and a slightly settled, almost sagging look. The casual visitor will enjoy its splendor and churchly implements. For the more inquisitive, a guidebook is suggested.

Archaeological Museum. Beyond the church and near the high school is the handsome museum. The courtyard

Ekatontapyliani

There are also places like NICK'S HAMBURGERS, MIKE'S TOST, and JOHN'S TAKE–IT–AWAY. John's specialty is hot dogs to eat while on the beach. ARGONAUTS, center-town, has soft ice cream and rich desserts. Popular are large cans of iced fruit juices which you drink with a straw.

More sophisticated dining is available at places like SCOUNA'S, where the menu includes roast beef with lemon slices, fried squid, lobster, lamb steaks, stuffed zucchini. Beachside is KARTEPIVA for a thick-crust pizza. VASSILIS, a favorite with the Greeks, has delicious *boullabaisse* and *cannelloni*.

There are several discos where the astringent tone of the *bouzouki* shares time with rock. Also, the town has an open-air theater from which, if your hotel room is nearby, you will hear the audio whether you want to or not. Movies are over at eleven o'clock.

Shopping

The first floors of many houses have been made into shops. One of the most charming, plus being authentic Aegean, is the Archipelago. All objects for sale are handmade and include old embroideries, antique jewelry, and fine reproductions of old icons.

There are excellent ceramic studios; among them is Yria, well worth a visit. They will ship if you find something you can't live without.

Look especially for handsome handknit sweaters for men and the popular men's clogs.

Beaches

The beach to the south of town has tamarisk trees with branches curving, bending and embracing to form shade if you want it. Morning occupants seem to catch up on their sleep, their prone and oiled bodies glinting in the sun. The north side of town has a beach shared with the campers, who have their own facilities, including a refreshment stand.

During the summer, launches leave the main dock of Paroikia every twenty minutes for beaches spread along the island shores. It is illegal to swim in the nude. Very private places are *not* the beaches, but out-of-the way shorelines with flat-topped boulders for sun-warmed rock therapy.

Excursions

Naousa. The bus fills quickly with tourists and islanders, and the 20-minute ride is through a well-farmed landscape. You will pass *Moni Logavardas*, a monastery of sun-struck white. Men visitors only are permitted.

Naousa, formerly a notorious pirate's town, is now dedicated to tourism. The central square, shaded by an enormous eucalyptus tree, offers relaxing comfort while you slake your thirst or wait for a bus.

Houses have been spiced with bright colors on the twisting uphill walkways, but enough of the old remains to enchant the visitor. Just below the modern church that crowns the top of town is the MINOA restaurant for authentic Greek food. Or stop harborside for fishermen/yacht-type atmosphere and fish, lobster, octopus, and *retsina* menus.

There are boats waiting to take you to the beaches at Kolibithres, Langeri, Agia Maria, and Platis Ammos; also a tourist agency to help you find accommodations if you decide to stay. On August 23, the big festival has costumed natives, singing, food, dancing, all to celebrate the anniversary of a long-past naval victory over the Turks.

Marble Quarries and Lefkes. Take the Lefkes bus and get off at *Marathi*, where there are the remains of marble quarries from 1844. Walk down into

Naousa

the valley to the solid marble hill. Three shafts descend into it; if you go down the middle one, you can return via a connecting one.

Parian marble is famous. It has a dazzling granular quality, and if you hold up a sliver to the sun, you will see how magically it absorbs the light.

Back to the road to catch the next bus (or walk) to *Lefkes*, located on the eastern slope of the island's central mountain range. After exploring the charming town, you may wish to take a downhill, stone-paved path dating from Byzantine times that leads to Marpissa.

Marpissa and Pisso Livadi. The *Monastery of Ag. Antonios* and Venetian ruins are a half-hour climb above Marpissa. Inquire in Marpissa to make sure that the church is open. You'll see splendid views from this height.

Back in Marpissa, continue to Pisso Livadi via bus or the same Byzantine path.

Pisso Livadi is a fishermen's harbor with a good beach, several restaurants, and many summer homes of Athenians. Here are the soothing wash of the waves and seagulls swooping in intense blue sky.

Petaloudes. Petaloudes is your chance for a donkey-ride excursion. If that doesn't appeal, there are buses, or you can walk to the park-like area called *Petaloudes*, the Greek word for "butterfly." Petaloudes does have these fluttering, myriad-hued beauties at certain times of the year. The area has beautiful old trees, meandering paths, streams, and flowers. There are also a Venetian tower, a nunnery (*Christos Stodhasos*), and a summer café. The donkey path back to Paroikia (see map) zigzags steeply down through vineyards, olive groves with fine views of Paroikia along the way.

Pounta. A tiny village. It serves as a takeoff place for Antiparos. There is a café to serve you while the launch comes back from its crossing (six times daily) to Antiparos.

Ageria. The end of the bus line. From

here, you will need to hike to Drios. It is 8 km./4.8 mi., if you are hoofing it around the bend.

Antiparos. Tourist agencies promote an excursion to the caves. You can take a donkey up the 165 m./545 ft. to the summit and cave entrance. Walk four hundred concrete steps down into a cold, eerie, stalactite and stalagmite cave, covered with graffiti. Out in the sunshine again, the views of Sikinos, Folangandros, Ios, and Paros seem super-splendid.

Personal Comment

Tourism is a major source of income for Paros, but it is backed by the islander's sturdy conservatism, which provides the "Greekness" that charms the visitor.

A verdant land and a convivial people give Naxos an attractive vitality.

naxos

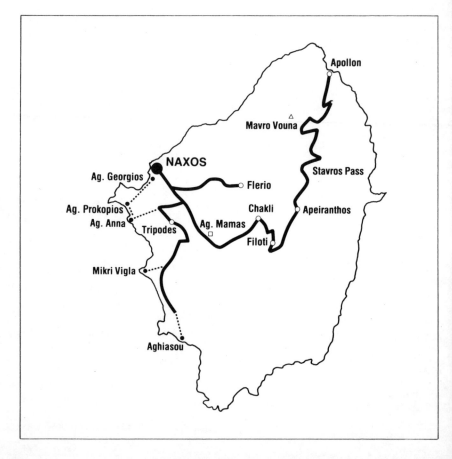

GETTING THERE

From Piraeus via Siros and/or Paros: 12 to 15 ships weekly.
From Ios and Thera: 5 to 8 ships weekly.
From Sikinos: 1 ship weekly.
From Amorgos and Rhodes: 2 ships weekly.
From Crete via Ios and Thera: 1 ship weekly.

DEPARTURES

To Iraklia, Shinoussa, Koufonissia, Donoussa: 2 ships weekly.
To Piraeus via Siros and/or Paros: 12 to 15 ships weekly.
To Ios and Thera: 5 to 8 ships weekly.
To Mykonos: Summer excursion boat daily.
To Crete: 1 ship weekly.

TOURIST TIPS

Naxos (Naxia) has an area of 448 sq. km./179 sq. mi. Its population is 14,201. No Tourist Police, but the Tourist Office, at the beginning of the landing dock, has a helpful staff to answer your questions regarding room and hotel reservations, youth hostels, camping, etc. Open 9:00 A.M. to 12:00 noon and 5:00 to 6:00 P.M. Public telephones are nearby. The bus and taxi station are in the same area. Bus schedules to inland towns are posted on the bulletin board outside the Tourist Office. A tour agency is at the Coronis Hotel. Cars, with driver service, are available. Cars, bikes, mopeds for hire. The post office has the OTE. Agrarian, National, and Commercial Banks of Greece have offices. Siesta observed. Excellent yacht facilities.

HOTELS*

(B) Ariadne (pension). (C) Aegean, Akroyali, Anessis, Apollon, Barbourni,

*See Part I, section on Accommodations, for explanation of hotel grades.

Coronis, Helmos, Hermes, Nissaki, Panorma, Renetta, Zeus, Kymeta, Chelmos. *Pensions:* Galini, Kondillis, Youth Hostel. Many rooms to let. *Beach hotels:* (C) Naxos Beach.

HISTORY

2000 B.C. Island inhabited from Proto-Cycladic times. *Seventh–Sixth Centuries B.C.* Island at the peak of power in the ancient world. Controlled the Cyclades with its fleet. Flourished as a center of sculpture and Ionic architecture. *490 B.C.* Persians sacked the Chora. Naxians fled to island interior. *466 B.C.* Island forced to join the Athenian League. It faded into background of Greek events. Remained a pawn during late Classical Age, Hellenistic, and Roman periods. *A.D. 1204* Island came under the control of Venice. *1207* Marco Sanudo captured the island. *1383* Crispi dynasty began. *1537* Ottoman Empire. Naxians bought their safety from Turks. *1821* Greek War of Independence.

Mythology

The small islet connected by a causeway to Naxia is the legendary location where Dionysos, god of wine, found Ariadne after she was abandoned by Theseus.

Prior to this event, Dionysos had been abducted by pirates who were going to demand a large ransom. Strange events took place on the pirate ship as it sailed away. Vines grew out of the deck and up the masts. The pirates became serpents, Dionysos made himself into a lion. The pirate-serpents slithered overboard and turned into dolphins. Dionysos resumed his human form, and the ship, aflutter with leaves and filling the air with flute music, wafted to the islet where Ariadne slept. He married her then and there, and later placed her bridal wreath among the stars where it is known as the Corona Borealis.

ABOUT NAXOS

Naxos, an emerald-green island set in a translucent sea, supposedly gave Lord Byron twinges of nostalgia and a longing to return to it. No doubt about it, there is much that favors a return *and* a first visit. A rolling splendor of landscape, webs of charming villages, warmly hospitable people, and enough adventure and romance in its past to spark the imagination.

If you are arriving by ship, you will have a good view of the town from the ship's deck. The farmers with their produce-laden trucks have lined up on the wide dock to await loading. Commotion amounts to high-key confusion. The dock officers shout orders, the truck drivers yell back, motors rev, arriving trucks rumble out of the ship's hold, departing trucks rumble in.

You will be swept along with the new arrivals to the end of the pier, which becomes an oasis of calm. Taxis await. The CITY OF NAXOS CAFETERIA, with outdoor, tree-shaded, frosty-white, wrought iron tables and chairs invites you to drop your luggage and sit down. Soft drinks and ice cream up front, meals to the back. It's the perfect place to await boat departures, pass the siesta hours, and enjoy the harbor sights.

This area is the beginning of the *Plateia* and, leading from it, the old areas of Borgo, Grotta, and passages up to the Kastro.

NAXOS TOWN

The exquisite little chapel on the harbor inlet is *Myrditiotissa*, built at the beginning of Marco Sanudo's reign in 1207. No more energetic or enterprising high-class pirate gave the Aegean area a busier time.

Borgo. The town has its sunny spots, bright with flowers, but the Borgo has a closed-in, medieval starkness. Once dank and dark, this area now has a marshmallow whiteness due, perhaps, to civic pride brought about by the island's stature as a National Monument. These ancient buildings contain meat markets, bakeries, vegetable stands, and the popular tavernas. These last-mentioned establishments are favorites with the farmers, who

Myrditiotissa chapel

Naxos from Naxia islet

like to whoop it up after the heavy work of shiploading their produce. Sociability is robust and earthy. Laughter comes easily as do singing and dancing. The tourist is invited to join in and, if you understand Greek, there is bound to be an amazing enrichment of the Greek sense of fun and humor.

Grotta. Those interested in archaeology may wish to explore the Grotta on the northern shores of town. Bronze sites have been revealed. A necropolis on a hill called *Aplomata* is just outside the Chora on the coastal road. Here are Mycenaean chamber tombs. Artifacts are also in the local museum.

Naxia Islet holds the ruin of an Ionic Temple. Standing in a jumble of marble is the northwest portal, 600 cm./ 20 ft. high, and 360 cm./12 ft. wide. The marble of the original temple became a quarry for churches, fortifications, and Kastro mansions in the Byzantine and Ottoman eras. Once the temple was thought to be dedicated to Dionysos, but today's archaeologists maintain that it was a sanctuary to Apollo. Sad to say, a hostile wire fence keeps you at your distance; however, with special permission, you can still get close.

Kastro. The Kastro turns its aged walls toward the Chora. Twisting streets will lead you under archways and up stairways to a splendid Venetian tower-gate, the only one of seven that remains in its original form.

From the Kastro, Marco Sanudo reigned as Duke of the Archipelago and Sovereign of the Dodecanese Islands. He founded the dynasty that he and his heirs held until 1383, when a soldier of fortune, Francisco Crispi, took over. The Crispi dynasty ruled until the sixteenth century, a total of 360 years.

Today, the Kastro remains apart from the Chora. Venetian families reside in splendidly restored mansions. Their church is Roman Catholic. The pavement in front of it has family coats of arms. The past remains close to families with Venetian names, the last survivors of the Duchy of the Archipelago.

Museum. Within the Kastro walls is the museum, the former French School founded in 1627. It was the finest free school in the entire Aegean, with both Catholic and Orthodox students. It was here that the great Greek writer, Nikos Kazantzakis, was a student in 1896 until his father roared in one stormy night and forcibly removed his son, fearing that he would become a Catholic.

Today, the museum has a well-lighted interior with an open, cool feeling and a definite sense of reserve. Cameras are not permitted. You will see a remarkable collection of Cycladic and Bronze Age marble figurines, considered the world's largest. There are funerary marble bowls, Geometric pottery, Hellenistic and Venetian marbles, and small *kouri*. Outside on the patio is a stunning mosaic pavement from the Grotta area, plus an equally stunning view of the mountainous inland.

Harborside cafe balcony

Dining and Entertainment

Naxos is famous for its Citron liqueur. To make your first experience of it a remembered moment, try it at the second-floor restaurant, SANUDOS, above the Commercial Bank. Here, on a cool and canopied balcony, you can enjoy the liqueur's lemony sweetness with alternate nibbles of salted peanuts. Before you is the complete Naxos harbor, a wide expanse of vitreous marine blue. Beyond the breakwater, the waves are doing a sun-drenched romp while a sailboat, mast swaying in a stiff breeze, makes its way into the breakwater calm. A gull soars, swoops, dives. Way in the back of the restaurant, classical music is played softly.

The Chora has a superabundance of restaurants and cafés. None are really sumptuous or lavish, and most are family ventures. Food is served with simplicity, ingredients are fresh and robustly flavored. KASTRO, high up outside the east fortress wall, has a Venetian ambience. MELTEMI, portside, is a favorite with locals who know where to satisfy their panhellenic appetites. Many pizza restaurants have a devoted following. The Borgo capitalizes on its medieval surroundings with tucked-away cafés, intimate and candle-lit.

AG. GEORGIO'S beach restaurants are favorites. People drift from sea to sand to bamboo-covered cafés. During the passive siesta hours, you can sit around tables, play backgammon, talk, drink beer, or just stare into the distance. Evening dining and dancing is lively and spontaneous.

There are many bars: MARCO'S, STELIO'S, VASILO'S. The clientele sing, dance, and enjoy their own full-bodied, loquacious amiability.

The owner of DISCO ROCK, on the causeway, promises an unforgettable evening.

Shopping

In the Borgo are shops with copies of fine Greek pottery dating back to Minoan times; Byzantine, post-Byzantine, and Roman icon copies that are well painted; much antique jewelry, some real and some copied; handsome handwoven clothing and handknit sweaters; and straw baskets and hats.

Many shops are smartly arranged and "music while you look" is in favor. Harborside are a few galleries showing paintings and castings. Also harborside are many typical souvenir shops.

Beaches

Ag. Georgios, the in-town beach, is long and curving, but too shallow for good swimming. If you walk far enough in a southeasterly direction, you will come to sheltered sand dunes, great for privacy.

Hikers can use the causeway across the salt flats to a beautiful beach, Ag. Prokopios, where several rustic tavernas offer refreshing drinks. The next cove is Ag. Anna. This beach can be reached by a motor launch daily in summer. Tickets may be purchased at the Lemnos Shipping Agency. Beyond Ag. Anna's headland is a 5 km./3 mi. beach of pink-white sand. At its end is the headland, Mikri Vigla, a sheltered cove behind a rocky headland. Two tavernas here can serve you.

Excursions

Apollon. A bus or car trip to this village gives the best views of this exuberantly arcadian island. The road winds its way through farmlands, then climbs into mountain terrain. Beyond *Gallanado*, note the double church, separated by an arch; one side Catholic, the other Greek Orthodox. *Potomias* is a valley of villages and orchards. Here is the island's oldest church, Ag. Mamas, partially restored. *Chalki,* the island's central town, may tempt you to linger and explore its

Ag. Georgios restaurant and beach

beautiful walks and old churches. *Filoti*, largest interior town, has a Dionysian festival on August 15. (An island expression is "Raise hell in Filoti.")

Apeiranthos has old stone houses melding into the mountains. Its inhabitants were known for their folk poetry. Roomfuls of people recited in unison at weddings, wakes, and baptismals.

Stavros Pass. Here the view opens up to the curving seacoast and glinting sea. Go around another mountain, *Mavro Vouno*, where according to legend, the nymph, Koronos, reared Dionysos in a cave. It is still considered a sacred place. Hairpin curves are next, and go through a long valley to Apollon.

Apollon will tempt you to stay. Clear sky, cool breeze, crisp waves, friendly restaurants, pleasant rooms and a new hotel. The 600 B.C. *kouros* up the hill is not as finished as the one at Flerio, but worth the climb.

Flerio. Near this village is the Flerio Kouros, a noted island antiquity, dating from 575–650 B.C. The Kouros, although a National Monument, rests in a private garden a short walk from the highway. Half the size of the Apollon Kouros, it is more developed; the figure is nude, broad-shouldered, and narrow-waisted, with an inscrutable archaic smile. A second, lesser *kouros* is on a hillside above. He lies among marble stones, a fallen warrior hauntingly evocative of passing time.

Tripodes and Beaches. Tripodes is one of the island's most venerated towns. Hospitable tavernas are in the square. From the highway, there are paths and dirt roads leading to coastal beaches. A resort and beaches near Aghiasou are worth exploring.

Personal Comment

Naxos Town has much to interest the island-hopper but, if possible, devote at least one day to an inland trip. This will make your visit truly memorable.

other cycladic islands

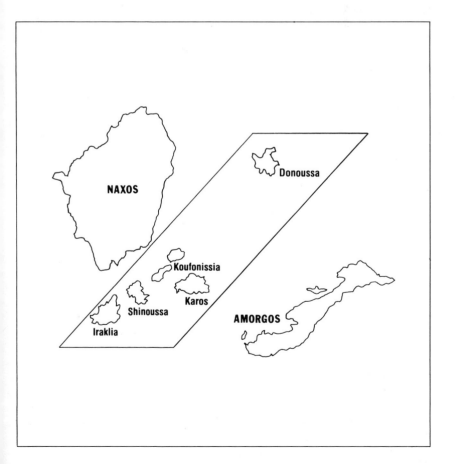

West of Amorgos and south of Naxos are several very small islands that may appeal to the camper and backpacker. They are served by ship once or twice weekly. Passengers are disembarked in small boats. A local ship makes the rounds between Naxos, the islands mentioned, and Amorgos several times weekly. Rooms are available in private houses. Iraklia and Donoussa have small guest houses. There are tavernas in Koufonissia and Iraklia. All islands have grocery stores and adequate water supplies.

Iraklia

(17 sq. km./10 sq. mi.) This island is an archaeological feast, with a multitude of undiscovered artifacts. The most important discoveries to date are of the temples to Tychi and Lofiskos. There are beaches and fishing; August 15 is a feast day.

Shinoussa

(9 sq. km./5½ sq. mi.) An old-time pirate refuge of uniquely beautiful landscape. It has two fishermen-type villages and a medieval tower at its highest point.

Koufonissia

(8 sq. km./4½ sq. mi.) Its towns are *Pano Koufo* and *Ano Koufo*, separated by a narrow channel where caiques and fishing boats anchor. It has beautiful beaches, quiet life, and hospitable inhabitants. August 15 is a feast day.

Donoussa

Near Naxos. *Stavros*, a clean little town, is on hilly, stony terrain. The small harbor holds the local caiques. Inhabitants welcome visitors, who will find golden beaches to laze upon.

Personal Comment

These islands are an opportunity to see Greek living in its purest island form.

amorgos

GETTING THERE

From Piraeus: 1 to 2 ships weekly.
From Rhodes via the Dodecanese Islands: 1 to 2 ships weekly.
From Naxos: Excursion boat 2 times weekly.

DEPARTURES

To Piraeus: 1 to 2 ships weekly.
To Rhodes: 1 to 2 ships weekly.
To Naxos via Iraklia, Shinoussa, Koufonissia, Donoussa: Excursion boat 2 times weekly.

TOURIST TIPS

Amorgos has an area of 134 sq. km./ 52 sq. mi. Its population is 1,822. Katapola has no Tourist Police. Regular police are stationed in the capital town, Amorgos (Chora). Presently, there are no cars, bikes, or mopeds for rent. Bus and a taxi meet arriving ships. Camping is allowed in out-of-town beaches, and in the area behind the school in Chora. There are no banks. Traveler's checks are cashed in Katapola, at Mavros General Market, midway along the harbor. The Market also carries yacht supplies. Katapola has a fine yacht harbor. The post office is on the quay; it also serves as the OTE. The bus from Katapola to Chora and Agiali runs several times a day. Siesta observed. Ship ticket agents serve as travel information agencies.

HOTELS*

Katapola: Pension Voula Beach, Pension Tazia, Pension Mavros.
Agiali: (C) Mekes (July–September). The island can accommodate about three hundred persons in private homes.

HISTORY

In antiquity, Amorgos had three important cities: Agiali, Minoa (Katapola), and Arkesini. Agiali was col-

*See Part I, section on Accommodations, for explanation of hotel grades.

Katapola

onized by Greeks, Romans, and Franks. Tiberius used it as a place of banishment for Vitrius Serenus. The nearby town, Tholaria, has Roman tombs.

Minoa was colonized by tribes from Samos. In the hills above the town are the scanty remains of a temple to Pythian Apollo.

Arkesini is on a rocky spur which formerly led in steps and terraces to the sea. Nearby is the famous watch-tower of Amorgos, the best specimen of Hellenic tower-art in the Cyclades.

The poet, Simonides, born on Kea, lived on Samos, and founded a colony on Amorgos.

When piracy was rampant, Amorgos had some of the cleverest.

KATAPOLA

An island town without a commercial hotel has a special atmosphere. Other than the yacht people, the visitors are mostly young travelers and seasoned Europeans who are content to live in pensions and rooms. This brings a closer association with Greek living and the much-promoted Greek hospitality.

Katapola has a quietness that is attractive. The harbor is a place of white-fronted restaurants and tavernas where, if you step into the coolness of the interiors, you are met with a friendly smile. Most of the tourists are young, tanned, and colorful in their short, shapeless cover-ups of such colors as brilliant purple, lime green, or watermelon pink. The men wear nothing more than their cut-offs or shorts; if they sling a towel over their shoulders, it could be yellow, even black. Against the whitewashed walls, they are all a feast of color.

The town follows a very large natural harbor, and there is a paved walk completely around it. On the far

Katapola town road

side is where the fishermen live and boats are built and repaired. An early evening walk around this bay will include a dramatic plunge of sun into the sea, the slow merging of the town into dusky shadows, a soft silence with only rhythmic sloshing of the waves on the narrow beach.

Dining and Entertainment

As the evening darkens, strings of colored lights glow in front of several restaurants. Near the landing dock is the PIRATE restaurant, with its conscious panache and sense of fun. The young chef has a spicy way with his specialties, and he makes a Pirate-burger with beef, cheese, tomato, and *tzatziki*, as well as a lamb, veal, or pork dish with wine, backed in a casserole with a pasta crust. Cumin, oregano, and hot pepper add zest. If this appeals, ask for *giouvetsi*.

At the town square are the restaurants AKROGALI and TO KAMARI. The latter is a favorite around five o'clock when *ravini*, butter cakes soggy with syrup, and *trigona*, nut-filled *phyllo*, will do wonders to satisfy those hunger pangs.

For a change of harbor scene, walk around the bay to MINI'S restaurant where the owner makes a succulent dish of butter beans flavored with salsa, onions, carrots, celery, and tomato. With this you may wish to try his *youvarlakia*, meatballs flavored with cumin and garlic and shaped like sausages.

The entertainment in this town is of your own making. The PIRATE restaurant has good jazz. There are one or two juke boxes, but mostly it's nature's music: wind in the trees, waves on the shore.

Shopping

Kitty's Gift Shop next to the post office has mod dresses and stunning wool sweaters. Europeans covet the spices that grow on the island, and you can buy them in the stores, or walk into the fields and gather your own tangy aromatic thyme, oregano, fennel, and sage.

Beaches

Nearest to town is Panteleimon. Motorboat schedule: every hour or so from the harborfront. This beach can also be reached by a hike around the entire bay. Nude bathing is permitted here if you so desire.

You can go by boat to Sarades Beach, a favorite with those who enjoy diving off the huge boulders. Finikes, with rocks and boulders, must be reached by boat also. Midway around the island is Ag. Anna, reached by bus.

Delivery service by donkey

From a promontory, you can see two little beaches about 90 m./300 ft. down, nestled in a landscape of monumental proportions. Agile as a goat, you scramble down and for a few hours enjoy the elements of sea and sky. The bus starts blasting its horn from far enough away to allow you to scramble up the path less like a goat and more like the person (puff-puff) you really are.

Excursions

Monastery Hazowiotissa. While you are in the Ag. Anna area, and have the proper cover-ups, you could visit the island's treasure, the Monastery Hazowiotissa. A rocky path high above the sea will take you to this monastery, which has been built into the precipitous mountainside. A monk will open the door and lead you to a reception room where you will be served coffee and a glass of water. He will then take you to the chapel, one of the most elaborately icon-covered in all of Greece. Many icons are embossed in gold and silver. Those on the sides of the altar have faces almost obliterated by reverent touching or kissing. This completes your visit, and you are shown to the gate. A breathtaking drop to the sea fronts this magnificently situated monastery.

Chora. The mountainous terrain of Amorgos would seem to have discouraged piracy; however, the islanders did have to build their capital on a bleak, windswept rock. Stay here for a few hours, and you will know what it is like to be cut off from the rest of the world. Friendly tavernas will help you pass the time until the next bus arrives.

Ormos Agiali. The island's second port; disembarkation by caique. The small town has a good beach and opportunities to explore Tholaria. There

Monastery Hazowiotissa

are Roman vaulted tombs. *Langada* is a fortified refuge from marauders of the past.

Festivals

August 15 is the big date; locations are Ag. Paraskevi for the south part of the island, Panagia Epanochori for the north. Included are food, dancing, merrymaking. Just mention this date to an Amorgiote, and his or her eyes light up. This is the island's biggest yearly celebration.

Personal Comment

During July, August, and the first part of September this island is crowded with Greek vacationers. Before and after that time, it will revert to its usual slow-paced lifestyle.

Renowned for the genial nature and hospitality
of its inhabitants, Ios is the perfect
"pleasure island" for young tourists and
those who are young at heart.

ios

GETTING THERE

From Piraeus via Paros, Naxos, or Siros: 10 ships weekly.
From Milos: 2 ships weekly.
From Tinos and Mykonos: 1 ship weekly.
From Paros: Daily excursion boat in summer.
From Crete (Iraklion or Ag. Nikolaos): 1 to 3 ships weekly.
To Manganari Bay: Caique daily in summer.

DEPARTURES

To Thera: Daily excursion boat.
To Sikinos: 1 to 2 ships weekly and return.
To Crete (Iraklion or Ag. Nikolaos): 1 to 3 ships weekly.
To Piraeus: 10 to 13 ships weekly.

TOURIST TIPS

Ios has an area of 105 sq. km./42 sq. mi. Its population is 1,270. It has no Tourist Police. A few taxis meet the ships. Some hotels have minibuses to meet arriving tourists. Good public bus transportation to Hora, the main town on the hill and to Milopota, a splended beach. Shipping and information offices are at both the harbor and Hora. Boats and donkeys can be rented. There are yacht facilities.

HOTELS*

Ormos Iou and Hora: (B) Psathi Beach Bungalows, Chryssi Acti (pension), Homers Inn. (C) Armadoros, Sea Breeze Hotel. (D) Acteon. (E) Avra.
Milopota (Beach): Pension Stavrakis.
Manganari: (B) In Athens, call 363–1614 for information. In Ormos Iou, contact local agent.

*See Part I, section on Accommodations, for explanation of hotel grades.

HISTORY

Prehistoric graves attest to early occupation. *129 B.C.* Roman occupation. *A.D. 120* Ios was a fief of the Venetian, Pisani. *1500* Frankish town in Palaiokastro. *1537* Island captured by Turks. *1821* Greek revolution. Island under domination of Otto, of Bavaria. *1832* Greek independence returned. *World War II* German occupation.
Note: Nearly four hundred churches embellish Ios, most of them built during the Turkish occupation when the island's excellent refuge from pirates gave it the name of Little Malta. Apparently, even pirates felt a need to placate the Deity and, when so moved, they built a church. Today, the churches scatter over the landscape in an array of pristine whiteness, jewel-colored domes, and diverse shapes.

ORMOS IOU (GIALOS)

As your ship enters the bay of this small port town, you see a glistening white, Cycladic welcome: the noble church of *St. Irene*. The town sprawls along the water's edge, and hotels, tavernas, and stores cluster around a small *plaka* which offers the tourists a gathering place, food, and a waiting place for departure. Luggage is piled helter-skelter, and the atmosphere is one of relaxed congeniality. Fishermen repair nets, others work on their boats quite in harmony with their tourist audience. If you're lucky, you may see an older man in native costume; baggy trousers, homespun coat, white ball atop his cap, and carrying a long stick used to prod a balky mule.

The arriving tourist without reservations must decide among accommodations located at the *plaka*, others with better views, one midway between the *plaka* and Hora, or those in Hora. All have certain advantages, but since the island is so small it takes little time to

Church of St. Irene

survey the situation. There are hotel booking agencies at the harbor to help you make a choice.

Ios has two mountains: Pirgos, 710 m./2,368 ft. high and Megalo, 702 m./2,342 ft. high. This verticality provides endless eye-catching vistas of sea, land, and sky. There is an excellent paved road between the port and Hora. Buses run hourly during the day and will stop to pick you up anywhere along the way, but full fare is collected. In the port, there is a small Memorial Park, and the beginning of a broad, balustraded stone stairway that meanders up to the Hora. Tree-shaded, it has the added allure of offering Ios views. Mule paths make shortcuts between the curves in the paved road, useful if you are a climber at heart. Either way, the stairs and paths cut the distance roughly in half. The last bus to return to the port leaves about 8:30 P.M. After that, it's a taxi or *mai ta podia* (on foot).

HORA

A Cycladic gem! Well worth the trip to Ios! At the church, with its gleaming blue dome, you enter a labyrinth of

pathways that crisscross, meander, rise on twisting steps, abruptly turn, or snake under arcades with old timbers that were part of the original fortress. Perhaps three or more pathways will converge. Which one to take? You can get lost, but only momentarily. Eventually, you will arrive at the minute town square where the islanders enjoy the tourists while sitting away the day, and the tourists soak up the Greek ambiance. A bakery sells delectables, some made by Ios housewives who pride themselves on their culinary extravaganzas. You'll also discover an exquisite little chapel, additional tourist services such as a ship ticket office, and even a bookstore with paperbacks.

Restaurants and tavernas are in good supply. ANTONIS' restaurant, in front of the church, has a charming setting, as does the nearby ACROPOLIS. One of the town's hilltops has an array of windmills formerly used to grind the island corn. Several restaurants here offer specialties ranging from Greek rice pudding to oriental pastries. The MILLS opens at 11:00 A.M., and you can dine to classical music at the RABBIT CLUB.

Music is an integral part of the Ios

experience. Rock, jazz, and classical share the scene. From the highest point near Hora is the IOS CLUB, where classical music is amplified by speaker systems until 11:00 P.M. After that, the sound is rock. The concert is listed each day on the village blackboard.

Nights on Ios are for enjoying, and the tavernas and cafés play their music loud and clear!

You can also climb to other points of town where the silence is absolute and the views of sea and sky are their own music.

Beaches

In Ormos Iou, there is a long, harborside, sandy beach (Gialos) with clear water, but small patches of seaweed sway lazily with the water's movement.

Hora

The popular beach is *Milopota*, where three sun-shaded tavernas offer food and beverages. Prices are set and the service is cafeteria-style. This sandy beach is on a long, curving bay. Bus service starts in the morning and ends at 5:30 P.M.

The bathers and sun-soakers have oiled bodies that glisten in the sun. Noticeable among young readers are books by Durrel, Miller, and Kazantzakis in several languages, proof that the "Greek experience" maintains its charm. There is music, of course.

Hiking Trips

Homer's Tomb. (Two-hour hike, one way.) Sturdy hikers who prefer to have a specific destination may wish to hike up over the north side of Mt. Pirgos where Homer was buried. Pliny called Ios *"Homeri sepulchro veneranda."* In 1770, a Dutch count, Paasch van Krienen, claimed the discovery of Homer's grave. Much skepticism accompanies his account. Others say, "Why not? He had to be buried somewhere." Marvelous scenery en route, and the Homer tradition gives a good feel to the day.

Palaiokastro. This Frankish town was built by Crispi in the fifteenth century. An arduous hike of two-and-a-half hours or a mule trip will bring you to a ruined town where the houses were built of white marble. Many walls are still standing. A marble quarry nearby supplied the material, but the marble was of an inferior quality compared with that of nearby Paros. A valley in this area evinces the existence of a Roman colony. Also nearby is the *Church of the Holy Theodote* where, in September, islanders gather for a great annual feast.

Plakatos is a three-hour hike to the north.

Personal Comment

If you enjoy afternoons on the beach, dining and dancing late into the night, mornings of sleeping in, then your stay could last and last. Two days are the minimum required to enjoy the local sights, sounds, and hospitality of Ios.

*An island of awesome beauty
and unanswered historical mystery.*

thera
(santorini)

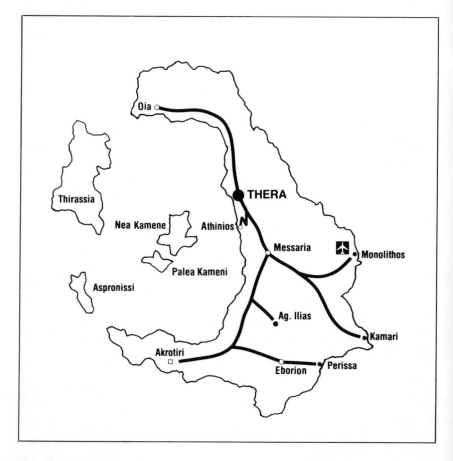

GETTING THERE

From Piraeus via Siros, Paros, Naxos, Ios: 2 to 10 ships weekly.
From Iraklion, Crete: 2 to 5 ships weekly.
From Ag. Nikolaos and Sitea, Crete: 2 ships weekly.
From Milos: 1 to 2 ships weekly. Summer excursion boats between Thera and Paros, Ios, Folangandros, Amorgos, and Amalfi.

DEPARTURES

Reverse of above.

AIR FLIGHTS

Daily between Athens and Thera, except Tuesdays. Seasonal flights from Crete.

TOURIST TIPS

Thera (Santorini) has an area of 76 sq. km./30 sq. mi. Its population is 6,500. No Tourist Police, but local Gendarmerie will serve your needs. Local buses connect with island villages. There are excursion buses to the Akrotiri site. Taxis, donkeys, bicycles, and mopeds are for hire. Buses and taxis meet arriving ships. In Fira (Thera), the bus, taxi, shipping office, and airline office are clustered together on the market street. Camping is permitted on the beaches. National and Commercial Banks of Greece have offices here. Siesta observed.

HOTELS*

Fira: (B) Atlantis. (C) Antonia, Kostas, Kacalari, Kamari, Galini, Panorama.
Messaria: (C) Artemidoros.

*See Part I, section on Accommodations, for explanation of hotel grades.

Firostefani: (C) Kafieris.
Perissa: Christina.
Beach Location: Olympic Villas and Apartments.
Many rooms to rent throughout the island.

HISTORY

3000-1500 B.C. Carians from Asia Minor settled the island. As trade flourished, they became influenced by the Cretan culture. *1500-900 B.C.* About 1500 B.C., the island was devastated by an earthquake and eventually was resettled by Phoenician traders. *900-323 B.C.* Dorian period. Colonists came from northern Greece. Theras, their leader, gave the island its name. *323-146 B.C.* Island was used by the Ptolemies as a naval base. *146 B.C.* Island became a Roman province. *A.D. 395-1210* Byzantine period. *1210* Venetian occupation. Marco Sanudo of Naxos gave the island to Jacopo Barozzi. *1537* The pirate, Barbarossa, conquered it. Eventually the Turks took it. They did not occupy it, but exacted taxes and tributes. *1832* Island became a part of Greece.

ABOUT THERA

All approaches to Thera are dramatic. Its crescent shape almost encloses a vast bay, the earth's largest caldera, 18 X 10 km./9 X 6 mi. The islets that form around the rest of the bay still have an active volcano which you may visit. Thera's cliffs are formidable, and the capital town, Fira, frosts them high above the landing dock. These cliffs are not stone, but layers of lava, ash, pumice, and slag. During daylight hours, they are bands of color: off-white, buff, red-brown, and pinkish-tan. At sunset, they become a fiery red, burnished with purple.

Mule track to Fira

FIRA

Ships that anchor in the inner harbor dispatch their passengers by motor launch to Skala Fira, where a zigzag mule track ascends the cliff. Those who ride the mules have an experience that bears many tellings. Climbing and descending the 587 steps is a lifetime career for the mules and a living for the muleteers who will vie for your business at the harbor landing.

There is bus service for those who land at Oia or Athinios.

North

To walk along the Fira's edge, high above the sea, will surely bring a tingle of excitement to even the most blasé traveler. Down below, the boats look like water beetles skimming the surface of the shimmering sea. The low-lying islands slumber peacefully for the present.

Your walk northward will bring you to Fira's museum with its locally found treasures including early

Cycladic figures, bases, pottery. Look for the seventh century Archaic Vessel decorated with Pegasus, a pelican, and charioteers. In the outer courtyard are Roman and Hellenistic finds. Closed Wednesdays.

Climbing upward, you will reach the Roman Catholic church where Queen Frederika founded a carpet-weaving school. Here, you can see fresh-faced, sometimes giggling young girls working at their looms and creating carpets that are works of art.

South

Returning to the center of town, and still keeping to the western edge, you will come to the new Orthodox Cathedral of *Panagia Ypapanti*, a domed and arched modern church. Try to see it at sunrise when a pink glow turns it into an opalescent extravaganza.

At this end of town, you can descend into narrow passageways that pass for streets. Try to get lost in them. In unexpected spaces between domes and belfries, arches and porticoes, you will catch glimpses of the intense blue sea. From a perch on a white roof, a black cat may watch you. An old lady, dressed in black, will flash a gold-toothed smile as she passes.

Or sit on a parapet and watch the antics of a frisky lamb, below. Sounds have an amazing clarity at this height. The ship's horn, the rooster's crows, the muted putt-putt of a fishing boat, a mule's bray are *living* sounds, but above and beyond all these is a vast and immeasurable silence.

Dining and Entertainment

"Vina Vecchi de Santorini, de prima qualita excellent." Yes, the wine is excellent, as the restaurant sign states. So is another wine labeled *Volcan*. There is a red *Visanto* and a white

Panagia Ypapanti

Fira

Nichteri, plus a liqueur, *Tsikoudia*, all made from grapes and grape leaves that flourish on this volcanic island. Restaurants are scattered; the most attractive are those with balconies and views of the sea. TAVERNA ARIS and the snack bar CANAVA are popular. So is the HOTEL ATLANTIS with bar, restaurant, and disco. The CANAVA plays classical music throughout the quiet siesta time, and loungers can enjoy this and the ever-changing symphony of the sea.

In the back streets, away from the tourist main drags, are the working-men's cafés complete with fishy, garlicky scents and pool rooms, bars, and strident Greek voices. Browse around; if you eat here, you may recognize your muleteer.

In summer, there are several discos open. There is one theater, open all year.

Shopping

Many shops sell creations made from the island's pumice, and quite hand-some jewelry, crafts, and clothing.

A civic endeavor—and open free to the public—is the E.P.S. (Exhibition of the Products of Santorini). All articles are for sale and include lacework, embroideries, wines, and nuts.

Beaches

You'll discover a new experience on beaches of black, volcanic sand. Perissa has the best sand, Kamari has black pebbles, and Monolithos is the furthest from town and the least crowded. All have bus service to them, and tavernas or canteens.

Excursions

Nea Kamene. A motorboat crosses to it daily in twenty minutes. A 30-minute walk from the landing will take you to Metaxa Crater. Here are gases and hot vapors, moon-type terrain.

Akrotiri. Excursion buses come here daily, or you can go on your own. At this site, a guide is necessary and a small fee is charged.

What happened to the Therans when disaster struck? During site excavations, no bodies of people or animals were found. Opinion suggests that minor earthquakes and pumice fallout prompted residents to flee.

Excavators (French, 1867–1871, and Greek, working since 1967) have revealed a Bronze Age town of an estimated 30,000 inhabitants and buildings two to three stories high, many with traces of balconies. The discovery proved that Thera was an important center of Cycladic civilization and Akrotiri a thriving community.

The frescoes excavated at Akrotiri rate among the most extraordinary works of Cycladic art ever discovered. Pictorially beautiful, they reveal and confirm facts about the lives of these unique people. Wall paintings depict battles, religion, sports, fishing, women's fashions, and community life. The sensitivity to design shows in floral patterns, birds, blossoms, and butterflies. These treasured frescoes have been removed and are in the Athens Archaeological Museum. (Perhaps, by the time you reach Thera, they will have been returned to the new Thera Museum.)

Ancient Thera. This city was in existence before 900 B.C. Ruins which the tourist can see date mostly from 300 to 145 B.C., when Thera was an advanced naval base from which the Ptolemies controlled the Aegean. It is best to take a taxi or bus to Ayios Ilias and walk from there to the site. You will be about 557 m./1,857 ft. above sea level, and the view is magnificent. One of the many islands in the distance is Crete. At the summit,

there is a small monastery (A.D. 1771), an eleventh century B.C. Byzantine church, and two chapels. Near the ruin, you'll see classical and archaic cemeteries being excavated. The ruins occupy a rocky spur of land. A guidebook will help you identify the great variety of buildings. There is some erotic graffiti and love messages of the time inscribed on the walls of one sanctuary.

Personal Comment

Mankind's fascination with the catastrophic has had full play on this Aegean island. Today, it slumbers peacefully in dramatic beauty. Spring and late summer are the best time to visit, thus avoiding the heavy cruise crowd.

Fresco from Akrotiri, now in Athens Archaeological Museum

small islands
for the
adventurous traveler*

Sikinos

Island has an area of 22 sq. km./9 sq. mi. Its population is 330. Sikinos rates 1 to 2 ships weekly from Piraeus via Ios. The harbor, *Ano Pronoia*, is the start of a trudge up the mountain to the Kastro, where there are pensions and private rooms plus camping, but no facilities. Restaurants and tavernas are ready to serve you.

Wisely, the Sikinotes have left plenty of room for dancing on the *plaka* of the church. Wedding celebrations can last five days.

In spring, the island is a botanist's delight, with its necropolis way up high, its wild beauty, and the shrill cry of birds which take flight at your presence. The island has gained the reputation of being "what Ios used to be."

Folangandros

Island area is 35 sq. km./14 sq. mi. Its population is 650. Cave enthusiasts

may be intrigued by this island on the Milos–to–Crete route, with ships 1 to 2 times weekly. Since ancient times people have poked into its unusual caves, *Faragaki, Chrysospelia*, and *Geogitsi*. They are reached by boat along a majestic coastline rising in some areas to 473 m./1600 ft. in height.

The main town, *Kastro*, sparkling white, is ready for visitors. There are rooms and small tavernas for your sleeping and eating needs. Field trips include the beautiful three-domed *Panagia* and a hike to Paleokastro for views of Crete. A second town, *Apano Maria*, has beaches and bays for lazy days.

Anafi

Island area is 38 sq. km./15 sq. mi. Its population is 350. This mere dot of land is your last Cycladic collectable on the eastward route via Sikinos or Thera, ships coming 1 to 2 times weekly. Legend states that Apollo raised the island to protect the Argo-

Backpackers

nauts from stormy seas when they returned from their search for the Golden Fleece.

Tourists are welcome in private rooms in the *Chora*, a Cycladic town of the usual narrow streets and white-washed houses embellished with fiercely brilliant flowers. Attractions include the *Kalamiotis Monastery*, sand-pebble beaches, a sunken city in the island's interior. The islanders make an excellent wine.

When you are ready, you can go onward to Crete.

western cyclades

*The first island of the Western Cyclades
remains steadfastly unaffected
by its proximity to mainland Greece.*

kea

GETTING THERE

From Athens: Bus #12 in front of the National Gardens to the Mavromateon bus terminal. Buses leave for Lavrion hourly. Take inland route.
Departure from Lavrion: 5 to 9 ships weekly. Once weekly (Friday) directly to Kea Beach (weather permitting), summer only.

DEPARTURES

To Lavrion: 4 to 9 times weekly.
To Kithnos: 2 to 3 times weekly.

TOURIST TIPS

Kea (Tzia) has an area of 103 sq. km./ 41 sq. mi. Its population is 1,500. The port town, Korissia, has Tourist Police, as does the capital, Kea (also called Ioulis). Taxis meet the ships. Kea Beach Hotel guests are met by the hotel bus. There is good bus service throughout the island. There are no camping facilities, but see Tourist Police for permission. The National Bank of Greece has a branch office in Ioulis. Except in the high season (July and August), restaurants close for the siesta. There is a shipping office in the harbor. Bike rentals are available in high season. Excellent yacht harbor in Vourkari.

HOTELS*

Korissia: (B) Tzia Mas (motel). (C) Tziamas, Karthea.
Kea Beach: (B) Kea Beach Hotel.
Ioulis: (C) Ioulis.
Pisses: (D) Akryliali.
Many rooms in private homes. See Tourist Police.

HISTORY

The island's closeness to Athens made it a center of learning. At the age of

*See Part I, section on Accommodations, for explanation of hotel grades.

seventy its citizens drank hemlock to remove themselves from society, a custom which made the island notable. *2000 B.C.* Four main cities: Ioulis, Karthea, Poiessa, and Korissia, all with great cultural development. *A.D. 5* Keans fought the Persians. *440* Byzantine period began. *1207* Dukes of Naxos owned the island for three-and-a-half centuries. During the Turkish occupation, the Keans paid tribute to both. *1821* Greek revolution.

In 1930, the huge and beautiful *kouros* was discovered on the site of ancient Korissia. It is now in the Athens Archaeological Museum.

Famous People
These include Simonides, born on Kea in 500 B.C., a poet and singer who knew the complete works of Homer by memory; Bacchylides, 500 B.C., lyrical poet; Prodicus, a philosopher, orator, and scientist; Theramenes, politician; Erasistratos, father of anatomy; Aristides, lawgiver; and Xenomides, historian.

KORISSIA

The ship's approach to Korissia is deceptive: all you can see are a few white houses scattered on the terraced hills, a lighthouse on a promontory. Then the ship enters a secluded bay and a two-street town nestled against the western hill is revealed. In the early evening's serenity, the red-roofed, white houses stain the placid harbor water with pink and white reflections.

Down through the years, the Keans have been complacent about the Piraeus ships passing them by. Even today, there is the feeling that the islanders have their own world within their larger Greek world. Only recently has tourism begun. Accommodations are improving, but the islanders are not to be rushed. The exception is the

Kea Beach Hotel on the far side of the island, a perfect hideaway.

Korissia has a splendid yacht basin. Sometimes, on a summer weekend, a hundred or more yachts will slip into its Vourkari Bay for a weekend of heady co-mingling. A memorable excursion experience for the tourist is to leave Korissia at dusk and walk to *Vourkari*. The tree-lined road opens up for glimpses of the sea, rocky bays, and undulating hills, all beginning to soften with the evening's darkness. The stars seem very close, and the air is sweet with the smell of acacia and camellias. Suddenly, around the last curve of road, will be the town of Vourkari, harbor ablaze with lights, the row of nifty-looking yachts lined up in full display, outdoor restaurant tables crowded with happy diners, joyous Greek music in the background. If you wish to join this Dionysian scene, there is always another table brought from somewhere, a willing waiter to serve you for an evening devoted to the spirit of music and wine.

Kea Kouros, now in Athens Archaeological Museum

KEA (IOULIS)

Bus leaves Korissia at 9:00 A.M. You will travel up a twisting, low-gear road where, in April and May, spring will manifest itself in tenderest leaf and brilliant flowering.

The bus heaves itself onto the level parking area outside the medieval gate of Kea, and you have three hours before the bus returns in which to enjoy one of the most charming hill towns of the western Cyclades. To your left, after you enter the gate, the donkey-wide street leads to the castle. The early morning a cappella choir of donkey brays, rooster crows, and bird chatter will accompany you as you climb the stony, twisting street to the castle ruin. This could be a leisurely

walk, for the views of the valley, the nestling town, and abundance of cascading flowers all demand their share of attention.

At the summit, you will be standing on the site of a temple to Apollo. It was wrecked to build a Venetian castle which, in turn, became material for Ioulis homes. Today, there is a (C) hotel with a magnificent view of Euboea, the sea, and the island beneath you. The breeze is fresh, the sun is warm.

Head down again to the town center, where the restaurants and shops cluster. To your right is a broad, level walk skirting the hillside that leads to the famous lion of Kea, offering another leisurely walk through the spring landscape where the riot of spring flowers is giving the bees a busy time.

The *Kea Lion* is about 8 m./28 ft. in length. Made of grey granite, it is believed to be an archaic work, prob-

Ioulis, view from castle

ably Palasgic. Long ago, it slipped from a stadium and is now comfortably propped in place. In modern art parlance, it would be called a "lion concept" and especially noted would be the sinuously curved back. Its resting place in that beautiful, bowl-shaped valley should keep it content into the endless future.

There is time for an *ouzo* and some *mezes* before the return to Korissia. You have a choice of tavernas, each with its own degree of loud male voices and Greek music. *Mezes* could be a plate with small pieces of fish, sausage, hard-cooked egg, cucumber slices, cheese, and little chunks of bread.

Lion of Kea

Right at the town's entry gate is an antique shop worth investigating. The museum is fine if you can find the man with the key. Next to it is the OTE. The Tourist Police are upstairs, and usually one of the staff speaks English. This is the place to go if you need a room because you are determined to stay awhile in this tucked-away, paradisiacal place.

Dining and Entertainment

In Korissia is the new chrome, glass, and marble ALONYSSOS restaurant, specializing in fish, beef, and Greek food. The UNITED EUROPE restaurant has a menu in three languages. In July and August, the TZIA MAS, on the beach, has restaurant facilities. Food is hearty, but perhaps these restaurants save their exceptional dishes for the July and August crowds. However, the island is noted for a bar-shaped dessert called *pasteli,* which is made with sesame seeds and thyme honey.

KEA BEACH HOTEL has a bar, restaurant, and disco. THE MEDUSA and CAVA are Korissia discos. The Vourkari restaurants are gayest at night.

Kean wine enjoyed fame in such faraway places as Constantinople. It's dark red, almost black, and you can find it in Vourkari's venerable fish restaurants.

Shopping

The best gifts in Vourkari are at the Vourkarini Gift Shop. Here you'll find unusual leather jewelry with finely polished stones and excellent weaving.

Beaches

Korissia and Yialiskari (on the road to Vourkari) can be reached by walking. Pisses and Kea Beach are best reached by bus or taxi.

Excursions

The dedicated hiker can explore the entire island on foot. Those who ride the bus will find it somewhat limiting, but satisfying.

The four ancient cities of the island are *Ioulis, Karthea, Poiessa,* and *Korissia.* Karthea, the most important, once had a temple to Artemis, Apollo, and Demeter. Today, the promontory ruins are marked by massive, fallen pillars and an ancient theater. Near Vourkari is *Ayia Irini,* excavated by the American School of Classical Studies. Pottery found there dates from 2500 B.C. It was in Korissia that the huge and beautiful Kouros, now in the Athens Archaeological Museum, was discovered.

Personal Comment

Ideally, Kea should be seen in spring when nature turns the entire island into a celebration.

*An island that has been
landscaped into an art form.*

kithnos

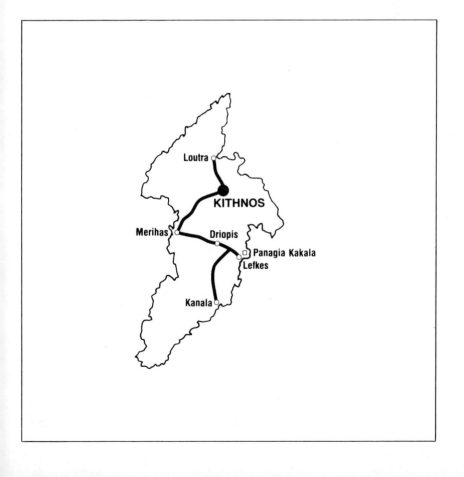

GETTING THERE

From Lavrion: 2 ships weekly.
From Kea: 2 to 3 ships weekly.
From Piraeus: 2 to 8 ships weekly.
From Serifos: 2 to 8 ships weekly.

DEPARTURES

Reverse of above.

TOURIST TIPS

Kithnos has an area of 86 sq. km./ 35 sq. mi. Its population is 1,500. There are no Tourist Police. Two buses and one taxi meet arriving ships. The office of a shipping agent is on the harbor. A bank agent operates from the food market. Store hours are uncertain except in the high season, June through mid-September. There is good bus transportation to island towns. Siesta observed, even by the dogs. Yacht facilities available.

HOTELS*

Merihas: (C) Possidonion. Many small, minimal apartments. Rooms with community kitchens.
Loutra: (C) Xenia, open June to September. (D) Hotel Othon. *Pensions:* Delfini, Katoulia. Rooms in homes.

HISTORY

Scanty Greek and Roman ruins, although the island was a strong military center in the Roman period. *198 B.C. to about 1000 A.D.* Island mostly deserted. Venetian Gozzadini ruled as an appendage of the Naxiote duchy. Turkish occupation. Iron ore mined. After mines went bankrupt, the island suffered a severe depression and declined in population.

*See Part I, section on Accommodations, for explanation of hotel grades.

MERIHAS

This port town is secluded in one of the island's many bays. Pre-season, April and May, the town's loudest sounds are lapping waves, voice echoes, and the revving of motors as fishing caiques and occasional yachts come and go. The harbor's unpaved road follows the curve of the bay where unusual trees called Armila pines send down their roots to sea-water nourishment. In random placement along the road are houses, cafés, restaurants, and a few stores. Short sidestreets dwindle away to patches of daisies and gorse.

Before the tourist season the town's timepiece ticks with inordinate slowness. June to September sees it jammed with Athenian and German tourists, and a holiday spirit livens the atmosphere.

Dining and Entertainment

GIALOS restaurant currently has a chef with culinary talents worthy of a first-class Athenian restaurant. You can eat inside, at tables on the veranda, or under the pines. KABAS, the largest restaurant, opens June 1. They have "Greek Musik every Nicht," so their sign states. The town has a few pizza places and little restaurants where you can eat under an arbor and savor your food along with brittle-bright Greek chatter.

Merihas' specialties are *koularia*, a kind of cookie-bun flavored with molasses and spices. Delicious. Near the bus stop is a small store where you can buy ice cream and frozen *galato-boureko*, cream pie in a *phyllo* crust. The local wine is good. Kithnos cheese and yogurt are special.

Excursions

Main roads from *Merihas* lead in three directions to the west side of the

Panagia Kakala, Lefkes

island. There are brief stops at each town, with several hours before the bus returns. It is best to check the schedule unless you intend to hike back.

Chora. Also known as *Kithnos*, the capital, this town is starkly white, bravely placed on a denuded hill, wide open to wind and sun. Notable are its five churches decorated with Byzantine-style frescoes done by the great hagiographer, Skordiles, around 1700 A.D. With persistence, you can find the caretaker with the keys. An unusual feature of the churches is that the Orthodox use one side of the church, the Catholics the other.

Loutra. A thermal spa, mentioned as far back as 1142, Loutra today is a mixture of spanking new buildings and those in shambles. There is a long length of beach, the north end used by the local fishermen. If you stay overnight, try to awaken to watch the sunrise. The Greeks sit outside for morning coffee and begin the day with this glorious spectacle.

Driopis. Driopis is nestled down into barren hills, a Cycladic town of narrow streets with many deserted houses. Near here are caves with old tombs dating from Roman times. Turks occupied the town for about ninety years.

Lefkes. The road ends at Lefkes, a town that is a summer place for Athenians. Houses rise up on tiers from a beauty of a beach and surround the church, *Panagia Kakala.* A big celebration is held on August 15. Away from the hurry of the world, the town occupants enjoy their holiday community, with folk dancing and feasts in the *plaka* surrounding their handsome church.

A Special Sight. For a never-to-be-forgotten experience, a bus ride should be taken from the east coast back to Merihas at sunset time. Now this almost-barren island becomes a piece of sculpture. Hills are backlighted by the blazing western sky. Up, down, and around, the road reveals a panorama that constantly changes as

Merihas fishermen

shadows darken the valleys. Most amazing are the endless, low stone walls which enclose irregularly shaped plots of land terraced with fields of golden grain. Built so long ago by colonizing tribes, these stone walls have beginnings lost in history, but today they could make any stone mason stand up and salute and any sculptor bow in reverence. Down the last hill to the port, the sea lies flat and blue. As you leave the bus, the driver smiles at you. He knows his island is beautiful, and he can see on your face that you know it, too.

Personal Comment

A springtime island for travelers who want a time with nothing to do. Midsummer, there is much to do.

serifos

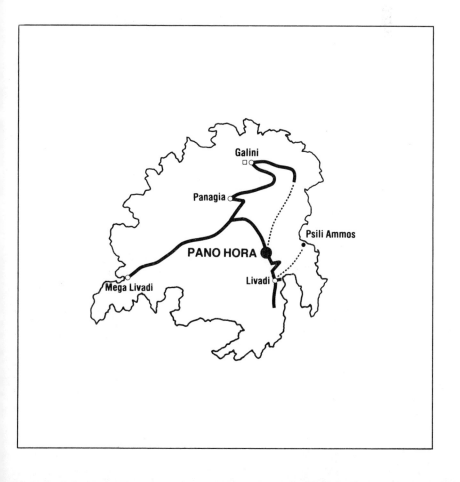

GETTING THERE

From Piraeus: 2 to 8 ships weekly.
From Kithnos: 2 to 8 ships weekly.
From Sifnos: 2 to 8 ships weekly.

DEPARTURES

Reverse of above.

TOURIST TIPS

Serifos (Seriphos) has an area of 70 sq. km./29 sq. mi. Its population is 2,000. Police are stationed in Pano Hora, the capital and upper town. There is a bank agent there as well as in Livadi, the port town. Ship ticket offices are in the grocery store next to the Serifos Gift Shop and in a store near St. Nickolas Church. There is camping at Karavi Beach, a 15-minute walk from town. A bus and several taxis go to Pano Hora. Siesta observed. The telephone kiosk is on the waterfront. OTE in Pano Hora. There are yacht facilities.

HOTELS*

Livadi: (B) Hotel Perseus. (C) Serifos Beach. *Pensions:* Kontes, Galanou, Goullelmos. (*Note:* New hotels being built.)
Pano Hora: Rooms.

HISTORY

First kings were Dictis and Polydectes. *7 B.C.* Island became a democracy. During the Persian wars, Serifos was a Persian ally, but during the naval battles of Salamis it revolted and re-united with Greece. *A.D. 146* Roman occupation, followed by Frankish and Venetian occupations. First iron ore mining began with the Venetians. Turkish occupation. Piracy was rampant. *1821* Civil leaders raised the flag of revolution and joined the Pan-hellenic struggle for freedom. In later years, the iron mines provided such meager living that many islanders left. Today, tourism is bringing a measure of security and prosperity to the people of this charming island.

Mythology
Danae, daughter of Acrisius, King of Argos, bore Perseus, who was fathered by Zeus. To punish her, Acrisius placed Danae and Perseus in a large chest and cast it into the sea. It came ashore on Serifos where King Polydectes received them. When Perseus was grown, King Polydectes ordered him to kill the monster, Medusa, hoping to get rid of Perseus so he could marry Danae. Surprisingly, Perseus returned with Medusa's head, and found the King making love to Danae. Perseus turned them and all the islanders to stone. According to mythology, this explains the island's stony nature.

LIVADI

As the ship enters the protected harbor, the small town of Livadi is completely upstaged by the capital, *Pano Hora*, unquestionably one of the most dramatically situated towns of the western Cyclades. As you leave the ship and maneuver through the crowd of departing visitors, you will, of necessity, give your attention to Livadi. Pleasantly strung out for nearly a mile along a clean, sandy beach, it is shaded by Armila pines, their aged trunks painted white.

The town is a succession of water-front buildings that serve your eating, drinking, sleeping, and socializing needs.

Settled in and ready for a discovery walk, you will find the most activity near the fishermen's pier. Here, too, are yachts, in varying degrees of im-

---

*See Part I, section on Accommodations, for explanation of hotel grades.

Climb to Pano Hora

pressiveness. Numerous cafés and tavernas provide sitting space for friendly loafing and that special, guiltless Greek curiosity that is so attractive to the tourist.

About nine o'clock in the morning is the time to watch the fishermen return, spread their yellow nets on the pier and glean their catch of fish. The islanders come to buy; the fish is hand-weighed. There are a few little black-dressed ladies who sort through the nets for "pickings," their labors resulting in a nice handful of fish. (One wonders if the fishermen deliberately overlook a certain amount each day.)

Visitors to Livadi will find the day's pattern loosely arranged around morning hours at the various beaches and a late lunch, after which the town becomes quiet until about five o'clock. From then on, you can make your own variety of entertainment until the cock crows.

Dining and Entertainment

Several of the restaurants do not open until June when the town becomes crowded with visiting Europeans, many of whom return each year. For early travelers there is a satisfying selection of seafood places. MOKKAS and O. GIANNIA have especially tasty lobster.

The PIZZA RESTAURANT makes a Greek salad that undoubtedly will tempt you to return again and again. Also, their pizzas should satisfy the most discriminating tastes.

Tavernas serve beverages from early morning on. Afternoons, they supply a honeyed dish of fruit that goes well with Turkish coffee. There are three strengths of *ouzo* to try. The island has an excellent local wine but, by report, the islanders keep it for themselves.

Juke box music is available for evening dining and impromptu dancing. The BLUE OX is a popular disco.

Around six o'clock in the evening, at the north end of the town beach, you can watch young Greek men dash around in a fast soccer game to the accompaniment of their own enthusiastic whoops and yells.

Shopping

The town has several outstanding gift shops. The Serifos Gift Shop has pottery made by Dionisia, a young local woman. Bowls, cups, and dishes are decorated with Serifos designs of birds, ships, figures, and flowers. Sweaters are island-knit. Small, hand-loomed rugs feature ship designs. A former Serifos man makes the shop's silver jewelry. Ask to see the "eye of the sea" pendants. The shop's owner has traveled far afield to bring the icons from Mt. Athos and filigree silver over glass from Ioanina, near Corfu.

Another shop, Vatsalo, has delight-ful folklore scenes painted on wood, hand-embroidered linens, and finely glazed pottery. The young artisan who owns the shop also makes handsome bronze jewelry.

Beaches

The town beach is long enough to be uncrowded, at least in April and May. *Psili Ammos*, a 30-minute walk along a dry riverbed, up over an embankment, and down to a sandy beach, will give you all the privacy you may wish. The camping area, *Karavi Beach*, has a sweeping curve of bay that is a 15-minute walk from town.

Excursions

Pano Hora. For most visitors, the upper town is not to be missed. You can take bus, taxi, or stairway to the top. If it's Sunday, you can stop midway at a small chapel and light a candle in exchange for a small coin. The Pano Hora had its beginning in Roman times, and today its most important church, *St. John Theologos*, is built over the ruins of a Temple to Athena. Around A.D. 1210, pirates, led by Barbarossa, almost demolished the town. Today, it is a drift of snow-white houses leading up to a ruined castle which encloses the *Church of St. Konstantine.*

In the center of the town there is a small *plaka*, post office, stores, taverna, boutique, and the OTE.

An unforgettable view of Pano Hora can be seen from Livadi at night as you walk along the quiet, nighttime sea. In utter blackness, the Hora's lights hang like a low-lying constellation, its intricate design outdoing the heaven's show.

Moni Taxiarchon. This monastery, beyond Galini, could be the objective for a satisfying day of hiking augmented with spectacular views. From a distance, the monastery looks like a fortress with battlements, and it did serve this purpose when piracy was a threat. Today, it has a cheerful red dome emerging from the center, and the heavy exterior walls are a gleaming white. It is considered the island's most consequential monument despite

Karavi Beach and campground

its badly damaged frescoes. The important library is not open to the average visitor, but coffee is served by the hospitable monk who will show you certain areas.

If you return by the mulepath via Kentarchos, you will have a windy walk in space, light, and solitude edged by the Aegean dashing itself against the headlands.

Note: Mineralogists have been interested in this island for a long time. The islanders don't mind collectors taking "pocket-size" pieces, but they frown upon anything larger. The mines at *Mega Livadi* are beginning to be reworked.

Personal Comment

The pre-June and post-mid-September visitor has the advantages of the best weather, choice of accommodations, and lack of crowds. During these times, the two ships a week on the Piraeus–Milos route necessitate a stay of several days. For those who have plenty of time, how lucky you are!

*Sifnos' architecture has harmony without
uniformity, resulting in a "Cycladic" difference,
eye-catching and intriguing.*

sifnos

GETTING THERE

From Piraeus via Kithnos and Serifos:
2 to 10 ships weekly.
From Milos: 2 to 10 ships weekly.

DEPARTURES

To Paros: 3 summer excursion boats
weekly.
To Piraeus via Serifos, Milos: Reverse
of above.

TOURIST TIPS

Sifnos (Siphnos) has an area of 79 sq.
km./31 sq. mi. Its population is 2,000.
Regular police are located in Apollonia.
Although non-English-speaking, they
will scout up an interpreter. Kamares
and Apollonia have shipping agencies.
Summertime buses run every hour to
island villages. A bus from the town
square in Apollonia leaves for Kamares
two hours before ship arrivals. Five
taxis meet ships. Mopeds are for hire
near Hotel Anthoussa in Apollonia.
Next door is the OTE. The bank is in
a grocery store very near the Hotel
Anthoussa. A bulletin board in Apollonia Square lists ship schedules. Siesta
observed except in restaurants and
patisseries.

HOTELS*

Apollonia: (B) Apollonia (pension).
(C) Anthoussa, Kamari, Sifnos, Sofia.
Kamares: (C) Stavros, Pension Exilge.
Building of several new hotels in
progress.
Artemona: (C) Artemon.
Platy Yalos: (B) Panorama (pension),
Platy Yalos. Camping permitted.
Rooms to let in Kamares, Apollonia,
Artemona, Katavati, Kastro, Platy
Yalos, and Faros.

*See Part I, section on Accommodations,
for explanation of hotel grades.

HISTORY

Eighth Century B.C. The rich workings
of the gold and silver mines provided
the means for temples, civic buildings,
and the Sifnian Treasury at Delphi.
550-525 B.C. Kastro sacked, gold
mines exhausted. *338 B.C.* Philip of
Macedon conquered the island. *146
B.C.-324 A.D.* Roman occupation.
476 Beginning of the Byzantine
period. *1207* Annexed by Marco
Sanudo of Naxos. *1617.* Annexed by
Turkey. *1771-1774* Russian occupation under Catherine. *1880-1918* Iron
ore mines were operated. *1941-1944*
Italian occupation.

Mythology
Each year the gift of Sifnos to the
Delphic Apollo was a solid gold egg.
One year the islanders sent a gilded
stone. Apollo was so furious he sank
the gold mines into the sea, and the
island's name became a synonym for
dishonesty. (*Note:* Apollo's fury was
probably an earthquake.)

KAMARES

This port town has a hospitable
frontage geared to make the tourist
comfortable while awaiting departure
or recovering from arrival. Small tables
with Van Gogh-type chairs are placed
at random on a beachside *plaka* shaded
by boxed trees. The row of restaurants, tavernas, and souvenir shops are
open most of the day, dependent on
ship schedules. Kamares has a workaday, noncommercial pottery manufacturing shop on the street behind
the harborfront. The natural clay is a
rusty red, indicative of the iron-rich
soil of the island.

The sandy beach is extensive in this
almost landlocked harbor. It looks
placid and gentle, but it can be
whipped to a small fury by winds
sweeping down from the mountains.
Fortunately, they pass quickly, and

the swimmers, pedalo-riders, sailors, and wind-skiffers can get on with their pleasures.

APOLLONIA

For those who intend to base in the capital, there is a half-hour bus ride upward on a snaky road that reveals the island's fertility and intricately formed terrain. Apollonia was built on the site of a Temple to Apollo which, of course, included a vast and encompassing view of the sea. Today, elegance and unforced dignity rest lightly on this Cycladic town, which is scattered over the green hills like the petals of a windblown white flower. The hillsides are terraced; each house has its vineyard, orchard, or small garden.

The town center is more closely knit. To walk among the twisting streets is to be part of an enormous architectural sculpture, embellished with flowers, chimney pots, wrought iron, flagstone walks, and house windows filmed with real lace, plus open doorways made private by canvas curtains of orange or pink, even turquoise.

The day starts with a broadcast of chicken cluckings and cacklings from the surrounding hills, followed by the sound of delivery trucks racing around on the few available streets. You can open your shutter doors to the sun rising from the Aegean, and Apollo's light will immediately prance and dance right into your room.

Dining and Entertainment

Reputations have a way of emerging and clinging. Sifnos enjoys the prestige of culinary excellence. This you will have to discover personally. Indigenous to the islands are capers. If your visit is in spring, look for the tender new leaves in your salad. Barrel wine is

Apollonia

available. In fact, bottles are valuable, so if you have an empty one, take it to a wine shop forthwith.

Patisseries are in abundance. *Schlag* (whipped cream) has been adopted through the influence of German visitors. *Melopita-sifnopita* is an island specialty. Cheese and honey, sugar and eggs are baked in a pastry shell, liberally sprinkled with cinnamon, and served in a diamond shape. Below the Anthoussa Hotel, there is a café that displays a selection of desserts that defies you not to make a purchase.

Three restaurants are recommended for you to try: SOPHIA, CYPRESS, and THE GOOD HEART. Look for a new one, SKIPITARIS, which promises to be uniquely decorated. The islanders claim a specialty that tops all others. Start with a solidly formed utilitarian pot, add water, then many chickpeas, oil, copious amounts of onion, and bake slowly for many hours. A hearty dish for hearty people.

Placed at random on winding streets are small cafés definitely not geared to the tourist. A blend of Greek voices and Greek music has an excited, happy quality. Outside, there will be a vine-covered terrace to sit on; inside, the café is apt to be small of space and haphazard with its chairs and tables. Toward the back of the room, through a window filled with flower pots, can be a blazing, sunstruck view of the Aegean.

When you enter, the Greeks smile at you. They are pleased that you have taken the time to see their way of life along with the busier tourist-type cafés and tavernas.

A Greek priest in his voluminous black robes may enter. Immediately, room is made for him at a table. He orders his soft drink and enjoys conviviality that seems to heighten with his presence.

Shopping

Pots and potters date far back into history. Formerly, the Sifnos potters would move from town to town, supplying each with well-made earthenware and cooking utensils, all part of an ancient craft. Today, you can visit these workshops throughout the island. Glazes tend to stay with the dark reds blending into brown, plus a particularly strong green.

Boutiques and shops are above average, and the industrious Sifnian women design and make the unique dresses that are for sale.

Beaches

See *Excursions.*

Excursions

Kastro. 3.5 km./2 mi. by bus ride or easy downhill walk from Apollonia. The serpentine road follows terraced hills liberally embellished with chapels.

Your first view of the Kastro reveals an impregnable hill surrounded on three sides by the Aegean. The town sprawls around it in gleaming whiteness.

About a hundred years ago, this striking specimen of medieval fortification built by the Da Carogna clan in 1365 was crumbling into ruins. Today, the town has inhabitants who have reclaimed the old houses, live there, and cater to tourism. There is an old-world atmosphere of combined Venetian, Greek, and Turkish influence.

Many homes are three-storied with balconies. Be wary. You may be caught in the drip of a balcony-hung wash. Arched bridges cross over streets, offering entry into second stories. Outside steps lead upward, short tunnels provide shadows from the glistening white of the buildings, while vines soften the angular walls.

If you keep bearing left after you enter the town, you'll eventually arrive

Kamares potter

at the Kastro. Overgrown grasses, thistles, and wild flowers surround remnants of a few arches and stonewall rubble, all that is left of the Italian Dukedom which strove so hard to master the not-to-be-mastered Greeks. Back in the town, a taverna awaits. So does a bus, nearby.

Vathy. Town can be reached by boat from the harbor town, Kamares. It has a beautiful beach surrounded by high mountains and a pottery shop to visit. Situated on a rock jutting into the sea is the perfect Byzantine church: three transcepts, two domes, and an elegant bell tower, *Taxiarchis* by name.

Platy Yalos. A second island port and a resort area, it has the longest beach in the Cyclades. The hotel has a bar, restaurant, and roof garden.

Artemona. Recommended for nightlife aficionados. Even the monasteries serve food and wine to their guests after vespers on festival days.

Faros. Ruins of mines and vestiges of ancient Sifnos.

Chryssopigi. A particularly beautiful Panagia on a tongue of land jutting into the welcoming waters of the Aegean. There is bus service to Chryssopigi from Apollonia.

Personal Comment

If you are collecting Aegean Island "gems," you may wish to include Sifnos as one of your treasures.

milos
kimolos

*Milos is an island with many
curiosities of nature.*

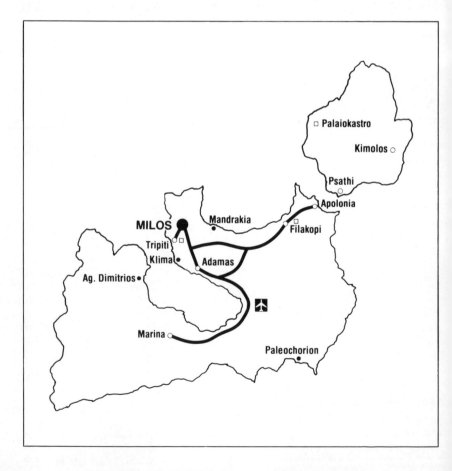

MILOS

Mandrakia

Tripiti
Klima
Adamas
Ag. Dimitrios

Marina

Paleochorion

Filakopi
Apolonia
Psathi

Kimolos
Palaiokastro

GETTING THERE

From Piraeus direct, or via the Western Cyclades: 2 to 12 ships weekly.
From Ios and Thera: 2 to 3 ships weekly.
Between Milos and Kimolos: Daily excursion boats or fishermen's caiques.

DEPARTURES

Reverse of above.

AIR FLIGHTS

Four times weekly between Athens and Milos. Olympic office in Milos is on Adamas Milou St.

Wood carving, San Triada church

TOURIST TIPS

Milos has an area of 160 sq. km./ 61 sq. mi. Its population is 4,503. Tourist Police in Milos, upper town. In Adamas the information center is in the Afrodite Shop on the harbor. Shipping agencies are nearby. Ten taxis meet the ships. The bus and taxi station is at the opposite end of harbor. Buses go to outlying towns hourly in high season and at 1½-hour intervals otherwise. Bikes and mopeds are available to rent for those who get to the rental place early. Commercial Bank of Greece has offices. Ninety percent of the island's accommodations are in the port town, Adamas. For camping and room information inquire at the Afrodite Shop. Siesta observed, except in snack cafés. Adamas has an excellent yacht harbor.

HOTELS*

Adamas: (B) Venus Village, Adamas. (C) Chronis, Corelli. (D) Delfini, Hotel Georgaritas. Rooms in private homes.

*See Part I, section on Accommodations, for explanation of hotel grades.

HISTORY

Island had Early and Middle Cycladic Bronze Age civilizations. *1600 B.C.* Island united with King Minos of Crete. *1100 B.C.* Dorian invasion. *416 B.C.* Athens attempted to subdue the islanders. Speeches known as the Melian dialogues took place, followed by Athenian invasions. Melians of military age were killed, women and children enslaved. Athenians colonized the island. Island became very wealthy and rated with Delos and Paros in artistic excellence. *A.D. 1677* Capsi, the corsair, made himself ruler of the island. *1697* Advent of the steamship destroyed island's economy since it was not needed as a stopping place. *1799* French used the island to train their corsair pilots. *1836* Crown Prince of Bavaria bought remains of the Roman Theater to protect it from oblivion. *1912* Cretan refugees arrived. *World War II* Allied naval base.

The Venus de Milo
The Melians purposely buried their statues, and in 1820 a farmer unearthed the Venus and three statues of

Hermes. Immediately, the area became a hunting ground for treasures. The Frenchman Brest was in residence at the time and successfully bargained for the Venus to be sent to the Louvre in Paris.

ABOUT MILOS

The island curves almost completely around its imposing majestic harbor. It is an island of gorges, valleys, and mountains where volcanic activity has created steam caves as effective as any Turkish bath, great yawning caverns, tufa rock in steeple form, and a mineral-rich soil. Mining is extensive. The remainder of its terrain is unused except by shepherds. Olive trees grow wild; so do cabbage and thyme. Oleanders choke any water course. As you ride along its minimal paved road, you will see tufa caves, many with doors that suggest living quarters or storage.

ADAMAS (ADAMA)

This port town has a crusty ruggedness. Trucks rumble along the harbor main street with their loads of alum, sulfur, pumice, or perlite. At the main dock, the long barges await loading. The tourist is advised to ignore all of this and, instead, to sit in repose under a leafy, vine-covered arbor or in the shade of the pines while enjoying views of Milos' glorious harbor. With skillfully balanced trays, waiters from across the street scurry back and forth with beverages and desserts.

Behind the harbor, the town rises on steep streets with a mixture of Cycladic charm and mediocre modernity. Outstanding are two churches which will delight the connoisseur of Byzantine art. *San Triada*, one half-block up from the bus stop, has been made into a museum. Among other treasures are thirteenth and sixteenth century icons brought from Crete by refugees. If you missed Skordiles'

Adamas arbor for diners

Icons, San Triada church

work on Kithnos, you will have your chance on Milos. San Triada has Skordiles plus icons from the Skordiles and Atrita schools of religious art. A priest is there to explain the church treasures.

A second church, *Ag. Ioannis*, is high on the hill, open usually 6:00 to 8:00 P.M. Here, the priest will show you the church's art collection and tell you that it rates first in the Cyclades and fifth in Greece. Look for the naive and charming interpretations of Biblical fables in the small icons at the front of the church. *Jonah and the Whale* is especially delightful. Both churches have excellent courtyard mosaics.

Dining and Entertainment

Harborside restaurants include AN-TONIS, its blue wooden tables covered with white oilcloth. The chef makes a distinguished *moussaka*, puts fresh mint in his *keftedes* (meatballs), and uses liberal amounts of sharp Milos cheese on his pastas. CAVE D'AMORE accompanies its food with loud Italian music. It offers a choice from its Snack Bar, Cafeteria, or Pizzaire. HOTEL ADAMAS has the best views of the harbor from its upper street level, plus an appetizing selection of the usual Greek cuisine. The town's most elegant dining is at the VENUS VILLAGE HOTEL. The chef may feature aubergines in various combinations, and artichoke hearts *a la polita*, in egg and lemon sauce. Their recommended wine is called Venus. Prepared lobster is sold by the kilo, and for dessert "a la Milo" the chef suggests green and purple grapes, sweet melons, or ripe figs.

Dining along the waterfront can last long into the night and become happier, louder, and more convivial as the hours pass.

Shopping

Plaster casts of the Venus de Milo, *ad infinitum*.

Beaches

The most convenient beach fronts the Venus Village Hotel. Wind-surfers and boats are for hire. Paleochorion Beach, as well as many coves, can be reached by boat trips. *Klima* is mentioned in *Excursions.* Other beaches to investigate are *Mandrakia* and *Ag. Dimitrios.*

Excursions

Plaka, also known as Milos, is the island's capital. As you sail into Milos Bay, you see the city cresting the hill, topped by the Frankish remains of its Kastro. A bus trip, hike by road, or along mule path, will bring you to hillside settlements topped by a row of windmills stubbornly defying complete disintegration. The capital has the police station, the OTE, a few stores, and the bus station.

Above you is the Frankish Kastro and a well-kept thirteenth century *Church of Thalassitras.* There is a good path up to it. Here, your views include the bay, Mt. Profitis Elias, and a coastline that raises the entire scene into the realm of the spectacular. Sunlight and shadow combine in Wagnerian grandeur. All the scene needs is an audience to appreciate it. For those not in the mood to climb, the same view can be seen from the front of the *Rosaria Church* near the *Folk Art Museum* and the *Archaeological Museum*. Both of these are closed on Tuesdays and during siesta.

Tripiti. The bus passes Tripiti on its way to the Plaka. Here, the hillside catacomb has tombs cut into the tufa rock. An estimated 1,500 tombs were excavated over the years in five galleries and their annexes. The tomb forms are borrowed from pagan ideas. They have curved and vaulted roofs, and a few inscriptions are still discernible. There are niches for lamps, but today the tourist has the advantage of delicate, twinkly lights lining the galleries and their annexes.

Down to the coast is *Klima* where a beach and a cool swim will make you feel very much alive.

Filakopi (Phylokope). Here are the remains of ancient towns excavated by the British in 1886–99. The dashing Flying Fish fresco came from this site.

Great archaeological importance stems from gleanings of this Early Cycladic and Middle Periods, plus a third city with Mycenaean influences. Historically important, too, to the ardent ruin enthusiast.

Apolonia. A small village, sleepy in the warm sun, with a few pine trees lining the beach, a few yachts lazing in the port, fishermen's caiques, a taverna where you can pass the hours in mental vacuity or hot discussion, plus a takeoff place for Kimolos. A boat leaves early each morning for Psathi port and returns about half-past-two in the afternoon. You can take your chances at catching a ride with a fisherman. They make the .8 km./½ mi. crossing several times each day. There are very few accommodations on Kimolos.

Kimolos. (55 sq. km./25 sq. mi., population 1,090.) This chalky, arid, and almost barren island supplies a white powder used as a base for aspirin and cosmetics. Whiteness dusts the island over a base of thin brown soil streaked with varicolored rocks. Where it is adaptable to vegetation, wheat is grown. Much of the area is archaeological-sacred to protect still unearthed treasures. Its many caves were used in former years by pirates who bivouacked there and debauched with the booty they had taken from the Turks.

The town of Kimolos is on a hill reached by a paved road from Psathi, the port. There is no hotel, but about fifty rooms are available to rent. Athenians have built summer houses, and a favorite hangout is NIKKO'S CAFE. It is also the busiest. Food is plain, heavy on the rice and snails, very light on the fresh fruit and

vegetables. A reservoir supplies the water.

The island will appeal to hikers who can explore the unusual terrain, hot thermal springs, abandoned stone bathtubs with running hot waters, mines and stony beaches, and the *Palaiokastro* topping a sharp hill with ruined fortifications.

Personal Comment

Milos and Kimolos are for the traveler with plenty of time who enjoys the unusual.

VI
crete

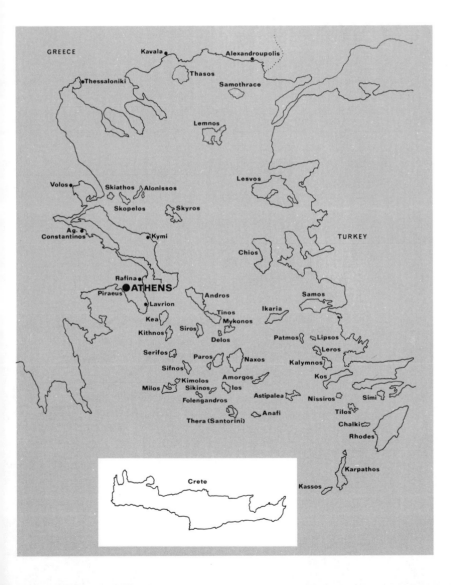

GREECE

Kavala

Alexandroupolis

Thessaloniki

Thasos

Samothrace

Lemnos

Lesvos

Volos

Skiathos Alonissos

Skopelos Skyros

Ag.
Constantinos

Kymi

TURKEY

Chios

Rafina
Piraeus ●ATHENS

Andros

Samos

Lavrion

Tinos
Mykonos

Ikaria

Kea

Kithnos Siros

Delos

Patmos Lipsos

Leros

Serifos

Paros

Naxos

Kalymnos

Sifnos

Amorgos

Kos

Kimolos

Milos Sikinos Ios

Astipalea

Nissiros

Simi

Folengandros

Tilos

Thera (Santorini)

Anafi

Chalki

Rhodes

Karpathos

Crete

Kassos

*"Out in the dark blue sea there lies a land
called Crete, a rich and lovely land."—The Odyssey*

crete

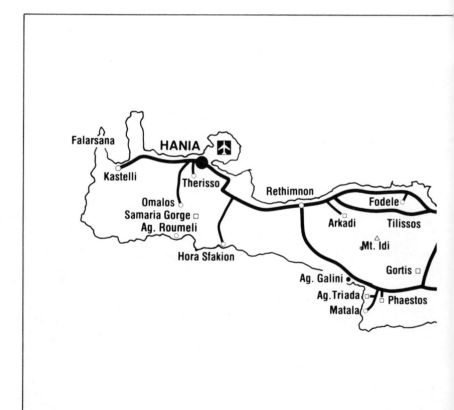

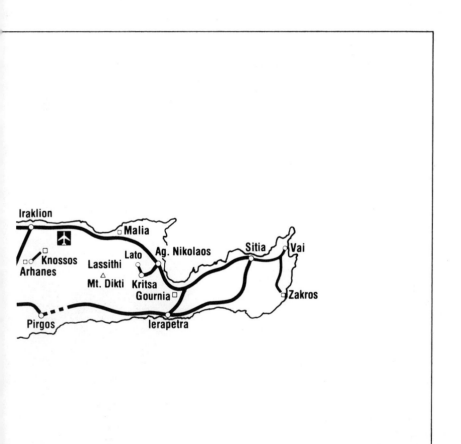

GETTING THERE

From Piraeus to Iraklion: 10 ships weekly.
From Piraeus to Hania: 4 ships weekly.
From Piraeus to Kastelli: 2 ships weekly.
From Milos to Ag. Nikolaos and Sitia: 1 to 2 ships weekly.
From Thera to Ag. Nikolaos and Sitia: 1 ship weekly.
From Rhodes via Karpathos to Ag. Nikolaos and Sitia: 1 to 3 ships weekly.
Note: Certain ships stop at Siros, Paros, Naxos, Ia, Ios, and Thera. Check with travel agent or shipping clerk.

DEPARTURES

To Piraeus: Reverse of above.
To Thera from Iraklion: Local summer line 4 times weekly.
To Rhodes and Milos: Reverse of above.

AIR FLIGHTS

Daily between Athens, Iraklion, and Hania.
Between Iraklion and Rhodes in summer; also Thera and Mykonos.
Iraklion air links with London and Frankfurt.

TOURIST TIPS

Crete (Kriti) has an area of approximately 14,520 km./5,214 sq. mi. Its population is about 460,000. Tourist Police: *Ag. Nikolaos:* 7 Omirou St. *Hania:* 44 Karaiskaki St. *Rethimnon:* 214 Arkadion St. *Iraklion* has a regular police force. G.N.T.O. offices: *Hania:* 6 Akti Tombazi. *Iraklion:* 1 Xanthoudidou St.

Each of these towns has numerous tourist agencies that arrange trips to archaeological sites, and places, and towns of scenic and historical interest.

Regular bus service reaches all places of tourist interest. Cars are for rent in the four main cities, as well as in Ierapetra, Sitia, and Malia. Bicycles and mopeds are available also. There are yacht supply stations at the north coastal cities. For mountain climbing and camping information, contact the Tourist Police or the G.N.T.O.

The four main cities have offices of the National, Commercial, Ionian, and Popular Banks of Greece. All have the OTE. Siesta observed except for some places serving food.

GENERAL INFORMATION

Modern and traditional entertainment can be found in the larger cities and towns. Popular and local Cretan dancing and singing are featured. There are endless beaches devoid of crowds. Fishing can be arranged with boat owners in most seaside towns.

Festivals include the June Cherry Festival and the July Wine Festival in and near Rethimnon. August has the Raisin Festival in Sitia. October has the Chestnut Festival in the Hania district. Visitors are always welcome at local weddings.

Minoan bull,
Iraklion Archaeological Museum

HOTELS*

Iraklion (Heraklion): (A) Astir, Astoria, Atlantis, Creta Beach, Xenia, Zeys. (B) Castron, Cosmopolit, Esperia, Mediterranean. (C) Dedalos, Domenico, El Greco, Galini, Iraklion, Knossos, Olympic, Prince, Faedra, Mirabello, Park, Pasiphae, Poseidon, Selena.
Ag. Nikolaos: (L) Minos Beach, Mirabello Village. (A) Hermes, Mirabello, Ariadne Bea, Coral, Polydoros. (C) Akratos, Alkistis, Delta, Du Lac, Kreta, Kronos, Rea.
Hania (Chanea): (A) Kydon. (B) Doma, Lissos, Porto Vene, Samaria, Xenia. (C) Aptera Bea, Chanea, Cypros, Dictynna, Ellinis, Elyros, Kriti, Lucia, Plaza.
Rethimnon: (B) Ideon, Xenia. (C) Braskos, Park, Valari, Monos.
Sitia: (B) Sitian. (C) Alice, Crystal, Itanos, Sitia.
Malia: Ikaros Village, Kemos Beach, Sirens Beach, Malia Beach, Grammatikaki, Zeys.
Ierapetra: (C) Atlantis, Crete, Lygia. Many (C) and (D) hotels, pensions, and private rooms on the island.

HISTORY

Neolithic Period (6000-3000 B.C.) First inhabitants may have arrived from Asia Minor. They lived in caves and open settlements. Artifacts include stone and bone tools. Female figurines indicate a cult of the Mother Goddess. *Minoan Period (3000-1100 B.C.)* This was the period made famous by Sir Arthur Evans and his archaeological activities at Knossos. *1700 B.C.* Catastrophic disaster. Palaces and town sites destroyed. After rebuilding, the island entered its greatest stage. *1700-1450 B.C.* The buildings that survive today are from this period. Trade with other countries

was established, and a great prosperity ensued. *1450 B.C.* Total destruction, cause unknown, but conjectured to be the great explosion on Thera. *1450-1380 B.C.* Recovery at Knossos and partially at other sites. *Geometric and Archaic Periods.* By the eighth century B.C., the Dorians occupied the island. A flourishing artistic life developed in jewelry, statuary, pottery, polychrome amphoras, clay votive plaques. *Classical, Hellenistic, and Roman Periods (Fifth Century-67 B.C.)* Frequent intercity warfare. Aristocratic families dominate. *Medieval and Modern Periods (Fifth-Ninth Centuries A.D.)* Byzantine culture flourished. After the Fourth Century Crusade, the Genoese ruled until the island was sold to Venice, which held it for 400 years (1210-1669). Turkish occupation caused life to reach an abysmal level. *1898-1913* Island became a part of Greece. *1941-1944* German occupation.

CRETE'S
THREE MAIN PALACES

Three palaces were built about 2000 B.C. in the central section of Crete. *Knossos,* on the northern shore, was ideally placed for trade. *Phaestos,* to the south, was open to trade from Egypt and Libya. *Malia,* to the east, was the third palace. Knossos dominated and maintains its popularity today with tourists because of the reconstruction work of Sir Arthur Evans.

All three palaces have common architectural features, including a dominant central court and a large informal court on the west wall. Decidedly Minoan in character, the palaces had privacy, domestic amenities (plumbing!), gardens, and flower beds. Many columns were incorporated into the designs. There was a deliberate creation of light and shade areas, enclosures and open

Model of Knossos, Iraklion Archaeological Museum

spaces blended into a lively harmony. The spirited frescoes, with their feeling of playfulness, the use of animal, sea and flower forms, sexually-alluring women and slender, masculine men are unique. Always one senses excitement and the delight Minoans felt towards their bodies, their activities, and their portrayal of life.

Horns of Consecration, Knossos

The palaces served as religious centers of their domains. They were surrounded by markets and many large residential estates. Nearby were the ports and fishing villages. The palaces housed royalty and those who participated in court life. Rituals involving Minos, the bull, were part of the life pattern. The palace had administration offices, tax-collecting facilities. Storerooms housed decorative, large-bellied jars where oil, grains, wine and precious goods were kept.

Palaces were not fortified, for the general atmosphere was peaceful, yet they did have substantial outer walls designed against looting. One senses that life at that time was peaceful and orderly. A lively and sophisticated

228   Crete

Olive grove

society existed. Skilled craftsmen contributed to a high standard of original art creations and frescoes. The ideals and material conditions were three thousand years ahead of anything in Europe.

Landsmen became wealthy from the products of the soil worked by the peasants. Merchants made fortunes by exporting olive oil. Overseas trade flourished. On eastern and central Crete, the density of population left less than ten open miles between seaboard country towns, markets, workshops, ports, and mansions of the well-to-do. The island seems to have been a demi-paradise.

What mysterious happenings ended it? Earthquakes? Seismic history is complicated and uncertain. Did the violent eruption at Thera damage Crete? Did the tidal wave that followed the eruption destroy Cretan ports, towns, and palaces near the sea? Did the fallout of pumice-ash destroy the earth for crops and grazing? Was the final end due to fires, internal revolution, and sacking by mainland Athenians?

Scholars are writing books, archaeologists are still unearthing new evidence. No absolute has been stated; the mystery still remains.

eastern crete

AG. NIKOLAOS

This festive little town hugs the inner shore of Mirabello Bay. When tourism took hold, many foreign investors built hotel complexes in the nearby areas. Soon Greek shoemakers were making sandals for tourists, women spun yarn to sell, and Greek families ventured into the restaurant business.

Ag. Nikolaos

Foreigners opened sophisticated shops and eating places. Hotels catered to their European clientele.

Today, the atmosphere is light-hearted and, after a day of sun and surf, it is the harborfront that attracts the crowds. Here among the murmur of foreign tongues, the well-primed tourists swirl their *retsina* in their glasses and settle for an evening of talk and dining with perhaps a late evening fling at a discotheque.

Excursions

Kritsa. The glorious Cretan mountains rise up behind Ag. Nikolaos, and a short bus ride will take you to Kritsa, a weaving and craft town. Its main street is festooned with articles. Its tavernas solicit your patronage. Under an enormous plane tree, a sign states, "Eat our yogurt with honey. We have the best!"

An agreeable walk from Kritsa is to the *Church of Panayia Kera* which has

fourteenth and fifteenth century frescoes, the finest on Crete.

Lato-Goulas. This archaeological site is a one-hour walk from Kritsa; a car can approach it quite closely. The Doric ruin covers two hilltops and their saddle. The view of Mirabello Bay is fabulous. A picnic is suggested.

Ierapetra. Reach it by bus across the narrowest part of Crete, believed to be an overland trade route during Minoan times. Ierapetra is a year-round resort. The beach is lined with feathery tama-rack trees, plenty of attractive restaurants, and café–bars. At *Koutsounari*, along the coast, there is a Cretan-style bungalow village.

From Ierapetra you can drive along the southern coast to *Gortis*, with a short detour between *Vianos* and *Pirgos*.

Gournia. You will catch a brief glimpse of Gournia when your bus turns inward to go to Ierapetra. This ruin dates back to 1600 B.C., when it was a thriving trade and commerce city (in contrast to a palace city such as Knossos). Excavated among the cramped little houses on narrow streets were articles such as carpenter's kits, chisels, and forges. Art objects found in the Agora suggest that a Mother Goddess was worshipped. These findings are in the *Iraklion Museum*. When Minoan power declined so did Gournia. An American archaeologist, Harriet Boyd, excavated here in 1901–1904 and is credited with getting Gournia back on the map.

Sitia. This town is an alternate port to Ag. Nikolaos for island-hoppers who are traveling east and west; it is also the route from Thera.

Sitia is a fishing village which has sprouted some comfortable hotels. Less touristed than Ag. Nikolaos (as yet), it has a quiet, lazy-day atmosphere and is attractive to people who like to hang around and participate in harbor life. Here, the fishermen play the *bouzouki* and sing for their own enjoyment.

Palace of Zakros. East of Sitia is *Palaikastro*, where a turn to the south will take you to *Ano* and *Kato Zakros*. Through an olive grove and a gorge known as the *Valley of the Dead* (Minoan cave burials) is the Bay of Zakros. Here is an excellent beach backed by a banana grove. In the north corner is the *Palace of Zakros*, regarded as the fourth greatest Minoan ruin.

If this excursion is not for you, the treasures unearthed may be seen in Room VIII in the Iraklion Museum.

Vai. This tropical-looking beach has palm trees and a cafe that serves meals in summer. It can be reached by land, but much more enjoyable is an excursion group by boat from Sitia.

The following three attractions can be reached from either Ag. Nikolaos or Iraklion:

Lassithi. This lushly alluvial plain is surrounded by mountains and made unique by an estimated 10,000 windmills used when the wind is up to irrigate the farmers' fields. When the sails are whirling, the effect verges on the psychedelic.

Mt. Dikti. At Lassithi you are high in the mountains, but to go to the *Dictaean Cave*, a hard climb, you will need to go higher. Persistence and dynamite opened a fissure in the mountain and revealed a hidden chamber. Found were countless votives, proving that it was once a place of cults and worship. Allegedly, Zeus was born there; other places have made the same claim.

Malia. Not as dramatic as Knossos and Phaestos, this place is agreeably situated between mountains and sea. From the village of Malia a road leads through banana groves to the seashore, where holiday hotels and a fresh sea breeze may tempt you to stay.

The *Palace of Malia* that exists today dates from about 1450 B.C. Pre-existing palaces had suffered destruction. For dedicated "Minoan" enthusiasts this archaeological site should not be missed.

rural crete

Visitors by the thousands come each year to see and marvel at the remains of the Minoan civilization and to admire its ancient modernity. This pil-grimage may suffice, but to leave without a glimpse of Cretan life today is to see an unfinished whole. The islanders who live beyond the boundaries of tourist attractions are little touched by the island's ancient past. Theirs is a life of the land and sea. They have been characterized as tough, fearless, quick-tempered, and given to intercommunity feuds. They are also warmhearted, curious, and hospitable. They enjoy the reputation of being the liveliest dancers. If you stop in one of their villages, you will most likely hear, *"Ela. Kathise."* "Come. Sit down."

Here is a different harmony from the outward world, an almost dreamlike distortion of the visitor's personal reality. Refreshing!

Cretan mountain men

middle crete

IRAKLION (HERAKLION)

If you arrive by ship, you will dock at the New Harbor, grandly embellished with a Venetian castle and the *Lion of St. Mark*. Today, Iraklion is an architecturally scrambled, dun-colored city, a focal point for cruise ships, and the home of the world's largest collection of Minoan art. If your days for sightseeing are limited in Iraklion, you may wish to give the following priority: *Archaeological Museum.* Open weekdays 8:00 A.M. to 1:00 P.M., 3:00 to 6:00 P.M., Sundays 10:00 A.M. to 1:00 P.M. Closed Monday afternoons. The collection is housed in a fine modern building near Liberty Square. Guided tours are available; an official guidebook can be bought. The museum's small-scale reproduction of Knossos (see photo page 228) helps to make a mental base for your later on-the-spot experience. The frescoes in the museum are the originals.

Fountain Square. This area has cafes and patisseries. Especially active is the *volta* time; this is a good place to see Iraklion's youth on parade. *Morosini's Fountain* is a city treasure, as is the *Basilica of St. Mark*, nearby. Here is an exhibition of frescoes copied from Cretan churches.

Venetian Wall. Take a jaunt along a fifteenth century wall considered the strongest in the Mediterranean world. Smooth and rough going. *Martinengo*, the southern bastion, has the grave of Nikos Kazantzakis (1883–1957), a rewarding pilgrimage for those who know his writings.

Morning Market. Several blocks long, on 1866 St. This is an experience not to be missed for its color, crush of people, and the sight of all those good things to eat.

Cathedral of Ayios Menas. In the square of Ayia Ekaterini. A contemporary of El Greco, Michael Damaskino's collection has six masterpieces brought from the *Monastery of Vrondisi*, high up on Mt. Idi.

Excursions

Knossos. The Palace of Knossos is 5 km./3 mi. southwest of Iraklion and can be reached by buses that leave every 20 minutes from *Plateia Kormarou* at the harbor gate. Tour agencies arrange guide tours and have their own buses. The Palace grounds are open from 7:30 A.M. to 1 P.M., and from 2–6 P.M. On the highway, near the entrance, is a string of restaurants.

Without doubt, this is the most ancient city of Europe—not Greek, but

Knossos Palace excavations

Matala Beach (*Photo courtesy Melanie Heims*)

Minoan. Sir Arthur Evans, the archaeologist with seemingly endless enthusiasm and funds, was responsible for the excavations that he began in 1900. Today you will walk past a sculpture of him on a pedestal as you enter the grounds. It is early morning, a wisp of spider web may be floating from his serenely poised head.

Tours are fine, but somewhere along the way try to be in a quiet spot just by yourself and introspectively enjoy the mystique of this amazing site.

Gortis (Gortyn). This significant city flourished during the Hellenic period (1100–66 B.C.). Today you can see the considerable finds in the museum, and wander through fields where hidden objects nestle among tall grasses.

The importance of the city extended into Christian times, and even authorized St. Paul to convert Crete to Christianity.

Phaestos (Phaistos). One should not go to Phaestos without walking up the grand staircase and enjoying a royal and grandiose feeling of drama. Then you can turn and enjoy the view that deserves the raves it receives. Second in importance after Knossos, it flourished during the same period and had a similar architectural plan. In the deeper layers of excavations, some remains from the Neolithic Age were found.

Ayia Triadha. You can walk from Phaestos; the bus will take you a bit nearer. This exquisite ruin was the *Royal Villa*, circa 1600 B.C. It is conjectured to have been used as a summer residence for an important prince or the kings of Phaestos. Truly exceptional works of art such as a double ax, vases, frescoes, and inscribed tablets (in the Iraklion Museum) indicated a high degree of culture existed.

Matala. Caves and swimming at the

port town of Matala. Unique and intriguing are the caves in the high sheer cliff that rises up from the broad, grey sand beach. Some of the caves are large enough to incorporate steps, benches, fireplaces, windows, and doors.

South from Matala are grottos and caves—an invitation to ardent scuba divers and snorkelers.

Agia Galini. A touristy town with hotels and beaches edging mountains that rise up in Cretan ruggedness.

From Galini the road branches off to Rethimnon and the western part of Crete.

western crete

Hania (Chanea). Arrival by ship is at Souda Bay. Hania is Crete's capital and is proud of its hospitality and tourist amenities. The town is divided into the old and new. By far the most colorful is the old town waterfront with its Venetian buildings of creamy lightness, highlighted with vivid pinks, blues, and ochres, plus red-tiled roofs. At sunset the whole area turns golden. Seen from a boat, the reflections of the entire scene gleam and glow with a shimmering intensity.

Restaurants, cafés and patisseries cater to tourists. Points of interest include the museum, a number of churches with "built-on" minarets, the remains of the Fortress Wall, gardens, parks, a market modeled after the one in Marseilles, and an outstanding Museum.

Excursions

Rethimnon (Rethymno). Reached from the north coastal highway or from an island route of mountain foothills. Rethimon proves to be an old and charming town edging a vast expanse of beach. It has a mixture of Venetian and Byzantine buildings, plus iron-balconied houses that have been taken over by Crete's intellectuals to make their own select community.

The town's museum is a 17th Century Venetian loggia. Its citadel, known as the *"Fortrezza,"* is one of the best-preserved Venetian buildings in Greece.

A main attraction is the old harbor area where restaurants and cafés have made themselves decorative with colorful umbrellas and brightly-painted chairs. Fish dinners are favorites. *Kefi* abounds among the yacht people and tourists, who linger long into the night hours.

Monastery of Arkadi. From Rethimnon there is a rewarding trip to this monastery, which has become the supreme Cretan symbol for their centuries of fighting tyranny and invasion. In its isolated mountain position, it has served as a meeting place for partisans and resistance movements.

During the Turkish occupation, Cretan fighters blew up the monastery's powder magazine rather than submit to the Turks. An estimated 1,000 Cretans and 1,800 Turks perished. Today, the anniversary of the event is still observed with solemn religious services at the monastery and games, singing, and dancing in Rethimnon.

Rethimnon harbor

The restored monastery is an amazing conglomerate of styles dating from 1587. This architectural celebration includes Baroque, Corinthian, Classical, and Renaissance styles.

Theisso, Kastelli, Falarsana. These areas are easy day-trips from Hania, and include (Therisso) driving through a deep gorge, and swimming beaches for Kastelli and Falarsana.

Omalos, Samaria Gorge. For many travelers in Western Crete this area is the pièce de résistance. Go by bus to Omalos plateau, then descend and walk the 19 km./12 mi. to the sea at *Agia Roumeli*. The trip should be made between sunrise and sunset, but even better is to take a few days and camp along the way. (Mosquito repellent suggested.) Nowhere in Europe is there anything like this gorge. It's rough walking; the downward path puts all the stress on the back of the legs. There are places in the gorge so narrow you can almost touch both sides, and some walls are 2,000 ft. high. There are places where you have to wade through water, and places where the river goes underground. The gorge opens to the beach at Agia Roumeli where motorboats take the hikers east to Chora Sfakion or west to Palaiochora. Bus back to Hania.

Personal Comment

Inland western Crete has good rough terrain, mountains, isolated villages, lots of ruins tourists don't know about. Monasteries, fortifications, caves dating back to Neolithic times . . . whatever your adventures on Crete, there will always be more.

index

To the Reader: "Island information" includes Accommodations,
Getting There, Departures, History, Mythology, and Tourist Tips.